Table of Contents

D1497325

Preface

This book is the second in the Proven Practices in Higher Education series dedicated to sharing a collection of practices from a group of faculty members at a single university. City University of Seattle (CityU) is a small, private, nonprofit university primarily serving working adults in the Pacific Northwest, with satellite campuses in eleven countries on four continents. Through in-class, online, and hybrid delivery, CityU offers programs in education, leadership, management, technology, psychology, and general studies to students worldwide, many of whom would otherwise be denied access to education.

CityU is primarily a teaching institution; the institution has utilized technology in offering instruction for most of its forty years of operation, and has been ahead in its use of technology in education for that reason. Academic programs focus on delivering real-world skills, in an applied manner, that help students achieve professional goals. The vast majority of the university's faculty members are working professionals who are selected to teach what they do for a living. Over the years, one of the hallmarks of a CityU education has been the link to real-world applicability that comes from the connections that the university's seven hundred practitioner-faculty members bring to their classes.

While the university provides its faculty members with orientations and periodic trainings, faculty members often learn more by collaborating with their peers, sharing strategies for educating adults, and seeing the engagement that occurs from implementing these ideas. Over the years it has become evident that the university has accumulated a rich collection of valuable educational strategies that can and should be shared with teaching faculty from similar institutions worldwide. This is the driving force behind this Proven Practices series.

Most of the chapters in this book cover innovative practices that have been successful at helping adult students achieve their learning and professional goals. Rather than reporting on educational research and theory, these chapters generally cover teaching methodologies that CityU faculty members have successfully implemented. These practices are being shared so that other university instructors can also learn from these experiences.

As this book was coming together, four general themes emerged. The first theme is the importance of student engagement at all levels, and the roles that both students and instructors play in promoting and fostering this engagement. Instructors who are willing to assess their effectiveness and continually identify strategies that engage student populations (even as they change) will provide greater access to learning. Chapters 1, 2, and 3 integrate the student-engagement theme.

The second theme includes innovative ways in which students can authentically engage with their learning through real-life experiences and active involvement in internships, practicum opportunities, and professional association attendance. These experiences provide real-world application of learning, opportunities to interact with people who are engaged in their fields, and forums for raising challenging questions as members of a community of practice. These win-win activities need to be carefully designed, but provide rich experiences for employers, practitioner-faculty, and students. Chapters 4, 5, and 6 integrate the practical experience theme.

The third theme includes innovative practices in curriculum design and delivery. Designing courses and programs to honor student needs, prior experiences, and diverse pathways for learning has been shown to increase student satisfaction. Providing competency-based options, implementing universal design principles, and integrating technology features meet the needs of students today and further increase student satisfaction. Chapters 7, 8, 9, and 10 integrate the innovative design theme.

The fourth, and final, theme of innovative practices involves research strategies that are associatively applied in specific fields of studies. From lessons learned in the counseling and psychology industry to strategies applied in the training and development industry, authors have taken ideas from their fields and innovatively applied these practices in their teaching. The associative process provides new ways of engaging with students and developing as faculty. Chapters 11, 12, 13, and 14 integrate the research strategy theme.

If we are to believe that experience is the best teacher, then proven practices, developed through instructor experiences, have much to offer both novice and veteran educators. The insights included in this volume are offered with this goal in mind.

Kurt D. Kirstein
Craig E. Schieber
Kelly A. Flores
Steven G. Olswang

Seattle, WA
July 2013

Strategies for Engaging the Adult Learner

Kelly A. Flores, EdD, *Division of Doctoral Studies*
Timothy Sprake, MS, *School of Management*

Abstract

Students demonstrate their level of engagement in three ways: behavioral engagement, cognitive engagement, and emotional engagement. Instructors who proactively implement strategies to better engage their students enhance student learning and satisfaction in course work. Establishing shared responsibility between the student and the instructor is recommended to achieve higher levels of student engagement for adult learners.

Introduction

The landscape is rapidly changing in higher education, both for students and for instructors, in light of student and employer demands, financial challenges, and technological advancements. Students today have expectations for lower tuition costs and securing their education quicker than before. Instructors have the task of providing students with learning opportunities to meet their expectations for an engaging experience and achieve expected academic outcomes. Integrated technologies, evolving modes of delivery, and competency-based learning opportunities all affect the student experience.

While technology advancements provide multiple opportunities for increased interaction with students, the lecture format remains commonplace. Traditional forms of instruction, including the lecture format, are being challenged by adult learners because many of these instructional approaches do not provide students with as rich an opportunity to engage in learning at the level that they expect. Additionally, some instructors who integrate technology options do not employ optimal teaching strategies for the tool being used.

Unmet expectations have consequences. Students frequently talk with others about their learning experiences. If they have good experiences, they share these with others. Likewise, if classroom activities do not meet expectations, students share these negative experiences as well. This sharing of experiences affects the reputation of the institution in significant ways. Consequently, many institutions survey students on their level of engagement to measure students' perceptions of their experiences at the institution.

Defining Student Engagement

The National Survey of Student Engagement (NSSE) Institute for Effective Educational Practice (2013) describes student engagement both as (a) the time and effort that students apply to their studies and other related activities and (b) the resources the institution invests to organize the curriculum and other learning opportunities in meaningful ways.

In broad terms, engaged students take initiative, apply effort, and generally display positive emotions about the learning experience. "Students are engaged when they are involved in their work, persist despite challenges and obstacles, and take visible delight in accomplishing their work" (Schlechty, 1994, p. 5). Disengaged students do not produce their best work and often display passive behaviors such as boredom, anger, and anxiety.

They withdraw from learning challenges and even rebel against instructors and peers (Bomia, Beluzo, Demeester, Elander, Johnson, & Sheldon, 1997).

While definitions vary considerably, common themes emerge in the literature, providing potential frameworks for discussing strategies for student engagement. Three common themes are related to student engagement for the adult learner: behavioral engagement, cognitive engagement, and emotional engagement.

Behavioral engagement focuses on the extent to which students are actively involved in learning tasks with others (Harper & Quaye, 2008). Examples include respecting others, listening to instructors and peers, engaging in discussions, and participating in teams.

Cognitive engagement refers to the student's level of investment in learning and effort exerted to comprehend complex ideas or master difficult skills (Blumenfeld, Kempler, & Krajcik, 2006). Examples include the effort in understanding course material, completing assignments, critically analyzing information, applying concepts to real-world examples, and deepening insights through research and interaction.

Emotional engagement focuses on how students feel about the educational experience. (O'Donnell, Reeve, & Smith, 2011). Examples include students' level of excitement, interest, and enjoyment of their academic experiences.

These themes are broad and often overlap. One challenge for academic leaders is determining where to focus efforts for improvement. At institutions where the majority of students are adult learners, this adds an additional layer of complexity when challenging faculty to continuously improve student engagement.

Engaging the Adult Learner

Adult learners are operating in an environment where what they learn is often immediately applied to their work, career, and success. As such, these students have many expectations of instructors and the classroom experience. Adults are interested in the effective application of concepts learned in their course work (Honigsfeld & Dunn, 2006). Instructors would benefit from approaching the classroom environment with the characteristics of adult learners at the forefront of their minds.

Knowles (1980) stressed that adult learners need independence, self-direction, ownership of learning, relevant and applicable contexts, and sharing of life experiences as a source of knowledge. Instructors seeking to improve engagement of adult learners should ensure that course activities provide multiple pathways for learning and sufficient opportunities for discussion. Bocchi, Eastman, and Swift (2004) determined that adult learners should be "self-motivated and have self-discipline, initiative, commitment, time management skills, organization skills, and a willingness to participate in the class" (p. 247). Instructors should ensure that adult learners have these skills and characteristics and modify learning experiences accordingly.

Cercone (2008) recommended that instructors consider the following characteristics when designing learning experiences: (a) potential limitations such as preexisting learning histories or preferred learning styles; (b) a need to be actively involved in learning experiences and a possible need for support through coaching, resources, and other strategies; (c) a need for the instructor to act as facilitator to provide opportunities to share prior experiences; (d) a need to apply relevant learning to reality; (e) value placed on self-reflection and opportunities to test learning along the way; and (f) a desire for collaborative environments that promote dialogue, social interaction, and mutual respect.

Instructors are advised to evaluate the students in their courses to discover learning patterns, to permit self-directed learning among the students, to provide opportunities for the students to understand learning preferences, and to apply these preferences throughout the course (Honigsfeld & Dunn, 2006). Through interaction with the instructor and fellow students, adults learn from shared stories about successes and failures; they have the opportunity to explore concepts and learn from each other. When students come together to learn, instructors should strive to replace student passivity with active engagement.

Strategies for Increasing Student Engagement among Adult Learners

Instructors should monitor their courses for evidence of disengagement and proactively implement strategies for increasing engagement of adult learners. The following strategies for increasing behavioral, cognitive, and emotional engagement can be implemented to enhance the learning experience for adult learners.

Behavioral Engagement

Students demonstrate behavioral engagement when they are actively involved in learning tasks with others (Harper & Quaye, 2008). They are more behaviorally engaged when they are respectful in their interactions with instructors and peers, actively listening to diverse viewpoints, engaging in generative discussions, and effectively participating in teams. Evidence of behavioral disengagement can include distancing, independence (versus interdependence), and repeated tardiness to agreed-upon meetings. Other examples might include interrupting, side conversations, superficial responses, halfheartedness, and lack of participation.

Strategies for improving behavioral engagement among adult learners include:

Modeling expected behavior: Model respect by actively listening, acknowledging the value of student contributions, and honoring students' unique perspectives.

Promoting interdependence: Promote engagement between students by having them complete tasks together, share ideas with one another, or constructively challenge each other's positions with research support.

Providing constructive feedback: Provide explicit and constructive feedback to students on their interaction in the classroom, praising them for the areas in which they are performing well, and sharing areas in which they can work on improving.

Inviting interaction: Invite students to interact with each other by scaffolding ideas, highlighting connections between similar interest areas, and challenging students to resolve contradictory perspectives.

Cognitive Engagement

Students demonstrate cognitive engagement when they exhibit effort and investment in their learning experience (Blumenfeld, Kempler, & Krajcik, 2006). Students are more cognitively engaged when they exert significant effort into understanding complex course materials and completing assignments, critically analyzing information, applying concepts to real-world examples, and deepening insights through research and interaction. Evidence of cognitive disengagement can include lack of preparedness for class, superficial analyses, and basic responses to prompts. Other examples might include minimal application of content to personal and professional experiences and a simplistic approach to finding supportive research.

Strategies for improving cognitive engagement among adult learners include:

Encouraging critical analysis: Provide opportunities for students to identify opinions, underlying assumptions, and major ideas in readings or course work; have students critically evaluate each other's work and provide constructive feedback.

Personalizing summaries: Invite students to share key ideas learned, content they found most useful and relevant, and the questions that remain. Include these ideas in course summaries and announcements, addressing key questions.

Applying concepts to real-life scenarios: Share relevant case studies and real-life examples, and encourage students to do the same. Include additional resources (e.g., videos, websites, blogs, articles, or activities) to enhance learning and reinforce key concepts.

Promoting information literacy: Challenge students to support their positions, resolve controversies, and deepen their understanding through scholarly research. Model information literacy in discussions and summaries.

Emotional Engagement

Students demonstrate emotional engagement by how they feel about their educational experience (O'Donnell, Reeve, & Smith, 2011). Students are more emotionally engaged when they are excited about coming to class, interested in the content of the course, and enjoy the learning experience. Evidence of emotional disengagement can include absence from class, infrequency of participation, and a negative or critical tone in interactions. Other examples might include disinterest, indicators of boredom, and nonchalance toward the learning experience.

Strategies for improving emotional engagement among adult learners include:

Establishing personal connections: Reach out personally to students to find out what their goals, hopes, and expectations are for the class. Find out about personal and professional interests and find ways to establish personal connections.

Recognizing achievements: Praise students when they perform well, make improvements, respond to feedback, and when they lead by example. Where appropriate, praise publicly, and incorporate their contributions in course summaries.

Integrating students' goals: Find ways to integrate students' individual goals into the curriculum or discussions. Provide real-life examples that resonate with students and empower them to share their own examples to make connections.

Providing personalized feedback: Take the time to provide personalized feedback on the work students submit, and hold them accountable for incorporating feedback in future work. Invite students to discuss feedback and questions in a face-to-face or virtual meeting.

Shared Responsibility for Student Engagement

Accepting responsibility for student engagement is challenging and for good reason, especially in circumstances where factors affecting results are beyond an institution's direct control. Many businesses conduct *employee* engagement surveys for the purpose of identifying opportunities to retain the talented people they employ (Markos & Waltair, 2010). Questions cover a variety of topics. Some are areas where the employee's manager has a direct impact on the engagement level of staff. There are other areas where the manager's impact is far less direct. Outside influences that are beyond managers' control can have a significant effect upon the motivation and engagement of employees. For example, compensation and benefits are typically not within managers' control but have a measurable impact upon the retention of their employees.

Despite the lack of complete control, many business leaders hold their managers responsible for the engagement level of those who report to them directly (Duguay, 2010). One reason for this may be that employees respond more favorably in those areas where the manager has direct control; correspondingly they likewise respond less favorably in those areas when the manager's control and influence is limited. While they realize that engagement is a shared responsibility (Duguay), they recognize that the manager's impact is far reaching.

With adult learners, academic leaders should consider the parallels that can be applied to student engagement, specifically in areas where the responsibility resides for improvement. Like managers, there are influences that are far outside of an instructor's ability to control, that can and do clearly affect the student's level of engagement. Just as the manager is the primary link between the employees and the organization, the instructor is perhaps the most important link to the success and engagement of the students.

References

Blumenfeld, P. C., Kempler, T. M., & Krajcik, J. S. (2006). Motivation and cognitive engagement in learning environments. In R. K. Sawyer (Ed.), *The Cambridge handbook of the learning sciences* (pp. 475–488). New York, NY: Cambridge University Press.

Bocchi, J., Eastman, J. K., & Swift, C. O. (2004). Retaining the online learner: Profile of students in an online MBA program and implications for teaching them. *Journal of Education for Business, 79*, 245–253.

Bomia, L., Beluzo, L., Demeester, D., Elander, K., Johnson, M., & Sheldon, B. (1997). *The impact of teaching strategies on intrinsic motivation.* Champaign, IL: ERIC Clearinghouse on Elementary and Early Childhood Education.

Cercone, K. (2008). Characteristics of adult learners with implications for online learning design. *AACE Journal, 16*, 137–159.

Duguay, D. (2010). *Who is responsible for employee engagement?* Retrieved from http://www.humanresourcesiq.com/talent-management/articles/who-s-responsible-for-employee-engagement/

Harper, S. R., & Quaye, S. J. (2008). *Student engagement in higher education: Theoretical perspectives and practical approaches for diverse populations.* New York, NY: Routledge.

Honigsfeld, A., & Dunn, R. (2006). Learning style characteristics of adult learners. *Delta Kappa Gamma Bulletin, 72*(2), 14–31.

Knowles, M. (1980). *The modern practice of adult education: From pedagogy to andragogy* (2nd ed.). Englewood Cliffs, NJ: Prentice Hall.

Markos, S., & Waltair, V. (2010). Employee engagement: The key to improving performance. *International Journal of Business and Management, 5*(12), 89–96.

National Survey of Student Engagement (NSSE). (2013). *What is student engagement?* Retrieved from http://nsse.iub.edu/html/about.cfm

O'Donnell, A. Reeve, J. M. & Smith, J. (2011). *Educational psychology: Reflection for action* (3rd ed.). New York, NY: John Wiley & Sons.

Schlechty, P. (1994). *Increasing student engagement* Missouri Leadership Academy.

How to Engage a Group of Diverse Adult Learners in a Way That Also Raises Rigor and Increases Learning

Paul C. Robb, EdD, *Albright School of Education*

Abstract

Typically, we teach the way we were taught unless we can learn new approaches to pedagogy. The literature on adult learning can guide meaningful, practical pedagogy that catalyzes the process of constructing meaning and the improvement of student learning. Moreover, when the quality of learning opportunities improves, underrepresented populations are more likely to benefit. Transformative change (Mezirow, 2000) in individual learning requires new approaches in thinking in how one can engender growth and learning with adults. This suggests that adults desire active versus passive learning that is also practical. Learners construct new knowledge that builds upon their prior understanding and experiences. Learning can be enhanced by what is termed "sociocentric," rather than egocentric thinking, when learners share ideas, inquire, and solve problems together and address the constant human need for dialogue (Brookfield, 2003; Garmston, 1997). By implementing simple strategies that create conditions and opportunities for adults to construct meaning, it is quite possible for cognition and understanding to improve significantly.

Introduction

Colleges and universities in the United States enjoy a reputation throughout the world of offering high-quality education. Indeed, it is a healthy industry by many measures: 70 percent of the world's Nobel prize-winners work in U.S. universities, twenty of the top rated twenty-six universities in the world are in the United States according to the Times Higher Education World University Rankings, and more than 764,400 foreign students attended U.S. universities during the 2011/2012 school year, a record number and nearly 6 percent higher than the previous year (Doughty, 2013). Clearly, it has the reputation of high quality and rigor.

It is not a stretch to claim that the present higher education system succeeds in some measures. Yet, while our country espouses democracy and cultural pluralism, college admission, retention, and graduation rates for historically marginalized students indicate predictably fewer opportunities for success. The graduation rates for African American and Latino students are significantly lower than their white and Asian counterparts (Carey, 2004). As the need for a postsecondary education becomes greater than ever before, the economic disparities resulting from the variance in educational attainment are a matter of equity and pragmatism for our society.

Academic Traditions

University faculty members were very likely successful students in an educational system that valued the dominant Western cultural norms such as competition and independence while devaluing other culture's norms such as cooperation and interdependence. Since we typically teach the way we were taught, it is not unreasonable to assume that the default teaching style found in most university classrooms favors members of the dominant culture over other groups (Ginsberg & Wlodkowski, 2009). Moreover, considering the recent advancements in learning theory, one can argue that some time-honored academic traditions may not result in the highest quality of learning, regardless of one's cultural experiences. Yet, traditions of questionable value continue, even within an industry that proudly promotes new ideas and academic freedom.

Dating back over eight hundred years, academia draws upon the rituals of medieval times and religion. At the heart of most university classrooms is the lectern, so steeped in tradition and formality and not unlike the church pulpit from where the Bible was placed. In the middle ages the word "lecture" literally meant reading aloud from an authoritative text. People believed that knowledge and truth came from above. Books were scarce and many people were illiterate. At the universities, teachers dictated the texts to students. Although the advent of the printing press brought significant changes to the world, the university tradition of dictation and note taking persisted for many years following, as if nothing had happened (McLuhan, 1962). Another vestige of the Middle Ages is the flowing robes and chevrons worn by faculty and graduates, indistinguishable from the attire of many clergy.

Learner-Centered Education

In the Information Age, accelerated by technological advances, students not only have unprecedented access to information but also may participate in the co-construction of websites. Today's students, more often than not, possess their own mobile devices capable of retrieving recorded lectures to be played back at an increased speed for efficiency and convenience. Furthermore, a new research-based paradigm shift in higher education calls for a learner-centered rather than a content-centered approach. The end goal of a course is no longer simply to increase a student's amount of knowledge, but also to change the student's way of thinking and conceptualizing within the real world context. In other words, faculty members are now considering how to facilitate the process of learning. Moving from the "sage on the stage" to the "guide on the side" role confronts traditional faculty identities and roles. For some, this new paradigm challenges the control and power of being the sole content expert. This shift also requires a new set of skills to accompany the change in philosophy (Saulnier, 2009).

The literature on adult learning suggests the need for making meaning and constructing understanding as a critical learning component. For many learners, this requires active versus passive learning. Students need to discuss what they are learning, relate it to their prior knowledge and experiences, wrestle with discrepancies, and determine how it applies to their lives. Learning as a spectator sport that entails memorization and recall is much less rigorous and often irrelevant. Although lectures should not be necessarily rendered obsolete, their effectiveness alone, or in large doses for enhancing learning is questionable. For instance, some research suggests that a lecture typically results in a 5 percent retention rate over twenty-four hours (Sousa, 2001).

Recently some attention has been given to university instructors who have "flipped" their class by sending the lecture and/or readings prior to the class session so that the class can be used for students to question and interact with the instructor regarding the material. Though this strategy has potential for increasing student engagement and understanding, there are also downsides to the model. An instructor without strategies to engage more than one student at a time may miss the opportunities for all learners to participate. Discussions dominated by a few students and the instructor would only reinforce the competitive and individualistic model for learning. Others students might ascribe to the traditional construct that the lecture is the center of higher learning and the additional class time is remedial. By not seeing the additional time in class as productive or necessary, they might simply skip the sessions.

Adult Learning

For many, learning is most effective when students work together. The "sociocentric" approach, in contrast to an egocentric approach, invites rich thinking and new understanding through sharing ideas, inquiry, and solving problems together. Public discussion and thinking out loud increase an individual learner's capacity and adds to the collective knowledge of the group (Garmston, 1997). Even at the graduate level, students explaining the concepts to each other, using their own understandings, language, and assumptions are often more effective than the instructor who has a

different level of experiences, understanding, assumptions, and orientation. Probably the best analogy would be to recall the frustration of not
comprehending the explanation from a "computer nerd," a "math whiz,"
or a car mechanic who explains a concept or procedure either too quickly
or who uses unfamiliar terms and unfamiliar concepts. Yet, when a peer
who has successfully captured the essence of a concept explains, it can be
better understood.

Adult learners are diverse in their learning styles. That alone could
discourage any instructor's desire to change to reach all their students.
Yet, similar to Supreme Court Justice Potter Stewart who proclaimed,
"I know it when I see it," in reference to pornography, adults recognize
effective instruction and facilitation that result in substantive, relevant
learning experiences. Yet, unlike the Supreme Court that struggled with
defining pornography, there is a body of research that does identify
the components. Although there may not be a definitive list of adult
learning principles, there is plenty of agreement and overlap between
lists. The following is a partial list compiled from articles, research
reports, dissertations, and textbooks on adult learning (Brookfield,
2003; James, 1983; Merriam, Caffarella, & Baumgartner, 2007; Mezirow,
2000; Garmston, 1997):

1. Adults are motivated to learn by a variety of factors.
2. Active learner participation in the process contributes to learning.
3. Content should be presented in a variety of mediums and formats.
4. Content interspersed with opportunities for processing creates personal relevance, facilitates construction of meaning, and
   increases retention.
5. Experience of the learner is a major resource in learning situations.
6. Collaborative opportunities for processing and problem solving
   through interaction and learning from peers increase engagement and conceptualization.
7. A comfortable supportive environment is a key to successful
   learning.

Changing practice and implementing adult learning principles
into university classrooms promise deeper levels of understanding, increased amount of retention, with greater numbers of students. Students who will benefit the most from a learner-focused and

sociocentric approach are the historically underserved populations. For instance, several independent studies of college students have concluded that Native American and Latino students prefer sociocentric learning conditions with opportunities for "active and concrete learning experiences" (Sanchez, 2000). Though we know that a certain arousal and activity is necessary to stimulate cognition, we also know from research and experience that stress acts as a major block to learning. A comfortable supportive learning environment is also particularly important to underserved populations who have legitimate reasons to believe that the environment is not conducive for all learners. Although offering culturally responsive learning environments is complex and multifaceted, shifting to a sociocentric, learner-centered approach will address many of the challenges.

Repertoire of Effective Strategies

Building a repertoire of effective strategies to increase student engagement and learning, for which there are many, is a reasonable starting point. The following strategies are but a handful of examples of how instructors can begin to shift the focus and outcomes of their classes:

Establish Norms and Use a Parking Lot. In order for students to feel safe and take risks, it is recommended that norms be established at the outset of the course. The norms address expectations, how the class will fully participate in discussions, address criticism, and complaints. The parking lot is to be used to put aside complicated or peripheral issues that require longer reflection or attention outside of class.

Instructor Role:
1. Offers ideas for course standards and invites student input.
2. Facilitates discussion, relegating less relevant or more complicated topics to the "parking lot" for reflection and later discussion.

Student Role:
1. Join in establishment of basic norms.
2. Feel free to invoke the norms throughout the course

Assessment:
1. Do students respect each other's time and feelings?
2. Can the instructor accept questions/challenges without derailing the curriculum by using the parking lot?
3. Is there an environment of psychological safety with room for diverse opinions?

Take Attendance by Giving a Survey. The purpose of giving a survey is to inform or influence discussion or lecture. The survey can appear online before the class, be given out at the beginning of class, or be in PowerPoint.

Instructor Role:
1. Prepares questions that cover opinions formed from a common reading or other information sources.
2. Directs one or more students to compile the results and report them to the class. Asks for comments on the results.
3. Uses the survey to monitor attendance, if needed.

Student Role:
1. Reply anonymously to ensure frankness, but check off their name from class list.
2. Make statements of analysis, evaluation, or judgment regarding the survey results.

Assessment:
1. Are students reflecting more on readings or other information sources?
2. Are the students confident that the instructor values their prior knowledge but at the same time expects objective analysis and reflection whenever possible?

Think-Write-Pair-Share. In a lecture-format classroom, pausing at ten-minute intervals for at least two minutes or more of processing improves the level of student engagement and understanding. Think-Write-Pair-Share is a protocol for students to reflect, analyze, and collaborate with other students in response to an instructor's prompt in a lecture or during other times in the period. The prompt might be a slide in a PowerPoint, a point in the lecture, or an excerpt from a reading.

Instructor Role:
1. Choose a prompt from one of many possible sources and direct students in a timed thinking period, a writing period, and then a sharing with one or two partners.
2. Circulate throughout the class reading over students' shoulders and eavesdropping on the conversations.
3. Ask a few students to share their reflections or those of their partners.

Student Role:
1. Focus on one or two points that the instructor deems significant or perhaps complicated.
2. Have a chance to share their impressions, and perhaps their doubts, about the meaning of the material at hand.

Assessment:
1. Are students connecting the new information with their prior knowledge?
2. Are the students learning to air their questions, or criticisms, in an open manner?
3. Is the instructor catching misinterpretations and confusions before they become embedded in students' minds?

Anticipation Guide. The learning from a lecture or presentation can be greatly enhanced by incorporating an Anticipation Guide that measures student knowledge and understanding prior to and immediately after a presentation. The before and after responses are on the same sheet to help students see the relevance and development of their learning. It is also an effective organizer to keep the instructor on track to cover all of the items earmarked earlier.

Instructor Role:
1. Keep it simple. Choose the most important concepts and keep it to ten or fifteen questions.

2. Choose a few questions or statements that are likely to surprise the students. Part of the advantage of using a guide is to show the students how their ideas change.

Student Role:
1. Answer the questions before receiving instruction.
2. Read/listen to the material, and then answer the questions again, noticing when their answers are different from before.

Assessment:
1. Do students connect their prior knowledge to new learning?
2. Does the instructor more accurately anticipate students' prior knowledge as well as areas of less familiarity?
3. Is the relevance of the presentation clear to students?

List-Group-Label. In a less formal setting, students are seated in groups around tables. List-Group-Label is a protocol intended to help students get an overview of a large body of material and concepts by organizing information into categories. This is done by allowing time for the students to process content through collaboration with peers in analysis and synthesis of the material.

Instructor Role:
1. Prepare a list of vocabulary items, which may denote concepts, descriptors, or artifacts of the course material or unit.
2. Each item needs to be printed beforehand or by students on a separate piece of paper such as three-by-five-inch index cards, Post-its, address labels, scrap paper, etc.

Student Role:
1. In groups, students rearrange the vocabulary items into categories. For example, for a World War I list, the words "gas," and "Big Bertha artillery" might be placed in a category named "weapons."
2. Each category must have at least two entries, and its name must not be repeated in any of the entries. For example, "democratic rights" would not be an acceptable entry in a category called "democracy."

3. Each group presents its list of labeled categories and category members.
4. In a class where there is strong student rapport, students can be encouraged, after each group has finished grouping and labeling, to challenge the other groups' thinking regarding the categories.

Assessment:
1. What student understandings do the categories suggest?
2. Are students working and participating together equitably and productively?

Carousel Brainstorming. In Carousel Brainstorming, students externalize beginning or intermediate knowledge by working together to plan, critique, or solve problems. The classroom can also be energized by a cognitive activity with physical movement.

Instructor Role:
1. Sets up topics on large papers posted around the classroom.
2. Forms the students into groups, assigns each group to one topic, and gives them time to record their thoughts, suggestions, analysis—whatever the topic calls for—on the paper. Calls the time and has the students rotate through the topics.
3. Each group is given pens of certain colors to differentiate them from other groups.

Student Role:
1. Work in their groups demonstrating their knowledge and analysis of the topic.
2. When finished, the student groups rotate to the next topic, adding their questions, comments, or suggestions on the next group's paper.
3. Students rotate through all the topics, adding information as they go.
4. Each group nominates a spokesperson who responds to the comments from the other groups.

Assessment:
1. Do students show curiosity about others' diverse opinions?
2. Do the students seem able to incorporate others' thoughts into their work?
3. Does the instructor begin to present material with the particular students' strengths and knowledge base in mind?

Jigsaw. Jigsaw is a text-based protocol in which difficult reading material is broken into sections and strategically assigned to various students. The instructor creates two types of groupings among the students: experts and teams. Each student belongs to an expert group as well as a team. Difficult material is broken into sections, each section assigned to experts. Once mastered, the sections are shared with the team.

Instructor Role:
1. Chooses a challenging reading that presents interrelated concepts or information.
2. Divides the reading into four to six more or less equally difficult sections, assigning each section to a different group of four to six experts (four reading sections = four expert groups; five reading sections = five expert groups, etc.).
3. Quizzes each team on their understanding of the reading either orally or in writing.
4. Assigns a group grade (to enforce team cooperation, many instructors give the team the lowest grade achieved by any one team member).

Student Role:
1. Understand who is in their expert group, and who is on their team.
2. At the end of a set period of reading, discussion, and analysis, the members of each expert group return to their team with the mission of teaching them the contents of their reading section. They are the "experts" on their section.
3. Listen to the rest of the members of their team as they instruct about their sections.
4. Ask questions of the other experts and, since the group grade will be based on the weakest member of the team, check for understanding among all the team members.

Assessment:
1. Are students learning to rely on their peers to help them better understand information?
2. Are students able to clarify doubts and questions with their peers?

Final Word. Final Word is a text-based discussion group protocol. It allows all students to participate equitably without interruption by following clear procedures. The protocol also enhances the quality of discussion by requiring students to reference the source that they are speaking about and comment on the content. The protocol also keeps the focus on one topic at a time.

Instructor Role:
1. Provides an article, film clip, newspaper article or some other resource for students to review.
2. Typically, this protocol works best for resources that represent an integration of past learning, not brand-new concepts.
3. Organizes the students into various small groups of three to four members.
4. Time the rounds so that each student gets equal time to talk.

Student Role:
1. Join into groups and number off from one to three or one to four.
2. The first student indicates a sentence or paragraph in the material that represented a particularly interesting idea, analysis, or interpretation.
3. Each of the other students, in turn, comments on that one sentence or paragraph, either enlarging upon the thought or critiquing the thought.
4. When the other students have all spoken, the initiating student closes the discussion with his/her reasons for the choice and possible change of thinking due to the other students' comments.
5. The process is repeated so that each student is the initiating student.

Assessment:
1. Do students show curiosity about others' diverse opinions?
2. Does the instructor notice improvement in the students' tendency to incorporate various points of view into their work?
3. Are all students sharing their thoughts more freely thereby producing more robust discussions?

Inquiry Approach to Data Interpretation. This approach allows students to indicate at the beginning of new material the extent of their prior knowledge, as well as make connections to new knowledge.

Instructor Role:
1. Choose a set of data points that are closely related to the new material. (e.g., regional variations in the United States of child mortality)
2. Lead the students in a discussion of possible interpretations of the data.
3. Illustrate the way a possible interpretation would lead to further questions and study.

Student Role:
1. Review the data points and jot down ideas for possible interpretations and/or conclusions.
2. Share their thoughts in a class discussion.

Assessment:
1. Does the instructor get a solid sense of the current background knowledge of class members?
2. Do the students experience a balance between the instructor's presentations and the student contributions? Is content balanced with process?

Simulation. A simulation is a learning activity that assigns roles to students and often presents them with a problem to solve. A simulation can fulfill the following purposes: reinforce inquiry learning, teach a chronology, teach connections, teach a concept, teach a process such as bargaining or interviewing, experience a different culture or mindset, and/or teach emotional intelligence. Some examples of emotional intelligence outcomes are learning to resolve a conflict, empathize, manage feelings, communicate appropriately under stress, and cooperate in a group. Designing and implementing a classroom simulation can range from focusing on a very short experience used to introduce a topic to a more complex learning activity. Longer simulations initially require more preparation time by the instructor to effectively implement. However, the outcomes are well worth the effort with students experiencing virtually firsthand the roles and issues being studied and engaging more deeply in the material because they feel they have leverage in the outcomes in the classroom. Rich discussions that follow are often reflected in higher retention of facts and concepts. These outcomes may motivate the instructor to create other simulations and continue the practice in subsequent courses.

Elements of a simulation:
1. Goals and objectives
2. Roles
3. Activities (what the participants do during the simulation)
4. Rules of interaction, special procedures, penalties
5. Parameters of the game (time allotment, behavioral rules)
6. Method of assessment (questioning, quizzing, presentations, earning points)
7. Rewards (points, prizes, privileges)
8. Debrief
9. Reflection
10. Reinforcement of the learning

Concerns of implementation:
1. What is the teacher's role?
2. Which elements of the simulation are flexible?
3. How to encourage participation by all students?

Conclusion

Changing to an instructional approach with the focus on the learner rather than the content is a paradigm shift. The rapid changes in our society and world demand that higher education be more responsive to citizens living in a pluralistic society. It is a moral imperative no less critical than the challenges of providing equitable education in the K–12 educational system. The changes required in such a shift challenge present practices, beliefs, and identities of higher education faculty. As with most changes, a simplistic understanding will bring about superficial change with little impact. Simply implementing a set of activities into the classroom will not guarantee change in student achievement. A thoughtful and effective change that improves student learning will need a deeper philosophical framework and a sense of coherence that undergirds instructional moves. Both the instructor and students will need to know what, why and how they are to participate throughout the course. The purpose of an activity and the connection to the course outcomes need to be explained in order for adults to fully appreciate and then participate. Instructors who take a growth mindset stance, willing to assess their effectiveness frequently and search for cause and effect relationships, will in the very least model learning for their students and very likely bring about a greater access to learning.

References

Brookfield, S. D. (2003). Racializing the discourse of adult education. *Educational Review, 73*(4), 497–523.

Carey, K. (2004). *A matter of degrees: Improving graduation rates at four- year colleges and universities.* Washington DC: The Education Trust.

Darling-Hammond, L. (1997). Quality teaching: The critical key to learning. *Principal, 77*(1), 5–11.

Doughty, B. (2013). Number of International Students Attending American Colleges and Universities Continues Rising. Learning English, Voice of America. Retrieved from http://learningenglish.voanews.com/content/article/1546399.html

Garmston, R. J. (1997). *The presenter's fieldbook: A practical guide.* Norwood, MA: Christopher-Gordon.

Ginsberg, M. G. & Wlodkowski, R. J. (2009). *Diversity and motivation: Culturally responsive teaching in college.* San Francisco, CA: Jossey-Bass.

Haycock, K. (2001). Closing the achievement gap. *Educational Leadership, 58*(6), 6–11.

James, W. B. (1983). An analysis of perceptions of the practices of adult educators from five different settings. *Proceedings of the Adult Education Research Conference,* no. 24. Montreal: Concordia University/University of Montreal.

McLuhan, M. (1962). *The Gutenberg galaxy: The making of typographic man.* Toronto: University of Toronto Press.

Merriam, S. B., Caffarella, R. S., & Baumgartner, L. M. (2007). *Learning in adulthood: A comprehensive guide* (3rd ed.). San Francisco: Jossey-Bass.

Mezirow, J. (2000). Learning to think like an adult: Core concepts of transformation theory. In J. Mezirow and Associates, *Learning as transformation: Critical perspectives on a theory in progress.* San Francisco: Jossey-Bass.

Sanchez, I. M. (2000). Motivating and maximizing learning in minority classrooms. *New Directions for Community Colleges,* 35–44.

Saulnier, B. M. (2009). From "sage on the stage" to "guide on the side" revisited: (Un)covering the content in the learner-centered information systems course. *Information Systems Education Journal, 7,* 3–10.

Sousa, D. A. (2001). *How the brain learns* (2nd ed.). Thousand Oaks, CA: Corwin Press.

Wenger, E. (1998). *Communities of practice: Learning, meaning, and identity.* Cambridge: Cambridge University Press.

Educational Theories in Practice

Kathy L. Milhauser, DMgt, PMP, *School of Management*

Abstract

Research has shown that both andragogy and heutagogy are relevant to the practice of management education and associated with adult learning and success (Hase & Kenyon, 2003; Knowles, Holton, & Swanson, 2005; Wlodkowski, 2008). This chapter includes a brief summary of how these educational theories have evolved and an example of how to situate these theories within the practice of management education.

Introduction

One misconception held by some adult educators is that teaching approaches that are appropriate and relevant for children are also appropriate and relevant for adults (Wlodkowski, 2008). Pedagogy is the term for the theory and practice of teaching children (Knowles, Holton, & Swanson,

2005). The pedagogical approach, when applied to the education of adults in topics related to management, is limited in its utility. This approach fails to engage the adult learner's prior experiences and current management contexts by placing emphasis on the role of the teacher as director of learning (Knowles, Holton, & Swanson). Further, a pedagogical approach typically does not reflect research into the motivation and engagement of adult learners (Wlodkowski). Finally, because the pedagogical approach is founded on teaching in a simulated environment, it fails to leverage the authentic opportunities adult learners often have to apply what they are learning in relevant ways (Gruenewald, 2013).

This chapter will introduce two learning theories for consideration when designing management education: andragogy and heutagogy. For purposes of this chapter, the term andragogy will be used to refer to "any intentional and professionally guided activity that aims at change in adult persons" (Knowles, Holton, & Swanson, 2005, p. 60). The term heutagogy will be used to refer to "the study of self-determined learning" (Hase & Kenyon, 2000, p. 3).

Andragogy

As previously defined, andragogy is the application of learning theory to the education of adults (Knowles, Holton, & Swanson, 2005). Andragogical approaches acknowledge the needs of the adult learner as distinct and evolved from the needs of the child, noting the developmental stage of the adult and the impact of maturity on motivation to learn (Wlodkowski, 2008).

Knowles (1970) defined six core principles that are relevant to adult learning. These principles address the adult learner's need for relevance and reinforcement of self-concept, acknowledge the adult's prior experience and readiness to learn, and include methods designed to orient learning to the adult's unique requirements and motivations. This model and others provide direction to educators in the creation of adult learning approaches that acknowledge the adult's development and maturity.

The topic of adult motivation to learn was differentiated from pedagogical approaches by Knowles (1970) in alignment with andragogical models. Further, Wlodkowski (2008) suggested a four-part framework for motivating adult learners with components of inclusion, attitude, meaning, and competence. Methods to address this framework included treating adult learners with respect, including them in decisions that affect their learning, ensuring clarity regarding the relevance of learning, and aligning learning experiences with the adult learner's own perspectives and values. Wlodkowski (2008) also found that the adult learner's perception of his/her own potential for competence was critical to motivation.

Heutagogy

Hase and Kenyon (2003, p. 3) suggested that heutagogy evolves from pedagogy and androgogy as a "natural progression" in the evolution of thinking regarding adult learning. Palloff and Pratt (2009) referred to heutagogy as an educational process of self-directed learning, asserting that in learning based on heutagogy, the focus of the learning is on the adult (vs. child), and that learning is constructed by the adult learner (vs. by the instructor). As adults apply what they are learning to their own personal context, they find their understanding enhanced by the situations within which they construct meaning.

The theory of heutagogy is closely aligned with constructivism, a concept first introduced by Lev Vygotsky in the early twentieth century (Wink & Putney, 2002). When teaching from a constructivist or heutagogical perspective, the task of the instructor becomes one of facilitation (Duffy & Jonassen, 2013). The instructor helps the learner to relate concepts to his or her prior experiences and current context in a way that the learner can construct his or her own meaning. Thus, a heutagogical approach requires more focus on the desired outcomes of the learning and on facilitating the learner's navigation toward those outcomes with experiences and applications that the learner co-designs. In contrast to a pedagogical approach based on specific activities and experiences designed by the instructor, a heutagogical approach is much more adaptive to the needs of the learner and requires that the learner be intimately involved in directing the approach to learning and application.

Hase and Kenyon (2003) asserted that learning only happens when the adult learner interacts with new knowledge and skills, integrating them into his or her experience. Hase and Kenyon further suggested that action research was especially well suited to support a heutagogical approach, stating "action research allows experimentation with real world experience where learning is in the hands of the participants" (Hase & Kenyon, 2007, p. 113). Proponents of the action research approach suggest that learning on the part of individuals and organizations is enhanced through a process of action and reflection (Lewin, 1951, as cited in Hase & Kenyon, 2000). This concept closely aligns with Revans's (2011) action research derivative, which he called action learning. In action learning, the focus is on bringing together a team of people to analyze problems, take action, and learn through reflection on results. Thus, action learning supports the learning of individuals as well as organizations (Marquardt, 2011).

Application of Learning Theories

A pedagogical approach has some merit in an adult learning setting. Knowles, Holton, and Swanson (2005) asserted that pedagogical approaches with high structure, clarity, and clear performance expectations could be effective when used appropriately in adult learning design. I applied my evolving understanding of learning theory to my work at City University of Seattle in the design of the capstone program for the Master of Science (MS) in Project Management. The program had previously employed a thesis as the capstone activity for students. In the redesigned action learning capstone, students instead assembled a team in their workplace to help them focus on a defined problem, and then they developed cycles of project work to implement in the workplace, reflected on the results of their efforts, and continued to replan and adjust their project approach.

Marquardt's (2011) model of action learning, based on the earlier work of Lewin (1951), Revans (2011), Carr and Kemmis (2003), and Hase and Kenyon (2007), was well suited for use in a project management program and was deemed to be a relevant and applicable model to follow in the capstone for the MS degree. E-portfolios were added to the design of the capstone for two reasons: to provide a tool to support students in application and demonstration of learning, and to support the university's requirements for providing evidence of outcomes to accreditation bodies. E-portfolios have been recognized as tools to support student learning as well as outcome assessment initiatives (Sweat-Guy & Buzzetto-More, 2007). Therefore, I selected the action learning and e-portfolio methods for their alignment with andragogical and heutagogical learning theories and their suitability to the curriculum and the needs of the students in this particular program.

The model deployed in the design of the capstone course was developed based on the work of Wiggins and McTighe (2005), which connects desired learning outcomes to methods for assessment and learning activities. Table 1 illustrates an example of how one of the components of this capstone (the e-portfolio) aligns andragogical and heutagogical learning methods.

Table 1. *Alignment of E-Portfolio with Learning Methods*

Required Assessment	Andragogical Methods	Heutagogical Methods
E-Portfolio	• Students base their action learning e-portfolio on an authentic project in a setting of their choice. • Students may create multiple portfolios for multiple purposes. • Assessment criteria are shared with students so that they understand how they will be measured.	• Students can choose to meet minimum requirements or be creative in the design of their portfolio. • Students direct the update of the portfolio as they take courses, selecting artifacts to demonstrate their best work. • Students complete reflections on their learning and adjust their project as needed throughout the capstone.

The andragogical methods described in Table 1 support the adult learner's need for relevance by situating the action learning within the context of the student's choice of settings (usually the student's current workplace). Students also have the opportunity to create multiple portfolios for various purposes, such as to support a job search or promote their work within their organization, further supporting the adult need for relevance and meaning. Further, the adult learner's need for inclusion and competence are supported by providing clear assessment criteria to guide the student's work. Heutagogical principles are also embedded in the action learning capstone through self-direction and reflection opportunities. In short, students have the choice of simply completing the action learning capstone as a course assignment or leveraging it as a career-enhancing opportunity. They also have the choice of which artifacts (assignments) from their MS program reflect their best work. Reflection and change based on what is learned are also integral to the heutagogical design of the action learning capstone.

Conclusion

The example described above demonstrates the benefit of combining andragogical and heutagogical learning methods to management education. This benefit was further reinforced by the clear alignment of the relevant assessments (andragogy), experimentation and reflection (heutagogy), and the evidence of student learning. During the design of the action learning capstone, I incorporated the theories and associated methods that were best aligned to the needs of my students.

Understanding and applying learning theories and associated methods is the primary work of educators. Being open to new ideas while also remaining grounded in established theories and methods is good professional practice.

References

Carr, W., & Kemmis, S. (2003). *Becoming critical: Education, knowledge, and action research*. New York, NY: Routledge.

Duffy, T. M., & Jonassen, D. H. (2013). *Constructivism and the technology of instruction: A conversation* (pp. 1–16). New York, NY: Routledge.

Gruenewald, D. A. (2013). The best of both worlds: A critical pedagogy of place. *Educational Researcher, 32*(4), 3–12.

Hase, S., & Kenyon, C. (2007). Heutagogy: A child of complexity theory. *Complicity: An International Journal of Complexity and Education, 4*(1), 111–118.

Hase, S., & Kenyon, C. (2003). Heutagogy and developing capable people and capable workplaces: Strategies for dealing with complexity. [Paper presented at The Changing Face of Work and Learning Conference, Alberta, Canada.]

Hase, S., & Kenyon, C. (2000). *From andragogy to heutagogy.* Retrieved April 5, 2010, from http:// ultibase.rmit.edu.au/Articles/dec00/hase2.htm

Holmes, B., Tangney, B., Fitzgibbon, A., Savage, T., & Mehan, S. (2001). Communal constructivism: Students constructing learning for as well as with others. *Proceedings of the 12th International Conference of the Society for Information Technology and Teacher Education* (pp. 3114–3119). Chesapeake, VA: AACE.

Knowles, M. S. (1970). *The modern practice of adult education: Andragogy versus pedagogy.* New York, NY: Associated Press.

Knowles, M. S., Holton, E. F., & Swanson, R. A. (2005). *The adult learner: The definitive classic in adult education and human resource development* (6th ed.). San Diego, CA: Butterworth-Heinemann.

Lewin, K. (1951). *Field theory in social science.* New York, NY: Harper.

Marquardt, J. (2011). *Optimizing the power of action learning: Real-time strategies for developing leaders, building teams and transforming organizations* (2nd ed.). Palo Alto, CA: Davies-Black Publishing.

Palloff, R. M., & Pratt, K. (2009). *Building online learning communities: Effective strategies for the virtual classroom* (2nd ed.). San Francisco, CA: John Wiley & Sons.

Piaget, J. (1974). *The grasp of consciousness: Action and concept in the young child.* Cambridge, MA: Harvard University Press.

Revans, R. (2011). *ABC of action learning.* Surrey, England: Gower Publishing Limited.

Sweat-Guy, R., & Buzzetto-More, N. (2007). A comparative analysis of common e-portfolio platforms and available features. *Issues in Informing Science and Information Technology Education, 5*(1), 327–342. Retrieved January 30, 2010, from http://proceedings.informingscience.org/InSITE2007/IISITv4p327-342Guy255.pdf

Wiggins, G. P., & McTighe, J. (2005). *Understanding by design* (2nd ed.). Alexandria, VA: Association for Supervision and Curriculum Development.

Wink, J., & Putney, L. (2002). *A vision of Vygotsky.* Boston, MA: Allyn & Bacon.

Wlodkowski, R. J. (2008). *Enhancing adult motivation to learn: A comprehensive guide for teaching all adults* (3rd ed.). San Francisco, CA: John Wiley & Sons.

Practica: Practical Learning Outside of the Classroom

Jean Ann French, DBA, *School of Management*

Abstract

Dewey's (1938) theory of "learn by doing" is the underpinning pedagogy for the practica course design discussed in this chapter. Experiential learning and other approaches similar to practica are explored for business curricula. CityU's instructional design and approach to practica is clearly defined, and research demonstrates how successfully learners are engaged in a relevant manner for real-life application of business management concepts and learned skills. Additional research provides corroboration of a global trend in adopting this method of practical learning.

Introduction

Practica (the plural of practicum), experiential learning, service learning, performance-based learning, problem-based learning, internship, on-the-job training, integrated business core, and work-integrated learning are related pedagogical approaches. All are based on Dewey's (1938) theory of "learn by doing"; however, each "learning" can mean something different.

Educational theorist John Dewey suggested that education can be an active, involved process through which learning can be achieved not just by observing or reading about something but by doing something with the phenomenon being studied (Hutchings & Wutzdorff, 1988). Dewey believed that by putting the learner directly in touch with the subject of study, reflection on the experience would result in learning (Keeton & Tate, 1978). The pedagogy is experiential learning, which is the foundation for each method of delivery identified. The variation of terms stem from which decade the concept originated, the authors, the universities where employed, and often the industry of affiliation. Since all terms describe experiential learning, they are often used interchangeably. Practicum is an umbrella term very similar to internship for acquiring "practical" experience. Shariff and Saad (2010) determined that a meaningful internship or practicum experience for today's business students is vital for both the institutions and industry.

Wesch (2009) challenged the traditional teacher-centered approach, arguing that students today retrieve knowledge much differently than even five years ago, accessing through laptops, cell phones, and iPods. Traditional classrooms "built to re-enforce the top-down authoritative knowledge of the teacher are now enveloped by a cloud of ubiquitous digital information where knowledge is made, not found." Behind this massive shift away from such a narrow focus on information, "there is still the question of 'what' is to be learned" (Wesch, 2009, para. 2).

Purpose of Practica

Practica are designed to prepare the student for the work environment and provide documented, practical experience that can be used in a professional portfolio for future employment. Empirical research performed on business school graduates revealed that those with internship experiences tend to be hired more quickly, receive a higher starting salary, and report greater job satisfaction than their non-internship counterparts (Knemeyer & Murphy, 2002). The practicum at City University of Seattle

(CityU) is similar to an internship in that the student is exposed to real-life problems in a company or nonprofit. However, one significant difference is that the MBA practicum student serves as a consultant rather than a short-term employee (intern). Silva (2008) stated that decades of research revealed that there is no reason to separate the acquisition of learning core content and basic skills from more advanced analytical and thinking skills.

Related Strategies and Activities

Before the practicum can be defined for CityU, it is appropriate for all related methods within this pedagogy to be identified. The foundation established with these terms is that experiential learning, service learning, performance-based learning, and problem-based learning are learning approaches or strategies, while internships, on-the-job training, integrated business core, work-integrated learning, and practica are the *activities* of learning. In an effort to explain the various methods of learning as they pertain to university-level business education, each related pedagogical approach is reviewed by the practica strategies and activities as they pertain to CityU's program.

Practica Strategies

Habermas (1971) introduced a domain of knowledge called "emancipatory," which states that through critical self-reflection, knowledge is gained, which is seen as a component of the constructivist paradigm. The following strategies offer the student the opportunity for critical and self-reflective processes that can elevate them to Habermas's level of emancipatory knowledge. An explanation is given for how the strategies are employed by CityU's practicum courses.

Kolb (1984) defined experiential learning as knowledge that is continuously gained through both personal and environmental experiences: (a) the learner must be willing to "involve themselves fully and openly without bias in new experiences"; (b) the learner must be able to "reflect on and to observe their experiences from many perspectives"; (c) the learner must be able to "create concepts that integrate their observations into logically sound theories"; and (d) the learner must be able to "use these theories to solve problems" (p. 30). Experiential learning is the foundation of the practicum experience at CityU.

Jacoby (1996) created a working definition of service learning as a form of experiential education that addresses human and community needs together with structured opportunities intentionally designed to promote learning and development. Different forms of service learning, such as community service and volunteerism are offered by colleges and universities as a vehicle for creating a learning environment that links campus-based learning experiences with the larger community (Strand, Marullo, Cutforth, Stoeker, & Donohue, 2003). The service learning strategy is often used as a practicum project with a nonprofit community organization or a department within CityU.

According to Nickel and Osborn (2010), performance-based learners are informed of performance expectations in advance of instruction. CityU students are operating under performance goals established by the curriculum design.

Problem-based learning is an instructional method in which students learn through facilitated problem solving. Student learning centers on a complex problem that does not have a single correct answer. Students work individually or in collaborative groups to identify what they need to learn to solve a problem (Hmelo-Silver, 2004). A practicum project often includes a problem that the student researches, analyzes, and resolves through a proposed solution.

Practica Activities

Practica activities are best described by Mezirow's (1991) learning domains: (a) instrumental, the gaining of technical knowledge and (b) communicative, the gaining of practical knowledge, which he borrowed from Habermas's (1971) three domains of knowledge. The following learning activities are less reflective in nature and more physically engaging.

Internships are a practical activity for learning within a period of four to twelve months where a student performs work for an organization. Often considered as OJT (on-the-job training) for white-collar jobs. Some interns are paid with a stipend, while many are unpaid. Practica activities are not day-to-day work assignments, rather the student "acts" as a consultant to an organization and does not "work" for an employer like an intern. Practicum activities include research, analysis, and writing.

On-the-job training is designed to help students acquire practical knowledge and develop desirable work attitudes and skills (Arroyo, 2011). This approach aligns with Mezirow's (1991) communicative learning domain. On-the-job training is frequently used for "hands-on" job functions such as engineering, hotel and restaurant management, and interior design, while the practicum student is not "on the job."

The integrated business core method of practical learning lets students run businesses as part of an integrated experience. Since the early to mid-1990s, several universities have integrated business core activities into their curriculum (Walker & Black, 2000), attempting to bridge the gap between academia and the world of work (Bell, 2010). The integrated business core is often composed of four fundamental business classes: Marketing, Finance, Organizational Behavior, and Operations/ Supply Chain Management. CityU's program has many similarities to integrated business core, but it is not as structured, nor does the student "work" on-site. The experiential learning component of a cooperative education or work-integrated learning program can complement classroom learning, and education thereby becomes a more holistic, three-party endeavor in which students, employers, and educational faculty work together to produce graduates who are more work-ready (Eames & Cates, 2011; Groenewald, Drysdale, Chiupka, & Johnston, 2011). Note: Other terms used interchangeably with work-integrated learning are cooperative learning and service learning (Freudenberg, Brimble, & Vyvyan, 2010). A typical feature of work-integrated learning is a partnership between an external organization and an educational institution in an effort to increase employability as well as practical learning exposure for the student, a potential employee in the making (Boud & Solomon, 2001). CityU's practicum courses are quite similar; however, CityU does not currently have formalized partnerships with organizations for the purpose of the practicum, nor does the student "work" at the business.

The remainder of the chapter is focused on how CityU utilizes practica in its MBA program. The strategies employed by CityU are performance-based in establishing goals and problem-based for researching and recommending solutions.

Practica at CityU

The objective of the CityU practicum is to provide an opportunity to apply what the student has learned throughout the MBA program. It is also an opportunity for the student to select an area of specialty to gain additional skills through a focused, time-limited project that adds value to a company or service organization. Throughout the process, the student employs a performance analysis approach to an identified, real world problem, whereby the student analyzes a business environment, identifies the root cause of an existing problem, implements a solution, and evaluates its impact (CityU, 2008).

Practica are formal sessions or programs that attempt to incorporate the basic professional skills demanded by an employer in an independent online setting. The practicum is often a limited project in a professional environment that provides hands-on experience in the field or industry chosen by the student. The client deliverable is focused on a project that could be implemented by the client. This session is closely monitored by the professor and a client contact called an on-site supervisor (CityU, 2008).

The Curriculum at CityU

The MBA practicum at CityU takes place over two quarters. In the first quarter the student identifies the client and crafts the practicum agreement with the practicum site supervisor with oversight from the practicum advisor, the instructor.

The goals of the CityU practicum involve (a) utilizing the MBA program content in challenging and meaningful ways; (b) applying knowledge, skills, experiences, and strengths to the work environment; (c) enhancing an electronic portfolio of MBA program accomplishments; and (d) developing professional skills and networking contacts.

The criteria for the practicum include (a) the practicum must provide a new and significant learning opportunity; (b) the practicum must be related to the academic degree and should integrate previous learning with a new learning experience; and (c) the practicum student must be supported by appropriate supervision (CityU, 2008).

The Practicum

The practicum requires the student to act as a consultant to an organization to research, study, analyze, assess, and ultimately recommend or report the findings. The report is the final deliverable, and the student does not produce or implement the recommendations. The practicum project is doable and narrow in scope. The student can take on a research or analysis project that the company or nonprofit does not have the staff or funding to accomplish, but the project is not critical to the operations and success of the organization.

Preferably, the practicum is not conducted at the student's place of business. There are certainly exceptions, which are approved on a case-by-case basis. If a practicum is available at the workplace, it must be in another department with a site supervisor who is not the student's supervisor, directly or indirectly.

A practicum analyzes secondary research data, as gathering primary research data is often too time-consuming and begins to take on the characteristics of an internship. Marketing plans are the more popular projects and can be narrowed down to segments, such as Competitor Analysis, Target Market Review, SWOT, Promotions, etc.

The Students

Currently the method is applied at the master's level in the School of Management over two quarters for a total of twenty weeks as a capstone course with the population being mature students. Students who have a specific emphasis, such as finance, marketing, or project management do not have the option for the practicum, as the capstone course applies only to an MBA without an emphasis.

The Practicum Advisor (Instructor)

The two-quarter practica are conducted in a fluid manner with the instructor being continuous and the quarters being sequential. The responsibilities of the instructor who oversees the work on the practicum from the university's perspective include:

- helping with logistical, procedural, and other issues related to the practicum
- providing final approval of site and project
- approving practicum agreement and nondisclosure agreement with signature required
- grading practicum report and report presentation
- providing assistance and advice (CityU, 2008)

The Client Contact—Practicum Site Supervisor

The practicum site supervisor plays a vital role in the success and quality of a practicum. The supervisor should be an experienced professional who has been selected by the site in collaboration with the university to oversee and evaluate the practicum student. The practicum site supervisor maintains regular contact with the student and should expect to spend one hour per week, on average, over the course of the practicum project.

The following is a general list of practicum site supervisor responsibilities. This list may change or grow, based on the planned practicum.

- Personal interview with the practicum student to discuss parameters of possible project that the student can undertake. It is important to discuss the site's contribution to the practicum student's learning, how supervision will be provided, and time commitments at the site.
- Informs the student of all relevant personnel policies and procedures.
- Meets with the practicum student during the first weeks of the practicum and develops the practicum agreement.
- Provides activities that are both challenging and consistent with the goals of the student.
- Provides the practicum student with any necessary training related to the experience. The training aspect of the program may also include relevant reading material, videotapes, or company manuals.
- Schedules regular meetings with the practicum student. These meetings provide an opportunity to evaluate the progress of the practicum student and to make appropriate adjustments. The

practicum Time and Activity Log should also be reviewed and signed by the supervisor at these meetings.

- Completes the practicum evaluation for practicum site supervisors at the end of the project (CityU, 2008).

The Client Selection Strategies

All students bring varied academic backgrounds and interests to the practicum. The student is required to identify the practicum site, also known as "the client." Students are responsible for creating a meaningful practicum. The careful selection of a practicum site is the most significant step in this creative process. Selection of the site must be based on the learning opportunities that it can provide related to the individual student's emphasis, and on the availability of appropriate supervision. Projects can often be difficult to find, and it is possible the students will need a long lead time to conduct the search (CityU, 2008). The instructor should be prepared to guide students in the right direction.

Selection may be done by pursuing community contacts such as classmates, instructors, current or previous employers, family, or friends. In many cases, students are aware of opportunities in the community. The practicum advisor, the instructor, is available to assist in determining the appropriateness of the site(s) under consideration (CityU, 2008). *The practicum advisor must approve any practicum site.* Students are encouraged to use and develop their own network of contacts for locating their sites.

Students may establish a practicum at the business or agency where employed. If so, the following three criteria must be met: (a) students are performing in roles other than their usual job; (b) new learning is related to their degree; and (c) supervision is provided by someone other than their current supervisor or manager.

The Documents

Documentation of the practicum is critical and serves as an essential learning experience. The nondisclosure agreement demonstrates a high level of professionalism, while the practicum agreement serves as a contract and a memo of understanding (MOU). In either case, the student is protected from potential misunderstandings if the documents are properly executed. The documents required for CityU's MBA practicum over the course of two quarters are:

Nondisclosure Agreement—This document is intended to ensure the practicum site supervisor that any data or materials used during the practicum will not be shared with any other organization without the site's permission.

Practicum Agreement—A contract between the student, the City University practicum advisor, and the practicum site supervisor. The agreement serves as a starting point for the project, clarifies expectations, and formalizes the process. Through the agreement, goals, objectives, and expectations are established for the pending practicum. The agreement also aids later in evaluating their experience.

Activity and Time Log—Should be completed each time the student works on anything related to the practicum. Logs will be maintained and turned in at the end of the practicum as part of the final practicum report, and the practicum site supervisor should sign the form. Any activities, such as research, communications, meetings, and computer work that pertain to the practicum are recorded.

Client Deliverable—Agreed upon by the practicum site supervisor and the student. It can be a report of any nature that is accompanied by a PowerPoint presentation to the supervisor alone, or to a group. Note: The client deliverable is not submitted to the instructor.

The Practicum Report—Summarizes and assesses the work that was completed during the practicum, which includes (1) description of the project and a problem statement, (2) summary analysis of steps that were taken to ensure that the practicum would address the site's needs, (3) possible solutions that were considered and ultimately selected, and (4) evaluation and overall impression of the practicum and its long-range effect on the selected site.

The Practicum Presentation—Summarizes the contents of the report and is presented to the instructor (CityU, 2008).

The Lessons Learned

The lessons learned through the implementation of these practica experiences can be synthesized into three categories: (a) selection of practica sites, (b) selection of projects, and (c) the students' experiences. The lessons learned outlined below include what works, recommendations on what to avoid in the selection process, and direct feedback from students about their experiences.

The Lessons Learned: Practica Sites

Practica sites are as varied as the students when it comes to location, industry, and size. They range from an Internet start-up company to major corporations such as Microsoft and Boeing, along with many nonprofit organizations. The lesson learned from start-ups and smaller companies centers around the stage of development. If a start-up business is past its first year and is organized sufficiently to accept a "practicing" MBA student to analyze an aspect of the business, then the company could be a good candidate as a practicum site. A business that is within the first year of organization is probably too young to spend the time supervising a practicum student, and the work that needs to be accomplished is likely to be operationally critical to its success. The student is learning and should not be put in the position of managing a project that could negatively affect the firm's assets.

The other end of the spectrum includes large corporations such as Nintendo, Microsoft, and Boeing. It is highly unlikely that a non-employee of these employers would have an opportunity to serve as a "practicing consultant." CityU has many students from major employers and several practica projects have been quite successful. To honor the client selection strategies of CityU's practicum program, the student must take on a project outside of his or her immediate department and avoid direct and indirect supervisory relationships. One of the benefits for the major corporation is an opportunity for cross training, expanding the knowledge base of an existing employee, and a fresh perspective from someone outside of the department.

Nonprofit organizations are one of the better options as a practicum site because they are usually understaffed and short on funding for research and business analysis. Nonprofit groups are also accustomed to overseeing volunteers. The downside of this site is that volunteers usually "produce" a service for them, while the CityU student needs to act as a consultant to research, analyze, and make recommendations on a project.

Public organizations such as schools, government offices, state and county services, and political organizations have historically had a more difficult time serving as a good option since time frames and schedules are often not adaptable to the student's two-quarter class. Other challenges involve privacy, policies, and risks. CityU (as a private university) has hosted a few students for their practica and has been quite accommodating.

The Lessons Learned: Practica Projects

The instructor plays a significant role when reviewing and approving the practicum project. It is imperative to keep the scope focused and manageable during a two-quarter time frame, which includes finding, identifying, researching, analyzing, and delivering the project.

Projects that are manageable with proper parameters include a review of existing business plans, marketing plans, labor analyses, customer base assessments, operations analyses, workflow analyses, product development costs, market analyses, financial trend analyses, cost of resources/materials analyses, strategic plans, and systems analyses.

Some projects are not suited for a "practicing" student consultant due to financial liability, legal responsibilities, and privacy issues for the company and the student. Types of projects that are not recommended are full business plans that include sourcing the information, marketing plans with deliverables such as logo design and brochures, and contract processes due to legal liabilities. Risk factors include students' liability to the organization for results of findings and implementation of the program by the corporation. It is critical for the instructor to scrutinize the Practicum Agreement between the student and the site supervisor, as it is virtually a contract. Therefore, a section on limitations with terms and conditions are necessary to protect the student.

The Lessons Learned: Student Experiences

The practicum is the solidification of course work theories that are put into direct application. Whether the recommendations are adopted or the study proves that the project is not doable, the student has a valuable learning experience in real time in the real world. Students have written glowing recommendations regarding the practicum course of study stating that it should be a requirement for all graduates and that it fully utilized all courses of study with direct application. Following are quotes from students who valued the practicum course:

"I found this class to be the most valuable course throughout my entire MBA program at CityU. I loved this whole practicum idea, and I learned more from my practicum than anything else. It was actually life changing (being able to take what I've learned throughout the program and use it to improve a real-life organization that I care about)." —Anonymous, Fall 2010

"I have learned a tremendous amount working through the practicum execution with Vine Maple Place (VMP) as my object. I have been looking at the nonprofit viewpoint and comparing it with the for-profit viewpoint that I am accustomed to, as well as applying the concepts that I have learned during my MBA career to the different business model. It has been exciting to work with VMP and their changes of direction. This has been an excellent experience for me, and I can definitely carry it forward in my business life." — Anonymous, Fall 2011

"The recommendations I made are being used in my organization. It has really opened doors for me and allowed visibility into higher levels of the organization. The practicum increased my confidence in my abilities and what I could contribute to Microsoft. I think that the practicum should be a requirement, not an option." —Anonymous, Summer 2010

"My feasibility study looked at improving quality standards for two Boeing vendors, one local and the other in Japan, to capture a larger market share. The practicum experience was excellent—a true way to apply MBA learning to a real-world environment that I found to be very beneficial." —Anonymous, Fall 2011

"These last two quarters have been challenging to say the least. I have had to operate independently and initiate and lead meetings with both my advisor at CityU and practicum site supervisor at Nintendo. I've grown from the experience and think the program should continue at CityU." — Anonymous, Winter 2013

These statements are evidence of success with better visibility for the students' employers after the project, and for others the practicum serves to enhance their work experiences for prospective employment.

Conclusion

Student feedback has confirmed that practicum projects are useful for teaching performance-based learning. When a student can complete a course and a degree plan feeling ready to take on a new career with new options, then the instructor and university can be confident that the curriculum is successful. Based on the feedback from practicum students since 2008, CityU's MBA practicum program has been successful and is meeting the needs of the students.

This study indicates that experiential learning outside of the classroom is a valuable commodity. Staff members at one of CityU's partner universities, University of Southern Queensland, share similar conclusions. The career services staff members recognize a correspondence between their programs of career development learning and work-integrated learning. This perception of correspondence is interpreted as a positive sign of the pragmatic implementation of theory in the practice of career development learning in higher education. Further, they interpret this relationship as a dimension of career development learning contributing to the overall objective of graduate employability through its curricular influence upon work-integrated learning (McIlveen, Brooks, Lichtenberg, Smith, Torjul, & Tyler, 2011).

Future improvements to CityU's practicum program would be to formalize partnerships with corporations and nonprofits for practicum projects similar to the integrated business core and work-integrated learning programs offered by other universities, rather than resting the responsibility upon students because the task is sometimes overwhelming and is quite time-consuming. By enlisting corporate partners for the practicum, a more uniform experience could be offered and the quality of the opportunity and supervision would be ensured.

References

Arroyo, R. A. (2011). Practicum performance in Singapore and the Philippines of hospitality students in a state university. *Asian Journal of Business Governance Business Education Section, 1*(1), 145–166.

Bell, C. (2010). The value of the integrated business core experience: Perceptions of recent graduates from Brigham Young University, Idaho [Paper 52]. *Department of Educational Administration: Theses, Dissertations, and Student Research*. Lincoln: University of Nebraska.

Boud, D., & Solomon, N. (2001). *Work-based learning: A new higher education?* New York, NY: McGraw-Hill Irwin.

CityU. (2008). *Practicum handbook for the MBA program*. Bellevue, WA: City University, Seattle.

Dewey, J. (1938). *Experience and education*. New York, NY: Collier Books.

Eames, C., & Cates, C. (2011). Theories of learning in cooperative and work-integrated education. In R. K. Coll & K. E. Zegwaard (Eds.), *International handbook for cooperative and work-integrated education: International perspectives of theory, research, and practice* (pp. 41–52). Lowell, MA: World Association for Cooperative Education.

Freudenberg, B., Brimble, M., & Vyvyan, V. (2010). The penny drops: Can work integrated learning improve students' learning? *e-Journal of Business Education & Scholarship of Teaching, 4*(1), 42–61.

Groenewald, T., Drysdale, M., Chiupka, C., & Johnston, N. (2011). Toward a definition and models of practice for cooperative and work-integrated education. In R. K. Coll & K. E. Zegwaard (Eds.), *International handbook for cooperative and work-integrated education: International perspectives of theory, research and practice* (pp. 17–24). Lowell, MA: World Association for Cooperative Education.

Habermas, J. (1971). *Knowledge and human interests*. Boston: Beacon Press.

Hmelo-Silver, C. E. (2004). Problem-based learning: What and how do students learn? *Educational Psychology Review, 16*(3), 235–266.

Hutchings, P., & Wutzdorff, A. (1988). Experiential learning across the curriculum: Assumptions and principles. *New Directions for Teaching and Learning, 35*, 5–19.

Jacoby, B. (1996). Service-learning in today's higher education. In B. Jacoby (Ed.), *Service-learning in higher education* (pp. 3–25). San Francisco, CA: Jossey-Bass.

Keeton, M. T., & Tate, P. J. (1978). *Learning by experience—what, why, how*. San Francisco, CA: Jossey-Bass.

Knemeyer, A. M., & Murphy, P. R. (2002). Logistics internships: employer and students perspectives. *International Journal of Physical Distribution and Logistics Management, 32*(2), 135–152.

Kolb, D. A. (1984). *Experiential learning: Experiences as the source of learning and development*. Inglewood Cliffs, NJ: Prentice-Hall.

McIlveen, P., Brooks, S., Lichtenberg, A., Smith, M., Torjul, P., & Tyler, J. (2011). Perceptions of career development learning and work-integrated learning in Australian higher education. *Australian Journal of Career Development, 20*(1), 32–41.

Mezirow, J. (1991). *Transformative dimensions of adult learning*. San Francisco, CA: Jossey-Bass.

Nichol, R. and Osborn, L. (2009). WIDS and Performance Based Learning. Waunakee, WI: Wisconsin Technical College System Foundation. *Worldwide Instructional Design System (WIDS) Division*.

Shariff, S. M., & Saad, S. (2010). Continual improvement in outcome-based education (OBE) for industrial practicum training program. *Business Management Quarterly Review, 1*(1), 41–51.

Silva, E. (2008). Measuring skills for the 21st century. *Education Sector Reports*. Washington, D.C.: Education Sector.

Strand, K., Marullo, S., Cutforth, N., Stoeker, R., & Donohue, P. (2003). *Community-based research in higher education*. San Francisco, CA: Jossey-Bass.

Walker, K. B., & Black, E. L. (2000). Reengineering the undergraduate business core curriculum: Aligning business schools with business for improved performance. *Business Process Management Journal, 6*(3), 194.

Wesch, M. (2009). From knowledgeable to knowledge-able: Learning in the new media environments. *New Technologies and the Scholarship of Teaching and Learning*. Washington, D.C.: Center for New Designs in Learning and Scholarship.

Professional Association Attendance as a Course Requirement

Erik Fretheim, PhD, *The Technology Institute*

Abstract

This chapter looks at the value of including a structured attendance at a professional association event as a mandatory course requirement. The requirement is compared to other approaches and how they support soft-skill course and program outcomes that are sometimes challenging to support in the curriculum. The paper discusses how the assignment can be structured and how the structure supports the intended outcomes.

Professional Association Attendance as a Course Requirement

At City University of Seattle (CityU), one of the institutional learning goals is that CityU graduates are lifelong learners. This, or a similar goal, is common among colleges and universities and for specific program outcomes. The challenge is finding ways to attain this goal, which needs to be obtained by introducing students to tools of learning and building beneficial habits. These habits cannot be artificial or unique to the academic environment or else they will simply fade outside of the schoolhouse doors. One technique to achieve this goal in a sustainable manner is to require the use of attendance at a networking event of a professional association. If well structured, this assignment has the potential for a significant impact on the student.

Professional Associations—Recognized Value to Students

Schools have long recognized the value of student and faculty interaction with professional associations. Faculty membership and participation have been recognized as a contribution to scholarship and have been a factor in faculty ratings and even consideration for promotion and tenure. Some schools, such as the University of California (University of California, 2006) use faculty memberships in professional associations as a factor in assessing the attainment of institutional goals. Weber State University, in its Health Information Technology Program, requires, as a part of faculty development, "at least one State or National HIM professional association meeting attendance" (Weber State University, 2012). Other universities recognize the value of faculty participation through the granting of time to attend professional association meetings and even the reimbursement of the costs of attendance and membership.

The value of student participation with professional associations is also well established in the educational community. Many universities host and encourage membership in student chapters and sections of professional associations directly related to their programs, such as the Institute of Electrical and Electronic Engineers (IEEE), the Association of Computing Machinery (ACM), The Accounting Association, Guerrilla Marketing Society, American Psychological Association (APA), etc. These student sections are "[b]ridging the gap between the academic and professional worlds" (Boston University School of Management, n.d.).

Generally, these student societies tend in one of two directions, student emulation of a professional environment and alumni/university friend networking-focused. The student emulation type of involvement often includes faculty and outside involvement. The focus is on projects and activities that put the students into leadership or other roles where they can practice their academic skills, often in a competitive environment. Sometimes these associations are even incorporated within a for-credit course. While these are highly valuable to the students as a learning experience and also provide them with an excellent source for networking for their next job, their value in instilling lifelong learning is more limited. In addition, the number of students participating in these experiences may be limited.

These types of activities are viewed by the student as a student experience, not as a lifelong learning experience. Once the competition is over, students leave the university, or they secure a job, thus the objective has been met and the incentive for continued involvement fades. Once students are in the "real world" applying what they learned in their emulation, they are in a new phase and no longer have the need to emulate; the activity is put aside.

The networking-focused student associations are also a valuable tool for students. In these organizations, the typical meeting features a guest speaker on a topic of interest and time designated for networking. Alumni and friends of the university are invited to these events and are encouraged to network and mingle with the students. In the best cases, such as in the Master of Accountancy Program at the Villanova University School of Business (Villanova University, School of Business, n.d.), students take a Networking Skills Workshop and then attend the alumni networking event as a part of a required professional development program.

As with the emulation approach, alumni/friends networking can be of great value to students, both in attending learning events outside of the classroom, in beginning to develop some networking skills and in potentially finding a first job. However, this approach also falls somewhat short of instilling a habit of lifelong learning; in the students' view it as an academic or preparatory activity that lasts only through graduation, or perhaps returning as alumni, rather than the beginning of a continuing professional habit.

Outside of these more formal programs, universities take steps to involve their students in professional association activities. Most, at a minimum, encourage student membership in professional associations. In some programs, such as the PsyD program in Clinical Psychology at the University of the Rockies (University of the Rockies, n.d.), students are required to join the professional association as student members. Many schools with mandatory class attendance allow students to attend professional associations in lieu of class. The Graduate School of Education at Pennsylvania State University even provides assistance, up to $150 for twenty students annually to attend conferences and other professional association activities (Graduate School of Education, n.d.). All of this is very positive for the student, however, it doesn't translate to all students; much of what they do is left to the initiative of the students themselves and the tie into continuing association is limited.

Given the recognition of the value of professional associations for students in continuing their lifetime of learning and development, it is important to look for a means which involves the full student population and which also builds a habit they will continue once they leave the halls of academia. To do this, attendance at professional associations as a mandatory assignment in selected courses is a viable option. To make the assignment more effective though, structure and reflection need to be added to the exercise. Two examples from two different courses will be used to demonstrate:

Example Assignments

The first example is from a course in Global Marketing at Northwest University. In this course the students were given the assignment:

> Attend two or more meetings of an international trade organization or similar event with a global orientation. During the course of the meeting, talk to and obtain a business card from at least five different attendees at each of the meetings. Following the meetings, provide a copy of each business card and a paragraph or two describing each individual. In the information explain why the person was attending the event, what the person does, and ways in which you may interact with the person in a business capacity in the future (Fretheim, 2010).

The requirements of the assignment were designed to ensure the maximum possible involvement of the student in the meeting. For example, it is unlikely that a student could obtain the cards or information about the people met without actually talking with someone. The minimum required number of cards ensures that the student doesn't merely connect with one person for the duration of the event. The exercise also reinforces the content of the course by requiring that the event be global in nature.

This assignment was conducted from 2005 to 2010 in an evening MBA course composed primarily of adult learners. In addition to the instruction, students were given a list of about twenty-five events during the course of the quarter and sources for discovering additional events. During classes, there was instruction and discussion on networking and its value as a business practice. Much of this was in the context of global cultures and being sensitive to issues such as the manner of address, the placement of the feet, and formalities of presenting cards in some cultures.

The second example is from the capstone courses in the Technology Institute at City University of Seattle. These courses, and some of their predecessors, have had an assignment that required students to participate in professional networking meetings since 2011. The requirement follows:

> Each quarter students will be required to attend a minimum of two professional organization meetings or functions related to the student's study. Examples of professional organization include IEEE, IEEE Computer Society, ACM, IAPSC, ISSA, etc. One of these two meetings may be a general business, or business networking meeting or function. The meetings or functions must be face-to-face engagements. However, in exceptional circumstances (deployed to remote locations, on assignment in Antarctica, etc.) the instructor may approve the substitution of online activities on an individual basis.

> After attending the event, the student will prepare a brief summary of the experience. The summary must include: Meeting Identification—Title, Date, and Location. Attendance—How many? What types of people? How many did you personally speak to? General Description (one to two paragraphs)—What was the purpose of the activity? Did anything exciting happen? Reflection (one to two paragraphs)—What did you take away from the meeting? How can/did participation contribute to your professional career? Would you attend another meeting (why/why not)? (City University of Seattle, 2012–13)

This assignment differs slightly from the MBA course assignment. First, there is no specific target given for the number of people with whom the student needed to interact. This is part of an overall orientation slightly away from networking and more toward professional development and continuous learning. The need to talk with people is still present though and is expressed through the questions the student is expected to respond to in their summary.

This assignment also varies in that it is generally given in an online course with limited mandatory discussions. The remainder of the course is used for student teams to work on the design, implementation, and testing of capstone projects. As a result, while there is some online discussion on networking and events, the discussion is more limited.

As with the other assignment, students are provided with a list of potential events and information on how to locate others. In this course the latter is usually more important as students are located around the country and around the world. Despite being an online course, the emphasis is on face-to-face events. One potential future change is to add a requirement for a third event in an online environment.

Like the other assignment, this one makes a point of the events and associations being related to the student's area of study. This is important from a networking and professional development perspective, and it puts many students outside of their comfort zone. These students may be enthusiastic about attending a general event with their friends and peers from their current experience, but in going to an event related to their studies, it begins the transformation process of students seeing themselves as a part of the profession they are studying.

Finally, the requested summary in the newer assignment is more reflective and focused on the event as a whole rather than the individuals encountered at the event. This is both more reflective of the nature of the types of students, and of the intent to strengthen the focus on professional development.

Comparisons to Other Approaches

The first observation is that both of these are mandatory assignments. While universities have long encouraged student attendance at professional activities, there is a significant difference between mandatory and optional approaches. With an optional approach, the students who do attend are those who already have the strongest self-confidence and willingness to try new adventures. Those who can benefit the most, from discovering something they may not on their own, from breaking out of their shell, or from developing their own self-confidence are the least likely to participate in an optional event.

Students who do not have this as a mandatory assignment can find all sorts of excuses for not participating. Some raise the issue of costs, but available no-cost events have been identified. Other students weigh the opportunity cost of time spent on an event in comparison to time spent on homework or, given the majority are adult learners, time spent with family. In those comparisons, the short-term benefits may appear to outweigh the longer-term benefits of professional association and continued learning. Making the event mandatory dramatically alters the equation.

Another question is the potential benefit of a professional association versus a student event. General observations have been that the students are much more positive and enthusiastic about their experiences with professional organizations. One would expect that regardless of whether the student is an adult learner or traditional student, the growing sense of becoming a part of a profession has significance.

In an online context there is an additional benefit of using the professional association. Online students are geographically spread. Even if the students were in the same area, the nonsynchronous nature of the courses means that there will be students who would find it difficult to attend a student event at a specific time. As there are numerous professional events available, both geographically as well as chronologically spread, students have more options to find an opportunity that better fits their schedule.

Several weeks ago, I was attending a professional conference that was also attended by a group of students from another university as a class trip. While it is unknown if the trip was mandatory, it was interesting to observe the behavior of the group. They came in together, sat as a group, and conversed among themselves. At one point a member of the group said to the instructor, "go do your talk to people thing, we'll be here." Finally, at the end of a very interesting technical presentation, the group got up and left together. They missed a significant portion of the value of the event.

The behavior of the student group is one that the design of the assignments attempts to avoid. First, it is not a group activity; it is an individual activity, though that doesn't preclude several individuals attending an event together. This has happened, although in these cases the students who attended together have had different experiences. This difference has been driven in part by the requirement to meet other people—either explicit or implied, and by the need to write about the experience afterward.

Student Reactions

The reaction of students to these assignments has been extremely positive in both courses. Some of the students enthusiastically approach the assignment from the beginning and fulfill the requirements early in the quarter. These are usually the same students who would actively participate in a voluntary program. The other extreme is students who wait until the very last week of the quarter. These students may raise issue after issue as reasons why they are not able to complete the assignment and do so only after they see no other way to avoid it.

Once they have broken the ice and attended the first event, even the most ardent of the avoiders has had no problem with attending another event and completing the assignment (other than locating the next event in a hurry). Some of these students have expressed in their course reviews or in discussions that this was the most valuable assignment in the course and one of the most valuable in their program.

Other than anecdotal feedback from students, there hasn't yet been a concerted effort to measure the success of the approach. Ultimately this would require feedback from alumni on their continued attendance at professional association events and a comparison with a control group. In the short term and as a potential tool for measuring a program outcome, a survey could be conducted of the students to check whether they have voluntarily attended events since the completion of the assignment.

Summary

Including required professional association meetings is an excellent way of providing support for program and course outcomes such as "lifelong learning" and "contribution to the profession" that are otherwise challenging to include as part of a curriculum. The mandatory aspect ensures that not only those students who willingly volunteer participate, but also those who tend to be less willing and who perhaps need the additional encouragement the most. Building careful structure and the need for reflection into the assignment ensures that engagement with professional organizations provides value to the student

References

Boston University School of Management. (n.d.). Student organizations: 2012–2013. Retrieved from http://management.bu.edu/undergraduate-program/life/organizations/

City University of Seattle. (2012–13). CS 495, Syllabus (p. 5).

Fretheim, Erik. (2010). Northwest University, Global Marketing syllabus.

Graduate School of Education, Penn. (n.d.). Funding to attend conferences. Retrieved from http://www.gse.upenn.edu/students/conference_attendance

University of California. (2006, January 1). *Human resources and benefits, at your service: Personnel policies for staff members*. Retrieved from http://atyourservice.ucop.edu/employees/policies_employee_labor_relations/personnel_policies/spp50.html

University of the Rockies—Colorado Springs. (n.d.). *Cost of attendance.* Retrieved from http://www.rockies.edu/admissions/campus_cost.htm

Villanova University, School of Business. (n.d.). *Specialized master's programs, master of accountancy, professional development*. Retrieved from http://www1.villanova.edu/villanova/business/graduate/specializedprograms/mac/professional_development.html

Weber State University. (2012, December). *Portfolio, HAS—Health Information Technology, assessment plan*. Retrieved from http://www.weber.edu/portfolio/has_hit_ap.html

The Benefits of Practical Experience: Using Reflective Practitioner-Faculty in Graduate Programs

Kate Quinn, PhD, *Division of Doctoral Studies*

Abstract

There are substantial benefits of a pedagogical cycle in which reflective practitioner-faculty use real-world application of skills to enhance adult student learning. By professionally engaging in the fields in which they teach, practitioner-faculty ensure that the skills and theories taught to students are current. Likewise, through professional projects, practitioner-faculty are exposed to real-world situations where clients require up-to-date professional services, similar to the work environments of many students. This prepares practitioner-faculty to assist students in finding real-world applications for what they are learning in class. As students actively engage with the new materials and practice skills, they raise challenging, real-world questions as members of a community of practice. These questions result in a critical reflection process among practitioner-faculty, which helps keep faculty current in their fields. Connections are made to both the academic model and the learning goals of one institution of higher learning.

The Nature of Professional Education

There are significant benefits of a pedagogical cycle in which reflective practitioner-faculty use real-world application of skills to enhance adult student learning. In this cycle, practitioner-faculty bring current professional knowledge to their teaching. They use this knowledge in connecting course work and skill development to the professional lives of adult students to enhance their engagement and therefore their authentic learning. By engaging in this manner adult students who have professional lives, reflective practitioner-faculty foster a synergistic cycle that further enhances both teaching and learning. Connections between the literature, personal reflections from one practitioner-faculty member, and both the academic model and institutional learning goals support the synergistic cycle proposed in the model.

The Reflective Practitioner model is derived from the work of various scholars who have connected the need for real-world experience to effectiveness in teaching and learning, particularly in professional fields (Branch, 2010; Chan, 2010; Eraut, 1985; Olson & Clark, 2009; Rømer, 2003; Schön, 1983, 1987). It connects the goals and nature of professional education, best practices in professional education, and the role played by reflective practitioner-faculty in providing effective professional education.

The role of professional education programs is to prepare students to be effective professionals in their various fields, meaning that students must be capable of reflecting on their experiences and of continuous learning and improvement (Chan, 2010). Preparation for success in professional careers means learning the professional knowledge of the field, including both the technical and practical knowledge. Technical knowledge is "capable of written codification," whereas practical knowledge is uncodifiable and "is expressed only in practice and learned only through experience with practice" (Eraut 1985, p. 119). Practical, or "tacit," knowledge is less certain and more complex, typically, than is the codifiable technical knowledge (Chan, 2010; Eraut, 1985; Schön, 1987). In professional education, learning codified skill sets only meets some of the needs of the professional preparation; practical experiences and knowledge are also required (Branch, 2010; Chan, 2010; Eraut, 1985; Maudsley & Strivens, 2000; Rømer, 2003; Schön, 1983, 1987). Maudsley and Strivens (2000) note that "professional knowledge must ultimately reflect client-focused outcomes" to adequately prepare professionals to be competitive in their fields (p. 538).

Professional knowledge comprises four different types of knowledge within the technical-practical dichotomy: (a) propositional ("knowing that") knowledge; (b) process ("knowing how") knowledge; (c) personal knowledge, especially pre-propositional impressions; and, (d) moral principles or knowledge (Maudsley & Strivens, 2000). Aspects that are capable of being catalogued and explained through writing are the technical aspects and the practical aspects are the "messier" aspects such as the "art" inherent in many professional processes (Maudsley & Strivens, 2000). For example, moral principles and knowledge might comprise the technical aspects of Internal Review Board (IRB) regulations and forms, as well as the practical aspect of the nuance of language in creating effective protocols that protect human subjects.

Eraut (1985) draws on the typology of Broudy, Smith, and Burnett (1964) for the four stages of professional knowledge acquisition: (a) replication, (b) application, (c) interpretation, and (d) association. Replication is simply replicating task performance or skill application. Application is being able to correctly apply skills or knowledge to new situations. Interpretation is correctly understanding situations through applied theoretical knowledge and applying appropriate skills, potentially in novel ways, to meet those situations. Eraut (1985) comments that "the interpretive use of knowledge also plays some part in that mysterious quality we call 'professional judgment'" and notes that it is different than mere understanding or application (p. 125). Associative knowledge use typically represents the conveyance of complex theories and concepts through metaphors and images in a clear and compelling manner (Eraut, 1985). At this level of knowledge acquisition, novice professionals are capable of not only understanding but also distilling complex concepts and information into easy-to-understand analogies or visuals for other professionals or clients.

Best Practices in Professional Education

Chan (2010) provides an overview of the professional education literature, which covers both "the nature of professional knowledge and its pedagogies," noting the consensus that "practical experiences are indispensable and experiential teaching and learning are the best ways for providing students with professional expertise" (p. 36). Five aspects have been put forth as necessary for experiential learning to take place. Experiential learning "(a) has experience as its foundation and stimulus, (b) involves learners actively constructing their experiences, (c) is a holistic process, (d) is socially and culturally constructed, and (e) is influenced by the socio-emotional context" (Boud et al., 1993, as cited in Maudsley and Strivens, 2000, p. 539). The cycle of experiential learning includes concrete experience; reflective observations on the experience; abstract conceptualization; active experimentation based on the experiences, reflection, and conceptualization; and, concrete experience as a result of the experimentation (Kolb, 1984, as cited in Maudsley and Strivens, 2000). This process is very similar to that of action research, which "cycles creative problem solving, implementation of practice, and reflective interpretation of that practice" (Maudsley and Strivens, 2000, p. 539). Eraut (1985) argues that the "quality of the initial professional education depends to a considerable degree on the quality of practice; and that in turn is influenced by the continuing education of the practitioners" (p. 131). This speaks to both formal (academic) and on-the-job learning on the part of practitioner-faculty members who teach in professional education programs. By having professional education faculty members as current practitioners in their fields, the quality of the opportunities for practical experiences is enhanced.

In addition to practical experience, interpretive or critical reflection is needed in "situations where experience is initially apprehended at the level of impression, thus requiring a further period of reflective thinking before it is either assimilated into existing schemes or experiences, or induces those schemes to change in order to accommodate it" (Eraut, 1992, as cited in Maudsley and Strivens, 2000, p. 539). Schön (1983, 1987) posited that professionals learn best through reflective practice, namely reflection-in-action and reflection-on-action. Building on this work, many scholars recommend reflective practice in professional education to enhance authentic learning (Branch, 2010; Pack, 2011; Rømer, 2003; Saltiel, 2007). Schön (1983) recommended a reflective practical experience (i.e., practicum) to best prepare professional students for their chosen careers. Chan (2010) defined practicums as "a designed form of practice for the purpose of teaching and learning" (p. 42).

Similar to practicum opportunities, proponents of situated learning claim that professionals best learn how to engage in their chosen practice by "solving problems in context" and working closely with experienced practitioners (Maudsley and Strivens, 2000, p. 537). In this way, "novices learn what to observe, what interpretations to link to observations, and what words and actions to use when conveying these both to clients and colleagues" (Maudsley and Strivens, 2000, p. 537). As Maudsley and Strivens (2000) note, this is similar to learning in "communities of practice." Communities of practice have been recommended as best practices for various doctoral programs deigned to prepare students for membership in professional communities, whether academic or professional (Leshem, 2007; Wenger & McDermott, 2002; Wenger, 1998a, 1998b). Graduate instruction through communities of practice is considered a "signature pedagogy" (Golde, 2007; Shulman, 2005), which are "the characteristic forms of teaching and learning . . . that organize the fundamental ways in which future practitioners are educated for their new professions" (Shulman, 2005, p. 52). This course structure actively engages students in their own learning, as they learn from the faculty member and each other, and is supported in the literature on professional education and leadership development (e.g., Conger & Toegel, 2003; Mumford & Manley, 2003; Olson & Clark, 2009). Maudsley and Strivens (2000) imply that situated learning happens only in in-service or apprenticeship-style learning opportunities and not in higher education classrooms, but this reflects back to the identified disconnect between higher education and the needs of professional communities (Eraut, 1985). In institutions where active practitioner-faculty help design curricula and structure learning opportunities, situated learning is possible.

Finally, Chan (2010) notes that professional knowledge is best transferred from other professionals to novice professionals through individual coaching and the vicarious experiences from the instructor. These enable students to reflect on experiences, whether first- or secondhand, and to think through ways to experiment for improved outcomes, leading to new experiences and further reflection.

The Benefits of Utilizing Reflective Practitioner-Faculty

Teaching, application, and acquisition of graduate-level research design skills all benefit from utilizing reflective practitioner-faculty, and these benefits should apply to any level of professional education that serves working adult students (Fig. 1). At the top of the model, reflective practitioner-faculty stay current for their teaching and professional practice. These teaching faculty are primarily employed as professionals in their fields and secondarily as faculty. Their professional work keeps them up-to-date in the issues and events of the field in which they teach. As practitioners current in their fields, these faculty are well positioned to create or refine course work and learning experiences that draw from real-world situations, similar to the work lives of their students (second component of the model). This, in turn, encourages and creates the space where adult students, who are also working professionals, raise real-world questions of the course material and learning experiences back to the class and the instructor (third component of model), leading to reflection and growth for the instructor and the students. That loops back to supporting reflective practitioner-faculty in remaining current in both their professional practice and their teaching. Each step in this triad supports student learning, shown in the middle. All aspects are described in detail below the figure, with connections to the supporting literature.

Fig. 1. *Model of the Benefits of Utilizing Reflective Practitioner-Faculty*

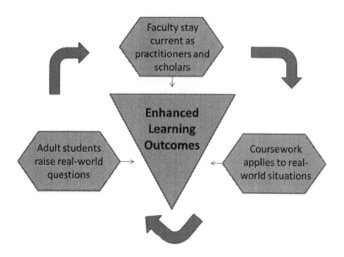

The first component of the model is a key benefit of using active practitioners as teaching faculty in professional education programs: they are current in their fields. Practitioner-faculty are teaching faculty who are employed full- or part-time as professionals, or are retired from professional practice, and who teach part-time in their field (Chan, 2010; Gappa & Leslie, 1993; Leslie & Gappa, 1995; Leslie & Walke, 2001; Tuckman, 1978).

Part-time faculty in higher education have received a fair amount of attention in the literature, including the changes in the demographics and use of part-time faculty (e.g., American Association of University Professors, 1980; Balch, 1999; Berberet & McMillin, 2002; Charfauros & Tierney, 1999; Conley & Leslie, 2002; German, 1996; Leslie & Gappa, 1994) and the satisfaction (or dissatisfaction) of part-time faculty (Antony & Valadez, 2002; Fulton, 2000; Gappa & Leslie, 1993; Unger, 2000). While some of this literature has either bemoaned the decline of tenure-track positions (Cooper, 2009; Finkin, 2000; Leatherman, 1997; Plater, 2008) or warned of the potential decrease in teaching quality and/or student learning outcomes resulting from utilizing part-time instructors (Balch, 1999), other scholars have detailed benefits of utilizing practitioner-faculty—particularly in professional fields (Chan, 2010; Fulton, 2000; Gappa & Leslie, 1993; Leslie & Gappa, 1995). At institutions such as CityU where the teaching model relies on practitioner-faculty, part-time instructors create less of a burden on the time allocation of full-time faculty, as has been found in settings with a bifurcated faculty of full-time tenure-line faculty and part-time adjuncts (Jacobs & Winslow, 2004).

Active practitioner-faculty must possess the four types of professional knowledge put forth by Maudsley and Strivens (2000) (i.e., propositional, process, firsthand impressions, and moral/ethical) to be competitive in their professional practice. As part-time teaching faculty, they are excellently situated to transfer this technical and practical professional knowledge to their students (Eraut, 1985; Rømer, 2003; Schön, 1987). Further, the wealth of knowledge these active practitioners bring about their professions into their teaching permits them to scaffold and assess the acquisition of this knowledge base. Practitioner-faculty are aware of the current events, issues, and complexities of their field (Chan, 2010), allowing them to keep the discussions and activities relevant. This awareness also positions practitioner-faculty members to facilitate productive reflection processes among their students as they gain professional experiences (Chan, 2010; Kennedy, 1987).

Chan (2010) found that professional students perceived their part-time teachers to be "more practical and in-tune with the trends and market" than were their full-time teachers (p. 43). Full-time faculty, even with active research agendas, face the challenge of remaining current in their professional fields and higher education, in general, and have been found to lack "appropriate structures for knowledge exchange between higher education and the professions" (Eraut, 1985, p. 117). These factors combine to create a disconnect between what many institutions of higher education are teaching and the needs of the professional communities for which they are preparing students (Chan, 2010; Eraut, 1985). Utilizing practitioner-faculty who are able to incorporate relevant experiences and facilitate the reflection process on these experiences helps to bridge the gap between theory and practice (Chan, 2010; Eraut, 1985; Maudsley & Strivens, 2000). Further, using practitioner-faculty facilitates the exchange of information between institution and professional community and helps to ensure that curricula are up-to-date and meet the changing needs of the professions (Eraut, 1985).

Additionally, practitioner-faculty are excellent coaches and mentors to their students, supporting them as they strive to attain the professional development necessary to further their careers (Chan, 2010). Practitioner-faculty typically have access to other professionals in their community of practice, who are valuable resources for students on their way to a higher rung of the ladder in the community themselves (Chan, 2010). In these ways, practitioner-faculty facilitate the transition into the professional community of practice for their students by being active members of the communities themselves (Chan, 2010).

The second component of the model connects practitioner-faculty expertise and awareness of the state of their field to the ability to structure learning experiences around real-world application of the skills and information being taught. As noted above, key elements of professional education revolve around active and engaged learning models that provide opportunities for students to learn from the experiences of their faculty while gaining new experiences themselves through controlled and supervised opportunities (Chan, 2010; Eraut, 1985; Rømer, 2003; Schön, 1983, 1987). Because of their connections to their professional communities, practitioner-faculty are able to translate current events and issues into relevant activities for their students. Additionally, practitioner-faculty are adept at creating learning opportunities based on the work lives and professional interests of their students, ensuring that course work is relevant. Specifically, practitioner-faculty are prepared to work with students to ensure that experiences and learning opportunities are co-created with the student and align with the personal and professional needs of each student.

Practitioner-faculty are not only able to design effective learning opportunities, but they are excellently situated to facilitate and monitor the learning of their students. Having gone through the stages of professional knowledge acquisition themselves, practitioner-faculty are prepared to work with students as they replicate what they are learning, apply what they are learning to new situations, interpret situations and apply knowledge/skills in innovative ways, and communicate concepts with others through imagery and other easily comprehensible styles. In the terms of experiential learning, practitioner-faculty are positioned to structure concrete relevant experiences for students, facilitate the reflective observations about the experiences by the students, work with students so that they productively conceptualize new and feasible approaches, and mentor the students as they actively experiment with the selected new approach and reflect on the process and outcomes.

Part-time teaching faculty who are practitioners in their fields can "easily relate theory to their practice" and are positioned to connect students to "cutting edge ideas and practice" (Chan, 2010, p. 39). Whether problem-based learning, experiential learning, or action research, connecting course work and application to the kinds of experiences students face in their work lives facilitates their active role in acquiring new skills and knowledge and helps close the gap between theory and practice, learning and doing (Billett, 1996; Chan, 2010; Conger & Toegel, 2003; Maudsley & Strivens, 2000).

Experience working with clients in various settings is often the best preparation for helping students, who have varied professional interests, find ways to apply what they are learning to their work environments. In cases where students are interested in changing fields, active professional practice enables practitioner-faculty to connect students with new opportunities to practice their skills beyond their current employment. As members of professional associations and networks, practitioner-faculty learn of new developments in the field and are able to bring these into classes. Additionally, in their professional roles, practitioner-faculty train new staff members in how to perform tasks and work with clients in the field. These experiences directly translate to work with students as practitioner-faculty find or create learning opportunities for them to practice new skills or concepts.

The third component of the model is the least covered in the literature: it is the synergistic effect of adult professionals raising real-world questions of their course work. As students process their course materials and engage in activities that have been intentionally structured to mirror real-world scenarios, they begin to pose thoughtful and engaging questions that frequently require faculty to be critically reflective on their professional activities in order to make any implicit or tacit practical knowledge explicit (Eraut, 1985). Reflection on the part of faculty significantly enhances teaching and learning (Hubball, Collins, & Pratt, 2005; Robinson, Anderson-Harper, & Kochan, 2001). Further, when faculty model for students the reflective process, it facilitates student reflection and enhances the transfer of professional knowledge (Eraut, 1985). Critical reflection is crucial to lifelong learning and continuous professional development (Eraut, 1985). Student questions may also lead to exploration or research on the part of the faculty member to determine an appropriate answer, potentially drawing on additional colleagues or resources. Finally, engaging with students in this manner helps faculty to communicate effectively what it is they do as practitioners, enhancing the ability to explain processes, procedures, and technical jargon of the field and, therefore, enhancing both teaching effectiveness and professional practice.

Performance in the professional role is enhanced by teaching activities. As professionals themselves, students raise very challenging and relevant questions of the professional knowledge being taught, particularly at the intersection of technical knowledge and practical application. In order to respond to these questions, faculty must reflect critically on the conceptual material and their practical experiences and be able to explicitly describe their findings. This also requires faculty to demonstrate competence in the highest stage of professional knowledge acquisition—the associative stage. Frequently, faculty must offer an easier-to-understand version of a concept to students or clients and practicing with one group benefits the ability to work with the other. Additionally, work with clients and with students forces practitioner-faculty to stay at the forefront of their field and on top of current events and circumstances. In these ways, roles as practitioner and faculty member reinforce one another.

Applying the Model

Connecting the prior concepts and discussion to the academic model and learning goals of an institution of higher education further demonstrates how utilizing practitioner-faculty benefits professional education. An example of one such institution practicing this model is City University of Seattle.

The City University of Seattle academic model has five components that support the learning goals across all courses and programs. The academic model is designed to ensure that learning experiences align with the mission, vision, and values of the university at the course and program levels (City University of Seattle, 2010). The components of the academic model are (a) a focus on student learning, (b) the use of professional practitioner-faculty, (c) ensuring curricular relevance to the workplace, (d) service to students, and (e) accessibility and responsiveness.

A Focus on Student Learning

City University of Seattle learning experiences are designed to support clearly articulated outcomes at the course, program, and institutional levels. Educational experiences are carefully designed by faculty to encourage self-directed learning within an appropriately defined structure of expectations. With the focus on applying theory to practical experience, learning activities form explicit links among the crucial abilities of an educated professional: critical thinking, self-exploration, and ethical practice. Multiple paths to demonstrating competency are available to learners when appropriate. Students are actively encouraged to define and take responsibility for their own contributions to the learning process, with the understanding that their engagement is critical for substantive learning to take place.   —CityU website

Reflective practitioner-faculty are well positioned to meet the learning needs of adult professionals continuing their educations. As discussed above, we are active in our professional arenas and able to quickly connect theory with practical experience. We have a solid, current understanding of the professional knowledge base, both technical and practical, that our students need to acquire. Enhanced by university supports for effective pedagogy, our understanding of our fields prepares us to recognize what our students already know, what they still need to acquire, and the best strategies to help them get there. We are well prepared to work with our students to ensure that they are thinking critically about how the course work and new skills or knowledge connect to their professional lives, how they are developing personally and professionally, and that they understand and utilize ethical practices.

Reflective Practitioner-Faculty

> City University of Seattle faculty are highly regarded practitioners who bring real-life experience to the learning environment. They consider students to be collaborative partners in the creation of learning opportunities. To support practitioner-faculty in their teaching roles, the institution provides orientation, training, mentoring, and coaching, all designed to foster a respectful and empowering learning environment. Faculty are rewarded for quality teaching and encouraged to continue their development as facilitators of learning.   —CityU website

In the traditional academic world, academic credentials tend to be valued higher than professional expertise or experience. In other words, my PhD makes me competitive for more positions in higher education than are open to my colleagues with more years of practical experience who hold only a master's degree. Combined with studies of part-time faculty that show negative findings related to student outcomes when compared to full-time faculty, part-time practitioner-faculty can be a hard sell to the accrediting bodies that approve professional education programs. I think this is an outdated prejudice that needs to be explored and put to rest. My two years as a professional evaluator prepared me better to teach research design than my doctoral training did. My on-the-job training as a professional working with clients—whether school districts, universities, or the U.S. Department of Education—gave me the practical experiences needed to understand how the theories I learned as a graduate student play out in the real world. My ability to transfer this knowledge to my students does not come from my academic credential; it comes from my status as a practitioner. Further, my doctoral program did not prepare me to teach, so I needed just as much support from CityU for effective teaching as did my colleagues without PhDs. Finally, incorporating practitioner-faculty into the core of professional education programs ensures that there is no disconnect between academic and professional communities.

Relevance to the Workplace

A City University of Seattle education is founded on carefully selected goals that are intended to provide graduates with up-to-date knowledge and practical skills required in the workplace, as well as a framework for continued development. Institution-wide learning goals that emphasize personal and professional growth are embedded in all programs offered at the university. The institution's current goals include professional competence and technical expertise, communication and interpersonal skills, critical thinking, ethical practice and community involvement, development of a diverse and global perspective, and lifelong learning. The overarching goals of a City University of Seattle education enhance the professional skills and knowledge of individuals who in turn add value to their organizations.   —CityU website

Reflective practitioner-faculty, who are actively involved in the same professional arenas that our students are coming from or going to, are the best positioned faculty members to keep the course work relevant to the workplace. Our knowledge and practical skills have to be up-to-date or we would not survive as practitioners, and we are excellently situated to share our technical and practical professional knowledge with our students. A common criticism of many academic programs is that curricular change is slow and that programs may be out of touch with the current trends in the market or professional communities. Having practitioner-faculty fully integrated into professional education programs ensures that the courses are flexible enough to quickly meet new professional needs, while including the fundamental skills and knowledge base of the profession.

Service to Students

City University of Seattle strives to provide a respectful atmosphere in which all students are valued for their contribution and individual needs are honored. A diverse and international student body requires a variety of services to support the learning endeavor. The university strives to be sensitive to students and their needs, to respond in a timely and professional manner to student questions or concerns, and to uphold high standards.   —CityU website

Practitioner-faculty, like their full-time academic counterparts, work with diverse clients, colleagues, and students. Practical experience working in diverse teams where members bring different skill sets, expertise, and styles of working transfers well to the professional education classroom. Increasingly, professional and academic collaborations cross national lines, preparing practitioner-faculty not only to recognize and meet different student needs but also to incorporate different skill sets and expertise of the students into the classroom. Similar to full-time faculty, who could be considered professional academics, practitioner-faculty bring a high level of professionalism to their interactions with students.

Accessibility and Responsiveness

The university is committed to making high-quality learning opportunities as accessible and responsive to the needs of our diverse student population as possible. This includes maintaining affordability, removing unnecessary barriers to entry, providing support for students with differing levels of educational background and preparation, and offering a variety of class schedules and modes of delivery.   —CityU website

Utilizing practitioner-faculty is central to keeping programs accessible and responsive to student needs. CityU attracts a diverse student body across its programs internationally, but a common element is the desire to enhance marketability and career-readiness. As noted previously, practitioner-faculty are well positioned to recognize the knowledge and skills already possessed by students, as well as their learning needs. Combined with entrance requirements and processes designed to assist students, rather than act as gate-keepers barring entrance to college, practitioner-faculty offering online courses asynchronously provide an exceptionally flexible opportunity for adult working professionals to return to higher education.

Alignment with Learning Goals

In addition to the academic model, many institutions of higher education have specified learning goals or outcomes that structure program and course development and implementation. In this way, curricular development and delivery are aligned to maximize the likelihood that students achieve the desired outcomes. To further demonstrate how well the reflective practitioner model supports effective teaching and learning, I have mapped the learning goals of the City University of Seattle.

Graduates Exhibit Professional Competency and a Sense of Professional Identity

> Our graduates bring to the workplace the knowledge and skills intrinsic to success in their professions. They understand the basic values and mission of the fields in which they are working. They are able to use technology to facilitate their work. They have an understanding of basic technical concepts and are able to demonstrate understanding through practical application. —CityU website

Practitioner-faculty are best prepared to transfer to students, and assess the acquisition of, the professional knowledge and skills students need to be successful in their target professions. As practitioners themselves, these faculty understand what it takes to be competitive and facilitate the transition for students into the professional community. Practitioner-faculty are well situated to craft learning activities that provide students with opportunities to demonstrate competency through practical application.

Graduates Have Strong Communication and Interpersonal Skills

> City University of Seattle graduates are able to communicate effectively both orally and in writing. They are able to interact and work with others in a collaborative manner as well as to negotiate difficult interpersonal situations to bring about solutions to problems that benefit all involved.
> —CityU website

Students learn the terms and communication styles of the profession from their practitioner-faculty members and practice conveying concepts through interactive lessons, preparing them to collaborate professionally in their fields. Having professional education programs structured such that students are learning as members of a community of practice, students enhance their interpersonal skills through a critical peer review process in which they give and receive feedback from their classmates and the practitioner-faculty. Practitioner-faculty members, as active members of the professional community, are positioned to model professional communication and interactions.

Graduates Demonstrate Critical Thinking and Information Literacy

> City University of Seattle graduates are able to think critically and creatively, and to reflect upon their own work and the larger context in which it takes place. They are able to find, access, evaluate, and use information in order to solve problems. They consider the complex implications of actions they take and decisions they make.
> —CityU website

As members of the professional community of practice, practitioner-faculty structure learning activities to provide students with experience thinking critically and creatively about how to apply knowledge and skills to new problems in the field. Further, practitioner-faculty introduce students to the professional resources and information to solve problems in the context of the professional field. As active practitioners, these faculty are also capable of assessing the performance of students and encouraging additional growth or development as needed.

Graduates Demonstrate a Strong Commitment to Ethical Practice and Service in Their Professions and Communities

> City University of Seattle graduates take responsibility for their own actions and exhibit high standards of conduct in their professional lives. They are aware of the ethical expectations of their profession and hold themselves accountable to those standards. City University of Seattle graduates are also active contributors to their professional communities and associations. They are informed and socially responsible citizens of their communities, as well as of the world. —CityU website

As noted above, moral practice and/or ethical knowledge are considered one of the four types of professional knowledge. As active professionals, practitioner-faculty possess this knowledge, apply it in their practice, and are ready to design learning activities through which students practice and demonstrate their acquisition of this knowledge. Further, as students move through the programs as members of a learning community, they further prepare themselves under the guidance of practitioner-faculty to be contributing members of professional communities of practice.

Graduates Demonstrate Diverse and Global Perspectives

> City University of Seattle graduates embrace the opportunity to work collaboratively with individuals from a variety of backgrounds, and to learn from the beliefs, values, and cultures of others. They realize that varied viewpoints bring strength and richness to the workplace. City University of Seattle graduates demonstrate an awareness of the interrelation of diverse components of a project or situation. —CityU website

Professional collaborations are increasingly international in nature, and with the international campuses of CityU, practitioner-faculty are well connected professionally and through CityU's resources to expose students to diverse perspectives. Further, CityU's practitioner-faculty establish learning opportunities through which students demonstrate broadened perspectives and awareness of different cultural values and beliefs. Related to broadened cultural understanding is the reflection process discussed previously; practitioner-faculty are able to guide students in reflective processes through which they can assess their own perspectives and attitudes as they are exposed to differing viewpoints.

Graduates Are Lifelong Learners

> In a world where knowledge and skills must be constantly updated, City University of Seattle graduates are self-directed and information-literate in seeking out ways to continue their learning throughout their lifetimes. —CityU website

The experiential learning and reflection process at the heart of acquiring professional knowledge and skills is itself part of a continuous learning cycle. In other words, the reflective nature of effective professional education fosters the continuous learning process, and practitioner-faculty help students develop these habits. Additionally, while students, they learn from practitioner-faculty members various sources of information and resources to facilitate self-guided learning. In this way, practitioner-faculty set students on the path to be effective lifelong learners and professionals.

Conclusion

The literature on best practices in professional education supports the utilization of practitioner-faculty. Practitioner-faculty possess the technical and practical professional knowledge of the field, as well as the practical experience and professional networks, to structure effective learning opportunities for students. At institutions such as City University of Seattle where offering continuing education to adult students is a priority, the practitioner-faculty model best serves students. As discussed here, the reflective practitioner-faculty model represents a synergistic cycle that begins with practitioner-faculty utilizing their professional experience, knowledge, and networks to connect course work to real-world application. Students who are also adult working professionals are then able to pose challenging questions about the theories and application. In response, practitioner-faculty must be reflective and explicit about their application of theory in practice. This process helps to enhance the practitioner-faculty member's ability to work effectively with clients by keeping them current in their fields and capable of effectively communicating with both clients and students.

References

American Association of University Professors. (1980). The status of part-time faculty. *Statements*.

Antony, J. S., & Valadez, J. R. (2002). Exploring the satisfaction of part-time college faculty in the United States. *The Review of Higher Education*, *26*(1), 41–56. Retrieved from file://c/Kate/Endnote/2002 Antony and Valadez.pdf

Balch, P. (1999). Part-time faculty are here to stay. *Planning for Higher Education*, *27*(3), 32–41.

Berberet, J., & McMillin, L. (2002). The American professoriate in transition. *Priorities*. Retrieved from http://offcampus.lib.washington.edu/login?url=http://search.ebscohost.com/login.aspx?direct=true&db=eric&AN=ED463698&site=ehost-live

Billett, S. (1996). Situated learning: Bridging sociocultural and cognitive theorising. *Learning & Instruction*, *6*(3), 263–280. Retrieved from http://proxy.cityu.edu/login?url=http://search.ebscohost.com/login.aspx?direct=true&db=ehh&AN=21628687&site=ehost-live

Branch, W. T. (2010). The road to professionalism: Reflective practice and reflective learning. *Patient Education & Counseling*, *80*(3), 327–332. Retrieved from 10.1016/j.pec.2010.04.022

Broudy, H. S., Smith, B. D., & Burnett, J. (1964). *Democracy and excellence in American secondary education*. Chicago, IL: Rand McNally.

Chan, J. (2010). The use of practitioners as part-time faculty in postsecondary professional education. *International Education Studies, 3*(4), 36–46.

Charfauros, K. H., & Tierney, W. G. (1999). Part-time faculty in colleges and universities: Trends and challenges in a turbulent environment. *Journal of Personnel Evaluation in Education, 13*(2), 141–151.

City University of Seattle. (2010). Self-study report. Retrieved from http://www.cityu.edu/pdf/Accreditation_2010.pdf

Conger, J. A., & Toegel, G. (2003). Action learning and multirater feedback: Pathways to leadership development? In S. E. Murphy & R. E. Riggio (Eds.), *The future of leadership development*. Mahwah, NJ: Lawrence Erlbaum Associates.

Conley, V. M., & Leslie, D. W. (2002). Part-time instructional faculty and staff: Who they are, what they do, and what they think. *Education Statistics Quarterly, 4*(2), 97–103.

Cooper, K. J. (2009). A disturbing trend. *Diverse: Issues in Higher Education, 26*(9), 20–21. Retrieved from http://search.ebscohost.com/login.aspx?direct=true&db=ehh&AN=42310525&site=ehost-live

Eraut, M. (1985). Knowledge creation and knowledge use in professional contexts. *Studies in Higher Education, 10*(2), 117–133. Retrieved from http://proxy.cityu.edu/login?url=http://search.ebscohost.com/login.aspx?direct=true&db=ehh&AN=19645305&site=ehost-live

Finkin, M. W. (2000). The campaign against tenure. *Academe, 86*(3), 20–21.

Fulton, R. D. (2000). The plight of part-timers in higher education: Some ruminations and suggestions. *Change, 32*(3), 38–43.

Gappa, J. M., & Leslie, D. W. (1993). *The invisible faculty: Improving the status of part-timers in higher education*. San Francisco, CA: Jossey Bass.

German, K. M. (1996). Part-time faculty: Identifying the trends and challenges. *Journal of the Association for Communication Administration (JACA), 3*, 231–241.

Golde, C. M. (2007). Signature pedagogies in doctoral education: Are they adaptable for the preparation of education researchers? *Educational Researcher, 36*(6), 344–351.

Hubball, H., Collins, J., & Pratt, D. (2005). Enhancing reflective teaching practices: Implications for faculty development programs. *Canadian Journal of Higher Education, 35*(3), 57–81. Retrieved from http://proxy.cityu.edu/login?url=http://search.ebscohost.com/login.aspx?direct=true&db=ehh&AN=20815234&site=ehost-live

Jacobs, J. A., & Winslow, S. E. (2004). Overworked faculty: Job stresses and family demands. *Annals of the AAPSS, 596*, 104–129. Retrieved from file://c/Kate/Endnote/2004 Jacobs and Winslow.pdf

Kennedy, M. M. (1987). Inexact sciences: Professional education and the development of expertise. *Review of Research in Education, 14*, 133–167.

Leatherman, C. (1997). Heavy reliance on low-paid lecturers said to produce "faceless departments." *The Chronicle of Higher Education, 43*(29), A12–A13.

Leshem, S. (2007). Thinking about conceptual frameworks in a research community of practice: A case for a doctoral programme. *Innovations in Education and Teaching International, 44*(3), 287–299.

Leslie, D. W., & Gappa, J. M. (1994). Education's new academic workforce. *Planning for Higher Education, 22*(4), 1–6.

Leslie, D. W., & Gappa, J. M. (1995). The part-time faculty advantage. *Metropolitan Universities: An International Forum, 6*(2), 91–102.

Leslie, D. W., & Walke, J. T. (2001). Out of the ordinary: The anomalous academic. *Report for the Alfred P. Sloan Foundation.*

Maudsley, G., & Strivens, J. (2000). Promoting professional knowledge, experiential learning and critical thinking for medical students. *Medical education, 34*(7), 535–544. Retrieved from http://www.ncbi.nlm.nih.gov/pubmed/10886636

Mumford, M. D., & Manley, G. G. (2003). Putting the development in leadership development: Implications for theory and practice. In S. E. Murphy & R. E. Riggio (Eds.), *The future of leadership development.* Mahwah, NJ: Lawrence Erlbaum Associates.

Olson, K., & Clark, C. M. (2009). A signature pedagogy in doctoral education: The leader-scholar community. *Educational Researcher, 38*(3), 216–221.

Pack, M. (2011). More than you know: critically reflecting on learning experiences by attuning to the "community of learners". *Reflective Practice, 12*(1), 115–125. Retrieved from 10.1080/14623943.2011.542080

Plater, W. M. (2008). The twenty-first-century professoriate. *Academe, 94*(4), 35–40. Retrieved from http://search.ebscohost.com/login.aspx?direct=true&db=ehh&AN=33966712&site=ehost-live

Robinson, E. T., Anderson-Harper, H. M., & Kochan, F. K. (2001). Strategies to improve reflective teaching. *Journal of Pharmacy Teaching, 8*(4), 49. Retrieved from http://proxy.cityu.edu/login?url=http://search.ebscohost.com/login.aspx?direct=true&db=ehh&AN=27645699&site=ehost-live

Rømer, T. A. (2003). Learning process and professional content in the theory of Donald Schön. *Reflective Practice, 4*(1), 85. Retrieved from http://proxy.cityu.edu/login?url=http://search.ebscohost.com/login.aspx?direct=true&db=ehh&AN=9428616&site=ehost-live

Saltiel, D. (2007). Judgment , narrative and discourse: Critiquing reflective practice, 1–12. Retrieved from http://www.leeds.ac.uk/medicine/meu/lifelong06/P_DavidSaltiel.pdf

Schön, D. A. (1983). *The reflective practitioner: How professionals think in action.* New York, NY: Basic Books.

Schön, D. A. (1987). *Educating the reflective practitioner.* San Francisco, CA: Jossey-Bass.

Shulman, L. S. (2005). Signature pedagogies in the professions. *Daedalus, 134*(3), 52–59.

Tuckman, H. P. (1978). Who is part-time in academe? *AAUP Bulletin,* (64), 305–315.

Unger, D. N. S. (2000). Academic apartheid: The predicament of part-time faculty. *Thought & Action, 16*(2), 61–64.

Wenger, E. (1998a). *Learning in communities of practice.* Cambridge, UK: Cambridge University Press.

Wenger, E. (1998b). Communities of practice: Learning, meaning, and identity. In R. Pea, J. S. Brown, & J. Hawkins (Eds.), *Learning in doing, 15* (p. 318). Cambridge, UK: Cambridge University Press. doi:10.2277/0521663636

Wenger, E., & McDermott, R. (2002). *Cultivating communities of practice.* Boston, MA: Harvard Business School Press.

Innovative Program Delivery: Performance-Based Education

Krissy Jones, MEd, *Albright School of Education*
Steven Olswang, PhD, JD, *Provost*

Abstract

Higher education today faces many challenges with less financial support from the government, rising tuition costs, and the greater public questioning the value of degrees earned. The increase of for-profit universities entering the market has added to these challenges by increasing the competition for student enrollment. Institutions everywhere are looking at alternative methods for increasing enrollment, meeting student needs, and providing high-quality and relevant programs that lead to increased degree completion and greater possible employment after graduation. One method rising to the forefront of postsecondary educational practice to help meet these demands is performance-based education. While performance-based education has been consistently implemented into K–12 systems and vocational education for decades, it is now increasing its visibility and support with postsecondary institutions all across the United States. This chapter will review the reasoning behind this increase of performance-based education, how it can benefit both the consumer and institution, and how it can provide students the skills and knowledge to increase their ability to positively impact the workforce environment.

Introduction

Higher education today faces many challenges including the increasing cost to students. In public universities, the decline in state contribution across the nation has led to double-digit increases in tuition, effectively pricing out entire populations from higher education access. In private colleges and universities, costs and associated tuition are also on the rise, making private higher education even more difficult to attain. Financial aid advisors in both public and private sectors encourage students to rely on support from the government increasingly from loans, making the debt load on students unbearable. The attempts to make higher education responsible to the consumer through rules like gainful employment have failed to this point, requiring students and their families to fend for themselves in an overcrowded market.

The entrance of for-profit universities into the market has only made the area more complex. With the promise of fast access and lower price to online programs, these too have run afoul of their claims, delivering instead low graduation rates and high government and accreditation scrutiny.

The total number of students entering higher education has declined in the last several years. In part this reflects the demographics of the high school graduation cycle, but also it reflects the economy and the costs of higher education. Even though numerous research articles suggest that the return on increasingly higher degrees in terms of earning power is significant, the cost of entry is preventing a large portion of the population from these benefits. Colleges enrolled 2.3 percent fewer students this spring than last, a steeper drop than the 1.8 percent decline reported by the National Student Clearinghouse for the fall (NSC Reports, 2013).

Less than 50 percent of all students complete their bachelor's degree in four years, and the U.S. Department of Education (DOE) calculates completion rates now on the basis of six-year data, reflecting the realization that students take longer to graduate. This longer completion rate also suggests that more students are stopping out to work, and more than half of students currently enrolled in college work twenty or more hours in addition to attending college.

This increase in completion time has necessitated the partial reinvention of the way academic programs are offered. The availability of online classes has skyrocketed, reflecting the reality that students cannot always leave work and life responsibilities to attend school. Many students are also exiting and re-entering higher education with work experiences. Acknowledging the value of these experiences and the related competencies, many higher education administrators are implementing competency- or performance-based education options. These new programs, which focus on student performance rather than instruction time, are quickly moving to the forefront of higher education and being offered at colleges and universities all over the world.

Origins

While performance-based education seems to have recently appeared with great magnitude in postsecondary education, its concept has been around for centuries in one format or another, historically being referred to as outcomes education or outcomes-based education. This type of educational practice has been largely used in K–12 education for decades and has also been a driving force in vocational and trade schools since the 1900s. Klein-Collins (2012) articulated the following historical facts about outcomes-based education in her article for the Council for Adult and Experiential Learning (CAEL). Outcomes-based education made its appearance into postsecondary education in the 1960s when the U.S. Office of Education funded ten colleges and universities to develop pilot training programs for elementary school teachers. By the 1970s, performance-based education programs emerged as important models for serving the increasing numbers of adults returning to college. At this time the U.S. Department of Education's Fund for the Improvement of Postsecondary Education provided significant grant support for adult learning programs to develop competency-based models. With progress linked to performance (rather than seat time) this new model for education offered many benefits to returning adults, including recognition of prior learning that adults had acquired through other institutions or outside sources (Klein-Collins, 2012).

This new approach to learning and completion of degree proved to be valuable and in demand; a vast increase of colleges and universities began recognizing prior experience. While many administrators of the traditional colleges and universities spoke intensely against this new form of learning and recognition, nontraditional innovative institutions began to rise and move to the forefront of postsecondary education around the world, bringing new focus to students' demonstration of learning.

Performance-Based Education

As the economy evolves, there is growing recognition of the importance of a well-educated workforce (Klein-Collins, 2012). Employers want clear and direct links between learning occurring in postsecondary education and skills needed to successfully complete workplace demands. Emphasis on seat time and courses completed through lectures is giving way to ability and skills gained through experience and completion of clearly defined competencies that directly relate to workforce needs.

Unlike traditional programs where the emphasis is on hours accumulated through seat time in lecture halls to earn credits toward a degree, performance-based education places the locus of control on the student and her ability to demonstrate learning through real-life performance tasks, similar to ones that workers would encounter in actual workplace situations. Students receive clearly defined competencies and must demonstrate their ability to meet or exceed them. The International Board of Standards for Training and Performance Instruction (IBSTPI, 2005) defines competency as, "a knowledge, skill, or attitude that enables one to effectively perform the activities of a given occupation or function to the standards expected in employment." The National Center for Education Statistics (NCES) for the DOE defines competency as, "the combination of skills, abilities, and knowledge needed to perform a specific task" (National Postsecondary Education Cooperative Working Group, 2002, p. 7).

As seen with both these definitions, competencies include both a means and an end. The means is the knowledge, skills, and abilities that students accrue while actively researching and learning through multiple facets ranging from listening, reading, researching, watching, discussions, and more. It is the building of knowledge and experience that is crucial for students to develop a deep understanding of content to begin applying this knowledge in diverse situations. The ability to effectively perform these new skills, applying the knowledge gained in a real-life workforce situation, for an employer, is the end to the means. The ends are often described in what many universities define as outcomes.

Outcomes are clearly defined expectations of the abilities that students must demonstrate proficiency in before progressing. Outcomes describe the "end" students achieve after completing the research and instruction provided. The amount and structure of outcomes ranges according to the program of study based on institutional and workforce needs. However, an essential requirement is that the outcomes must be clear, demonstrable, and directly relate to industry needs, workforce expectations, and the program of study. Outcomes are active descriptors of skills and abilities students must successfully exhibit to demonstrate learning rather than descriptors of what is to be taught. Outcomes relate directly to professional practice, rather than instruction as seen with objectives (Glennon, 2006). But the outcomes are the same for students in the regular curriculum or in a performance-based structure of learning; outcomes do not vary by mode of instruction as all students regardless of instructional format must be able to demonstrate proficiency in the outcomes. Outcomes can be written in various formats ranging from descriptive paragraph to detailed checklists, depending on the program. One example of an outcome is:

> Demonstrate understanding of the three major types of research methods: qualitative, quantitative, and mixed methods, including (a) how these are implemented correctly in current research, and (b) which research method is best for an intended outcome.

In this outcome, the focus is on the demonstration of learning acquired rather than the amount of time the student has spent in a class listening to the instructor speak about a story used and what was noted as important to remember. With performance-based education, there is less emphasis on how the student learns the material or which learning objects were employed in acquiring the knowledge. Nor is the student told how she must demonstrate the new learning in a given task. The emphasis falls more on the demonstration of learning and that the student is able to correctly demonstrate the application of the learning in the best way possible for that student.

Another benefit to performance-based education is that students develop the ability to process and apply new learning in a variety of situations, enabling them to successfully complete tasks in flexible and various formats. This furthers learning beyond simple recalling of facts to actual implementation of skills and ability. When students are given an outcome and rubric for assessment of that outcome, it enables them to take full responsibility for their own learning by determining the best course of action needed for them to complete the research, implement the new learning, and choose the best artifact to demonstrate this new learning.

It remains the responsibility of faculty members to provide guidance and support for students so that they can make informed choices about the learning objects available to successfully master the learning outcomes. Through interaction with peer groups, content experts, and program mentors, students are provided with multiple opportunities to collaborate, discuss, and expand upon previous experience, determining what needs to occur to ensure learning. These skills are crucial as flexibility and adaptability to meet workplace demands are highly sought-after skills in any corporation. As Klein-Collins (2012) stated, "The workplace now requires workers to be part of adaptable, effective working teams, and workers need to have much more than just technical skills, they also need to have adaptability, interpersonal competence, and the ability to deal with open-ended issues" (p. 10). These skills are in even more demand as the technology and the information age continue to advance exponentially.

Assessment

To ensure students have mastered the expected outcomes, they are assessed against the established standards of the course and program. One effective way to measure student learning and the ability to meet or exceed program outcomes is through the use of rubrics. Rubrics are assessment tools that provide detailed descriptors communicating expectations around the quality of completion on a task. By providing detailed explanations of expectations, rubrics enable students to have equal opportunity to succeed. While rubrics can be as simple as a checklist, all rubrics must contain criterion being assessed and the degree to which the student demonstrates meeting this criterion. The more detailed the descriptors for meeting each criterion, the more likely students will succeed. Rubrics are set like a table with the descriptors along the side and degree to which completion occurred across. A sample rubric for measuring student performance is shown in Table 1.

Table 1. *Sample Rubric*

Demonstrate understanding of the three major types of research methods: qualitative, quantitative, and mixed methods, including (a) how these are implemented correctly in current research, and (b) which research method is best for an intended outcome.			
	Developing →	**Emerging** →	**Proficient** →	**Exemplary**
Under-stand-ing	Artifact submitted: demonstrates a developing understand-ing by provid-ing a cited definition of 1 or 2 research methods, but does not include all 3 or any components for methods	Artifact submitted: demonstrates an emerging understanding by providing cited defini-tions of each methodology, but does not articulate major components for each method	Artifact submitted: demonstrates a clear understand-ing of each major research method and is able to clearly articulate the major com-ponents of each method along with when best to apply each method	Artifact submitted: demonstrates a solid understanding of each major research method and is able to clearly articulate the major and minor components of each method Student clearly relates each method to increasing current classroom practices
Imple-menta-tion	Artifact submitted: is not able to demonstrate correct implementa-tion of the research methods	Artifact submit-ted: demon-strates correct implementa-tion of 1 or 2 of the research methods articulates stu-dent's reason-ing to explain the use of the method(s) chosen	Artifact submitted: demonstrates correct imple-mentation of each research method articulates stu-dent's reason-ing to explain the use of each method of research	Artifact submitted: demonstrates correct implementation of each research method clearly and directly articulates student's reasoning for the use of each method of research and provides citations of current research as additional support
Inten-tion	Artifact submitted: does not state the rea-soning why the research method chosen was chosen	Artifact submitted: states the research method chosen, but not able to clearly articu-late why	Artifact submitted: clearly states the reasoning why the research method chosen is the best method to gather data needed	Artifact submitted: clearly and directly states the reasoning why the research method chosen is the best method to gather data needed and provides research citations to support reasoning

Through the use of a rubric, an instructor or evaluator can accurately indicate to what extent the student demonstrates proficiency in each of the indicators, assessing the areas of focus in the outcome. Highlighting the grading criterion to reflect the degree of completion for each indicator gives the instructor and the student clear and detailed information regarding performance. Rubrics are valuable in assessing student learning and informing students about instructors' expectations of them, empowering students to make the best choice for demonstrating their learning.

Value

Performance-based education is gaining considerable recognition from both students and employers looking to hire those students. When employers are interested in hiring a student, they do not seek out how many hours the student completed in a lecture hall or how many credits were tied to those hours. What they want is someone who can perform the required tasks to ensure organizational success. A student's competence is of greatest importance. Performance-based education goes far beyond the acquisition of knowledge; it develops the competencies needed to achieve the desired results. When implemented correctly, performance-based programs are of exceptional value because they are student-centered, flexible, and provide multiple avenues to demonstrate learning.

While performance-based education has been around for decades, it has only recently experienced a great surge in postsecondary education. Institutions are looking for ways to continue offering courses with less financial output. Using performance-based models for program delivery allows institutions to offer courses using mentors to guide students through completion based on student needs rather than instructors who would require students to attend daily lectures, regardless of the students' preexisting knowledge and skills. This type of delivery can substantially reduce expenses related to faculty pay and maintenance of physical classrooms.

Institutions that offer the performance-based model are positioned to acknowledge the skills a student learns outside of the classroom. This option can benefit students who are entering a program after attaining relevant experience in an employment setting. It also benefits students who are completing a program while working as it enables them to apply the knowledge and skills they are acquiring through the program in their current workforce setting. Recognizing prior work experience ensures that all students receive equal opportunity toward degree completion and omits the possibility of favoritism toward completion of the credit hour over experience gained.

In the spring of 2012, performance-based education received public recognition from the acting assistant secretary of the U.S Department of Education, David Bergeron, in his "Dear Colleague" letter. In this letter, he provides guidance to institutions that wish to continue receiving federally funded financial aid for performance-based and direct-assessment programs. Bergeron also states, "competency-based approaches to education have the potential for assuring the quality and extent of learning, shortening the times to degree/certificate completion, developing stackable credentials that ease student transitions between school and work, and reducing the overall cost of education for both the career-technical and degree programs" (pp. 3–4). Bergeron also recognized the collaborative efforts between the department, accrediting agencies, and the higher education community to encourage the use of innovative approaches such as performance-based education. This formal recognition, along with his commitment to collaborate with accreditation and other research bodies to identify promising practices and gather data to inform future practices is a tremendous step forward in advancing alternative and innovative educational practices.

External constituencies have begun to focus less on the nature of the form of the delivery method for programs and degrees, and more on the quality of the program and degree. Through performance-based education, higher education administrators can ensure program quality by critically evaluating students' ability to demonstrate proficiency in program outcomes in ways that are relevant and applicable to their fields of study.

However, creating quality performance-based programs will not occur without close connections among institutions of higher education and future employers. Through this partnership, administrators can develop purposeful outcomes to actively prepare today's graduates for our rapidly changing workforce. With half of all college graduates being either unemployed or underemployed, quality performance-based programs can help to restructure the nation's current economic status into a stronger, more viable economy that promotes hiring college graduates at a steady pace.

References

Bergeron, D. (2013). *Dear colleague*. Washington, D.C.: United States Department of Education Office of Postsecondary Education.

Chyung, S. Y., Stepich, D., & Cox, D. (2006). Building a competency-based curriculum architecture to educate 21st-century business practitioners. *Journal of Education for Business.* Washington, D.C.: Heldref Publications.

Glennon, C. (2006). Reconceptualizing program outcomes. *Journal of Nursing Education, 45*(2), 55–58.

International Board of Standards for Training and Performance Instruction (IBSTPI). (2005). Retrieved from www.ibstpi.org

Klein-Collins, R. (2012). *Competency-based degree programs in the U.S. postsecondary credentials for measurable student learning performance.* Council for Adult and Experiential Learning.

National Student Clearinghouse, NSC Reports (Spring 2013). *Term enrollment estimates.*

National Postsecondary Education Cooperative Working Group. (2002). *Report of the National Postsecondary Education Cooperative Working Group on competency-based initiatives in postsecondary education.*

Yen, H. (2012). In weak job market, one in two college graduates are jobless or underemployed. *Huffington Post.*

Universal Design of Online Classes

Rebecca C. Cory, PhD, *Division of Doctoral Studies*

Abstract

Universal design (UD) promotes designing with the greatest diversity of users in mind so that adaptations and accommodations are forethoughts, not afterthoughts. This concept, invented by architect Ron Mace, has been adapted to the education environment and applied to the "building" of both content and curriculum. By applying this framework, designers can create classes that are accessible to the greatest diversity of students. This paper explains universal design, gives ideas for using UD in an online class, and provides the author's reflection on her implementation of UD.

Universal Design and Traditional Design

The trend toward serving diverse students and diverse learning styles is one that has been increasing for a while. Universities and colleges are moving toward trying to serve students from different backgrounds and with different needs in more integrated ways. Traditionally, classes were designed for a typical student, and a teacher's style was based on the teacher's preferred way of learning. The typical student was often thought to be similar to Goffman's (1963) concept of a normative person, a heterosexual Protestant white male who is able in body and mind. A typical college student would also be one that is under twenty-five years old and a full-time student. The student that is returning to school after taking a job and raising a family does not fit such a normative profile.

Traditionally, colleges and universities would design for this typical student and create add-on programs, offices, and policies for anyone who had needs outside of the standard offerings. Disability services offices, multicultural student centers, and programs for gay, lesbian, bisexual, or transgender students all were created with the acknowledgment that these students were not being adequately served by the standard university offerings (Burgstahler & Cory, 2008).

Instead of designing for the typical student, this paper promotes the use of universal design for learning (UDL). The Higher Education Opportunity Act defines universal design for learning as follows:

> The term "universal design for learning" means a scientifically valid framework for guiding educational practice that:
>
> (a) provides flexibility in the ways information is presented, in the ways students respond or demonstrate knowledge and skills, and in the ways students are engaged; and
> (b) reduces barriers in instruction, provides appropriate accommodations, supports, and challenges, and maintains high achievement expectations for all students, including students with disabilities and students who are limited English proficient (Section 103.24).

Universal design for learning promotes designing courses and programs for students in such a way as to not need add-on "accommodations" or separate programming. The implementation of UDL creates a seamless environment for the student, where all students feel included and supported in the classroom and campus programs. UDL requires a process of imagining the greatest diversity of possible student, and designing a class or program to be accessible to all students. This renders afterthought or add-on programs and accommodations unnecessary. It is a framework for thinking about course design, and allows the instructor or designer to take responsibility for students who do not fit the structure of the class. Instead of blaming those students, UDL asks the designer to reimagine and redesign, incorporating those students.

Overview of Universal Design for Learning

Universal design promotes creating programs with the greatest diversity of users in mind so that adaptations and accommodations are rendered unnecessary, rather than add-on afterthoughts. This concept, invented by architect Ron Mace (Ostroff, Limont, & Hunter, n.d.), has been adapted to the education environment and applied to the building of both instruction and curriculum. The adoption of UDL as a paradigm for creating classes and curriculum has started to reach a wider audience since the Higher Education Opportunity Act of 2008 included references to UDL throughout the sections on teacher training, grant development, and, within those two sections, the use of technology.

The basic tenets of universal design for fearning (ULD), as developed by CAST (formerly the Center for Applied Special Technology) are:

- Providing multiple means of representation,
- Providing multiple means of action and expression, and
- Providing multiple means of engagement (CAST, 2011, p. 5).

These tenets allow curriculum designers and instructors to use a systematic process when thinking through the accessibility and universality of their courses. By applying this framework, designers can create classes that are accessible to the greatest diversity of students.

CAST has created a detailed framework for thinking about universal design for learning. Looking at the science of how the brain learns, CAST researchers have been able to correlate the different brain processes with different ways of providing instructional activities. UDL emphasizes creating options for students both to learn (the input and the processing activities) as well as to express their learning (udlcenter.org, n.d.). It moves us away from traditional models of lecture or reading for input and writing or tests for output of knowledge. It also ensures that instructors do not skip over the essential practice and processing portion of the learning process.

The repetition of multiple means as a way of framing universal design for learning encourages redundancy and duplication, in a positive way. A designer should note that what is intuitive to them is not always intuitive to everyone. Not every student thinks in the same way; therefore, adding some redundancy to the design will help make it feel logical to students even with different ways of thinking or organizing themselves. Building in some redundancies, so that students can always find the information they are looking for with little frustration, is good design.

UDL is, ultimately, a process, not a product (Burgstahler & Cory, 2008; Chisholm & May, 2009). A designer has to imagine the greatest diversity of students possible, and design for them. Then, when someone enrolls in the class who is outside the designer's original imagination, the designer expands her imagination and incorporates that person into the design of the class. The way designers change their class activities in response to the changing student body is not as an add-on accommodation or a onetime exception for that student. Instead, they expand the class materials for all students, giving everyone the new set of options.

Universal Design in the Online Environment

Universal design principles can be applied to the online environment as well as the in-person class. When designing a class, one could think about making it modality neutral, and creating aspects that work for students, regardless of the modality of instruction. UDL supports this in the online environment.

Technology can support UDL in many ways. When instructors provide information in accessible digital formats, then students can manipulate that material to meet their needs. For example, they can change the font, the font size, the color of the background or the color of the font. Students can also use software to have the information read aloud to them, or they can print the information and read it on paper. Accessible digital text provides multiple means of access for students (Chisholm & May, 2009). Accessible digital files are ones that are unlocked so that the reader can manipulate them; they also are marked up using headings to connote different sections, and with detailed *alt text* tags or detailed captions for all images. Many classroom-based faculty use computer software as a way to add UDL elements to their classes.

One of the best ways to make an asynchronous environment accessible is to make sure that the use of that environment is predictable (Chisholm & May, 2009). Blackboard and other learning management systems have some structures already in place that the instructor does not have the authority to modify. However, within the parts, the instructor can modify, and making the environment both predictable and redundant can make it more accessible. If the rubric for the first assignment is posted in the announcements, it is important for the instructor to make sure the rubric for the second assignment is posted in that week's announcements as well. Similarly, it is important for the instructor to post the link to the rubric in the announcement, the assignment area, and the discussion board. That way, students with different ways of thinking and different ways of organizing their course work will still find the information they need in a place that is logical to them.

Reflection on Challenges and Things I Learn as I Implement

When I recently created a new online course using the principles of universal design for learning, I found it harder than I had imagined. Perhaps it is the knowledge of all the details of the process, and the desire to do it all, right away, but I felt overwhelmed. I wanted to design a class that was perfect, and accessible to everyone. And I set out to accomplish that.

In the spirit of UDL, I looked to create a class that had multiple means of representation, multiple means of engagement, and multiple means of expression. Our university format typically has students read an article or book, discuss on a threaded discussion board, and write papers or create presentations. I wanted to increase the options for students. I enlisted some of the technology already accessible through Blackboard, and created a class wiki as a resource for the students both to contribute to and to learn from. I also included some presentations that students could access in real time, or later via recording. This allowed students who were able to attend to gain the benefit of immediate feedback and interaction. By recording these presentations, other students could benefit from the additional modality of learning and get the interactive piece through Blackboard discussions or individual emails. I created options for assignments, when possible, for students to present orally or to write a paper. I found reading that was engaging as well as other sources of input for new ideas—videos, blogs, popular media as well as peer-reviewed sources. Some accessible media was hard to find. There is no point in including a video if it is not also captioned. Vetting for quality and accessibility took time.

Additionally, I tried to make my online class both predictable and redundant. I created a Blackboard shell that was highly self-referential in order for students to be able to have multiple places that they can go to access the same information. The same information, such as the reading for the week, is posted in multiple places, like the course module for the week, the week's discussion board, and the class resources link.

Ultimately, I will never be able to be all things to all students. And I need to remember that UDL is a process. It is easy to follow creative ideas down one rabbit hole, only to realize that a whole category of students has been missed.

References

Burgstahler, S., & Cory, R. C. (2008). Moving in from the margins: From accommodation to universal design. In S. Gabel & S. Danforth (Eds.), *Disability and the politics of education* (pp. 561–582). New York, NY: Peter Lang.

Cast. (2011). *Universal design for learning guidelines version 2.0.* Wakefield, MA: Author.

Chisholm, W., & May, M. (2009). *Universal design for web applications.* Sebastopol, CA: O'Reilly.Goffman, E. (1963). *Stigma: Notes on the management of spoiled identity.* New York, NY: Simon and Schuster.

Higher education opportunity act of 2008. (2008, Aug. 14). Public law 110-315.

Ostroff, E., Limont, M., & Hunter, D. G. (n.d.). Building a world fit for people: Designers with disabilities at work. *Adaptive Environments Center.* Retrieved from http://humancentereddesign.org/adp/profiles/index.php

Udlcenter.org. (n.d.). Research evidence. Retrieved from http://www.udl-center.org/research/ researchevidence

Team Projects in Online Learning: Best Practices in Design, Implementation, and Evaluation

Elizabeth Fountain, PhD, *Division of Arts & Sciences, Division of Doctoral Studies, School of Management*
Kurt Kirstein, EdD, *School of Management*

Abstract

This chapter provides an overview of the emerging best practices in the design, implementation, and evaluation of team-based assignments in online learning, followed by suggestions for further research. As online learning has proliferated in higher education over the last decade, more students and instructors encounter the need to incorporate teamwork in the virtual learning environment. Team-based assignments are of high value in developing critical analysis skills, increasing engagement, and decreasing isolation, among other benefits; they also raise multiple challenges to implement effectively. A review of the literature notes several emerging best practices in curriculum design, instruction, and evaluation of teamwork in the online learning environment. Curriculum designers need to provide a supportive structure, clear expectations, and sufficient time for teams to engage in both the processes associated with socialization and trust building, and to complete the "product" assigned to the team. Instructors should engage early and often as teams go through their formative stages, and remain actively available as teams complete their work, should intervention be required. Finally, evaluation strategies that take into account individual contributions as well as the quality or completeness of the final team product are critical to encouraging the perception of fairness on the part of students. Overall, the benefits of including team projects in the online learning environment outweigh the challenges, making it worth the time and effort to include them in the curricula.

Introduction

Online learning has proliferated in higher education over the last decade (Mortgagy & Boghikan, 2010; Revere & Kovach, 2011; Prinsloo, Slade, & Galpin, 2011). Several factors drive the inclusion of team-based assignments for students in the virtual learning environment. In many fields, such as business, management, and leadership, developing skills as team members and team leaders is essential to achieving desired learning outcomes. The need for authentic assessment leads more academic leaders, faculty, and curriculum designers to incorporate teamwork in the learning activities and graded assessments for courses in these and other content areas. Students in online courses can feel isolated, and teamwork is one way to encourage and even enforce collaboration and communication.

Online team-based assignments serve multiple purposes, but they also cause multiple challenges. Team members must get to know one another and communicate in a virtual environment, in which they rarely or never meet in person. The instructor must monitor group progress, and evaluate teamwork fairly so that students who contribute the most to the success of the team project are recognized, while those who do not contribute are not able to benefit from the work of others. Another complication is the ever-changing array of technology tools available to assist in collaborative efforts; as soon as students and faculty become comfortable with one, new tools arrive that supersede their predecessors.

There is little direct research to help instructors and curriculum designers meet these challenges, but a review of the literature notes several emerging best practices that can be applied to team-based assignments in the online environment. These basic best practices can apply regardless of the choice or availability of specific collaboration tools, as they focus on the fundamental elements of supporting teamwork in a virtual environment. This paper provides an overview of the emerging best practices in the design, implementation, and evaluation of team-based assignments in online learning, followed by suggestions for further research.

Context: Student Engagement and Achievement in Online Learning

The inclusion of team-based assignments in online learning is taking place in the broader context of the need to improve the levels of student engagement and learning in online courses. Researchers and accreditors are recognizing the importance of engaging students as a prerequisite to higher-level learning (Alden, 2011; Association to Advance Collegiate Schools of Business, 2010; Prinsloo, Slade, & Galpin, 2011; Revere & Kovach, 2011), and a consensus is developing that higher levels of engagement in the learning environment and academic activities lead to greater achievement of learning outcomes. Collaborative teamwork is viewed as one important method of increasing engagement for online students, yet educators still encounter challenges in determining how best to engage students through this modality (Revere & Kovach, 2011).

In order to make learning experiences effective, especially collaborative learning experiences, designers and instructors need to focus on the ways in which these experiences connect to real-world applications, or the means by which instruction goes beyond "knowledge acquisition" and moves students to "knowledge application . . . and engaged discovery" (Revere & Kovach, 2011, p. 114). Supporting or even requiring higher levels of student-to-student interaction also has been shown to lead to higher levels of performance and satisfaction on the part of students (Alden, 2011; Revere, 2003).

Advantages of Team-Based Assignments in Online Learning

Increasing student engagement. Collaboration is one way to increase student engagement. In fact, researchers are discovering that students themselves want access to the means to collaborate with other students and faculty in their online course work as they do in face-to-face course work (Revere & Kovach, 2011). Group work can encourage students to connect with one another, facilitate the development of learning communities, and provide opportunities for students to "explore and expand their existing knowledge base together" (Revere & Kovach, 2011, p. 117); it can also help overcome the tendency for students who do not connect on a campus to feel isolated and disconnected. Students who participate in cooperative team learning tend to have higher motivation and a higher sense of classroom community (Yang, Cho, Mathew, & Worth, 2011).

Increasing relevance. Many students are in or plan to enter fields in which teamwork will be a regular way of doing business. The contemporary workplace is often structured around cross-functional teams, and many times, those teams operate with the support of online tools (Alden, 2011). Ensuring that students in online courses get exposure to and develop proficiency in team participation and leadership skills is one way to augment the relevance of their learning to the demands in the professional world.

Implementing authentic assessment. In addition to supporting a relevant curriculum, team projects and assignments provide instructors and program leaders with evidence of student achievement that lends itself to authentic assessment of student learning. Instead of asking students to read, reflect, or discuss the elements of team participation and leadership, students are required to actively engage in them, and to demonstrate their proficiency in the relevant knowledge, skills, and abilities (Green, Edwards, Wolodko, Stewart, Brooks, & Littledyke, 2010).

Enhancing critical analysis skills. As students co-create the team's project, they are joining together in a socially based construction of new knowledge and skills (Koh, Barbour, & Hill, 2010). By evaluating and assessing the contributions of each team member, the team collectively strengthens its members' skills in the areas of judging, valuing, supporting, or opposing different viewpoints. This supports the development of improved critical analysis skills and facilitates team collaboration, both of which will be valuable to graduates in a professional capacity. Elder & Paul (2010) point out that critical thinking skills are associated with the practices of clarifying purpose, establishing perspectives, and verifying assumptions leading to valid conclusions, all of which will be useful to the student in an academic team as well as in the workplace.

Developing virtual communication skills. Virtual projects require team members to develop a number of communication skills to compensate for the lack of traditional communication cues (Kirstein, 2011). Without body language, facial expressions, and voice inflection, students must learn to communicate with each other in a highly contextual manner where the bulk of the message is relayed in text-based communication such as email. Communication in such a virtual environment is a skill set that is learned and refined through experience, and these skills will serve graduates well as they enter the increasingly virtual workplace. In fact, this advantage of team-based assignments is specific to the online learning environment. While the other benefits accrue in face-to-face learning, providing a virtual environment for students to develop these skills mimics the conditions in which they are likely to find themselves in their professional environments. An argument could be made to include virtual learning "labs" for any student who is preparing to enter a profession that demands high levels of virtual communication skills.

Challenges of Team-Based Assignments in Online Learning

Lack of clarity. Because there is little or no face-to-face interaction and often limited virtual communication, online projects often lack a level of clarity in regards to how the goals of the team's project relate back to the course outcomes. This limits the extent to which the students see value and relevance in the projects themselves and, also, whether they feel a sense of motivation to overcome these obstacles in order to complete the project (Koh, Barbour, & Hill, 2010).

Additional factors that affect the clarity of team projects have to do with the project's deliverables and the roles of the individual team members. Unless the instructor is very clear about the specific deliverable the team is expected to produce, unresolved questions can impact a team's performance and cohesion and can lead to unproductive conflict. Yet, even more challenging is a lack of clarity about the role of each team member and what he/she is expected to contribute. Scherling (2011) indicated that teams often consist of a variety of personality styles, each of which may approach the team's task from a different perspective. Some will be highly motivated and may come off as pushy, whereas others may be content to let other team members do the bulk of the work. How teams deal with unclear expectations of each other's contributions can have a significant effect on the quality of their outcomes.

Using asynchronous collaboration and communication. In many online courses, students will not have the opportunity to meet in person. They might be geographically dispersed and/or have schedules that prevent face-to-face sessions. This means they will need to complete the tasks associated with the team assignment primarily using asynchronous collaboration, in which team members make their contributions at different times from different locations. In some cases, teams will be able to hold synchronous (same-time) meetings, though at a distance, using conferencing tools such as Skype.

This reality constrains the means of communication to text, for the most part; students must post drafts of papers or comments in an online discussion board, blog, or wiki. Therefore, they need to be able to communicate effectively in writing (Alden, 2011). Written communication can be informal, but must be accurate and precise. Asynchronous communication also requires clear task assignments and deadlines. Students may find it challenging to document group decisions, or even to come to a clear decision, when team members make contributions at different times.

Ensuring fairness in evaluation. Perhaps nothing is more potentially frustrating to the students and the instructors than determining fair means of evaluating (grading) student contributions to team projects. In some cases, instructors will assign the same grade to all team members, basing the evaluation only on the quality of the final "product" the team constructs. In the other extreme, grades are awarded only for individual contributions, leaving the team's final product out of the equation. Students do not want their grades unduly affected by poorly performing team members, but they also want the quality of their final product recognized and, if warranted, rewarded. The most common practice, therefore, is a combination of individual and team grades (Alden, 2011).

Best Curriculum Design Practices

In order to maximize the benefits and address the challenges of team assignments in online learning, curricular designers can implement several research-supported practices. First, the course documents should clearly define the team-based project and its deliverables; students should have a clear idea of what will be expected of the team. The method of evaluation for team members should also be clearly stated in the syllabus, as this will help to define the roles and actions of the team members early in the process (Koh, Barbour, & Hill, 2010). The team's task should be extensive enough so that every student has both significant work and a unique role as a member of the team (Lynch, 2010). The design of the project may even provide mechanisms for communication, including the tools that are available to the team as well as how the team can expect to interact with the instructor.

But a significant consideration of the design process for courses with online teams is to account for both process and project. Too often, sufficient time is allocated only for the team to complete its project without taking process time into account. Teams rarely hit the ground running; they need time to develop into a productive working unit. During this key phase of a team's experience, the team members will need to learn each other's strengths and weaknesses and develop a plan for how they will work together. The instructor may need to remain highly involved at the outset to make sure the team gets off to a good start. It may even be wise to assign a pre-project to help facilitate the team formation process so that it is largely in place before the team needs to turn its attention to its main project. Such a pre-project could include the development of a team charter that governs how the team will work together and what each member's role will be. Regardless of what process or pre-projects are decided upon, the design of the course needs to allow sufficient time for team process in addition to that which has been allocated for the project.

The importance of effective team interaction cannot be underestimated; perhaps the one factor, more than any other, that affects how well a team accomplishes its task is the level of trust that exists among the members. Trust is a key factor on any team and, like many other team aspects, trust evolves through a process (Beranek and French, 2011). Initially, trust is assumed through benevolence; team members believe that all members intend to make a substantial contribution toward the team's success. Trust is further built upon familiarity as team members get to know each other; following this, trust is reinforced based on observed results. In online team projects, trust can be slower to develop given the limited scope of social interactions that the team members experience (Beranek & French, 2011). Curriculum designers can build activities into the course that help facilitate the development of trust. These can include social activities that help develop familiarity and smaller projects that help the team members understand what they can reasonably expect from each other.

Best Instructional Practices

Instructors can choose from an array of strategies and tactics that will support students as they engage in team projects in online environments. Instructors need to be highly involved in the team as it forms and should remain involved in the team throughout its existence. At the outset, the instructor can provide coaching on the team formation stages (forming, storming, norming, performing) and conflict resolution. Sull (2012) suggests providing each team with a list of potential problems and the most common ways to address them. Scherling (2011) suggests that the instructor include tasks that will promote the development of interpersonal skills and conflict management as a part of the team's work. As a part of this effort, the team needs to consider expectations and the ways its members will address differences in work styles or team members who fail to perform. This is also the time when team members should be considering their roles (leader, contributor, scribe, etc.) and making conscious decisions regarding their method of participation. All of these activities are part of what has been referred to above as the team's process.

To highlight the importance of allowing the team to develop its process, Grinnel, Sauers, Appunn, & Mack (2012) describe three stages of a team's work that include socializing the team members, working on the individual tasks that make up the project, and managing the individual pieces of the project to completion. They measured the amount of effort that was dedicated to each of these steps at different points in the team's process. In the early stages of the team's project, the majority of all interactions and efforts were dedicated to socializing the team members with a smaller amount of time dedicated to the team's work. Over time, more effort was shifted to the actual project work they were assigned. This analysis demonstrates the importance of team process: until those processing steps are completed, the work required to finish the project will not receive the team's full attention.

During the early stages of the team's process, the members will decide how they will be led. Some teams may elect to appoint a single leader for the life of the project, but both Sull (2012) and Palsolé & Awalt (2008) suggest using rotating team leadership. This can be facilitated by asking the team to divide its project into logical sections and to appoint a different leader for each section.

As the team begins its work, the instructor can help the members establish good communication patterns so that nobody feels excluded. This may require a structured approach to help the team draw out the more reserved members and control those who may be overly active (Sull, 2012). Initially, the instructor may be very involved in the team's process but his/her involvement can taper off as the team starts to connect and develop effective working practices. The instructor should remain at least a limited part of each team until the conclusion of the project to provide rapid responses to inquiries and to intervene if problems occur.

Other suggestions for ways the instructor can help facilitate a team's development include (1) providing examples of good interactive processes so that teams can use them as a model; (2) providing a structured and fair way to allow team members to evaluate the contributions of their teammates; (3) allowing team members to evaluate the entire group process once the project is complete; and (4) integrating opportunities for self-reflection to allow team members to identify what has been learned through the team process and project. In short, instructors can best support online teams when they ensure that teams operate in a fair, productive, and equitable manner that aligns with the learning needs and motivations of each team's members.

Best Evaluation Practices

Grading student work in team projects in online learning requires creating a balance between recognizing the individual member's contributions and assessing the quality of the final "product." Alden (2011) evaluated common evaluation practices using seven criteria: validity of grades, ease on students, ease on faculty, encouragement of active participation, perception of fairness, utility for formative feedback, and impact on group dynamics (pp. 12–13). Based on results of surveys of faculty and students, Alden's findings show that students favor "records review," the analysis of actual log-ins, postings, comments, and other records of each individual student's contributions in the online environment as the method of evaluation for group work or teamwork. Faculty, on the other hand, showed a slight preference for portfolio reviews. Neither group favored the "shared grade," in which all team members receive the same grade. It seems both faculty and students want the results of teamwork to be included in the evaluation, and also want some means of ensuring that each team member's contributions are recognized and evaluated.

Instructors who want to apply these practices should take into account that both means of evaluation are time-consuming. Whether reviewing the "trace records" of student work in the online environment or evaluating the quality of artifacts included in a student portfolio, faculty will invest significant time and effort. Using automated reports from the online learning management system can assist in records review; and using clear and concise rubrics will make portfolio evaluation less burdensome (Alden, 2011; Revere & Kovach, 2011).

Other means of evaluation should be considered depending on the specific learning goals of the course. For example, if a learning goal emphasizes understanding of team dynamics, peer review might be appropriate (Alden, 2011). If the team is working on a cooperative project where each team member is responsible for a unique contribution to the team, then portfolio review may be the best option. However, if the team's project requires careful and close integration and collaboration, where team members jointly work on most or all sections of a project, then the shared grade may be appropriate.

Conclusion

As online learning becomes even more popular in higher education, the need to encourage student engagement and foster deeper learning in this modality will continue to grow. Team projects are an important component of most higher education programs, meeting the needs for student engagement as well as preparing students for the demands of the workplace. Yet, effective academic teams don't just happen, they take careful planning and diligent observation on the part of instructors and curriculum designers. Teams need time to establish proper social patterns and working practices in order to be ready to work on the actual project they have been assigned. Both the design of the course and the actions of the instructor can be important factors in ensuring that the development of team process is an effective and useful exercise that will lead to a successful online academic team project.

Further research on the most effective ways to design team projects for the online environment might follow discipline-specific pathways. Are there types of team projects that are more suited to management, leadership, education, science, or liberal arts disciplines? Additional exploration of instructional strategies that help students bridge the experience of teamwork in the online learning environment to the realities of virtual teams in the professional environment would also provide helpful context for faculty. Much work can be done to improve methods of evaluating teamwork to ensure these methods are responsive to academic demands (grading and fairness) and honor the spirit of authentic assessment.

Online academic team projects are here to stay and rightfully so. They provide students with a number of important skills and prepare them for the likelihood that they will become members of several global virtual teams at many points throughout their careers. The use of virtual teams is on the rise because they provide the benefits of multinational cooperation without the difficulty and expense of domestic and international travel (Kirstein, 2011). Considering the demands of the emerging global economy and the virtual nature of an increasing percentage of workplace activities, it is important that online academic programs play a role in preparing the workers of the future for the challenges they will face. It is equally important that such projects be designed and facilitated by instructors to help ensure student success.

References

Alden, J. (2011) Assessment of individual student performance in online team projects. *Journal of Asynchronous Learning Networks 15*(3), 5–20.

Association to Advance Collegiate Schools of Business (2010). *Eligibility procedures and accreditation standards for business accreditation.* Tampa, FL: AACSB International.

Beranek, P. M., & French, M. L. (2011). Team trust in online education: Assessing and comparing team-member trust in online teams versus face-to-face teams. *The Journal of Distance Education, 25*(3).

Elder, L. & Paul, R. (2010). Critical thinking: Competency standards essential for the cultivation of intellectual skills, Part 1. *Journal of Developmental Education 34*(2), 38–39.

Green, N.C., Edwards, H., Wolodko, B., Stewart, C., Brooks, M., & Littledyke, R. (2010). Reconceptualising higher education pedagogy in online learning. *Distance Education 31*(3), 257–273.

Grinnel, L., Sauers, A., Appunn, F., & Mack, L. (2012). Virtual teams in higher education: The light and dark side. *Journal of College Teaching and Learning, 9*(1), 65–77.

Kirstein, K. D. (2011). The effect of cultural dimensions on the development of intra-team trust in global virtual teams. In K. Milhauser (Ed.), *Distributed team collaboration in organizations: Emerging tools and practices* (pp. 64–81). Hershey, PA: IGI Global.

Koh, M. H., Barbour, M., & Hill, J. R. (2010). Strategies for instructors on how to improve online groupwork. *Journal of Educational Computing Research, 43*(2), 183–205.

Lynch, D. J. (2010). Application of online discussion and cooperative learning strategies to online and blended college courses. *College Student Journal, 44*(3), 777–784

Mortgagy, Y. & Boghikian-Whitby, S. (2010). A longitudinal comparative study of student perceptions in online education. *Interdisciplinary Journal of E-Learning and Learning Objects,* 6 (1), 23-44.

Palsolé, S., & Awalt, C. (2008). Team-based learning in asynchronous online settings. *New Directions for Teaching and Learning, 116,* 87–95.

Prinsloo, P., Slade, S., & Galpin, F. (2011). A phenomenographic analysis of student reflections in online learning diaries. *Open Learning 26* (11), 37–38.

Revere, L., & Kovach, J. V. (2011). Online technologies for engaged learning: A meaningful synthesis for educators. *The Quarterly Review of Distance Education 12*(2), 113–124.

Revere, L. (2003). An approach to improving student performance, assessment, and satisfaction. *Southwest Business Administration Journal 3*(1), 70–76.

Scherling, S. E. (2011). Designing and fostering effective online group projects. *Adult Learning, 22*(2), 13–18.

Sull, E. C. (2012). Keeping online groups dynamic, motivated and enthused! *Distance Learning, 9*(2), 66–69.

Yang, Y., Cho, Y. J., Mathew, S., & Worth, S. (2011). College student effort expenditure in online versus face-to-face courses: The role of gender, team learning orientation, and sense of classroom community. *Journal of Advanced Academics 22*(4), 619–638.

10

Next-Generation Teaching and Learning: Adopting and Adapting Web 2.0 to Pedagogy

Brian Guthrie, PhD, *RSW, Member Clinical Registry, Division of Arts and Sciences*

Abstract

Next-generation teaching and learning seeks to understand the student's experience of participation and collaboration in utilizing social media/Web 2.0 tools and incorporating these tools into a student-centered learning environment. This chapter will explore how the embedded principles of participation, collaboration, cooperation, and creativity inherent in social media/Web 2.0 tools can be applied to student-centered learning principles such as learner engagement, interaction in learning and learner ownership and management of learning. The discussion will detail how social media/Web 2.0 tools can be utilized to empower learners to contribute to the course material, formulate and express their own insights and opinions, construct their own understanding of material and connect concepts to personal experience on current events, and learn from one another in collaborative environments. In addition, the paper will discuss constructivism as a foundational perspective that supports the use of social media/Web 2.0 technology in the classroom.

Introduction

Almost thirty years ago Marshall McLuhan, a Canadian communication theorist, described how the world had been contracted into a village by electronic technology. In 1964 he wrote, "Today, after more than a century of electric technology, we have extended our central nervous system in a global embrace, abolishing both space and time as far as our planet is concerned" (1964, p. 3). In the 1960s the Internet as we currently know it was in its early stages of development. Originally called "ARPAnet," it was an experiment of the U.S. military to maintain communication systems in the event of a nuclear strike by developing a network of interconnected computers. A number of universities recognized the potential and power of networked computer systems and joined the experiment connecting their mainframe computers in order to enhance their research capabilities. In 1989, twenty-five years after McLuhan's vision of a global village, the Internet matured and evolved into the World Wide Web (WWW), a virtual world of interlinked documents and information accessible to anyone with a computer connection (Berners-Lee, 1989). In 1999, ten years after creating the WWW, Berners-Lee (2000) commented, "I have always imagined the information space as something to which everyone has immediate and intuitive access, and not just to browse, but to create" (p. 169). Today a simple click of a mouse button gains access to the WWW and a myriad of information pages, knowledge content, and knowledge experts.

With the advent of the twenty-first century, the discussion and debate about the affect of the digital age on education has evolved into a vision of twenty-first-century learning. Many educators imagined a learning environment that included virtual connections to other students and other teachers in other parts of the world. The formal structural hierarchy of the classroom wherein the teacher imparts knowledge and the student is the receptacle of that knowledge would be replaced by a global learning community with many teachers and multiple worldviews. Students and teachers would communicate and collaborate with peers and colleagues, interact with experts in their field, and participate in online courses from other institutions. Within the virtual world of the Internet, web applications would enable students and teachers to be actively engaged in real time, anytime and anyplace in a process of peer learning, exchanging ideas and creating new knowledge outside of the physical restraints of the classroom.

The WWW has made that vision a reality. The WWW, more commonly referred to as Web 2.0, is the current evolution of the Internet and consists of a variety of social media software tools that facilitate virtual interaction between individuals and allows information to be shared with other users having the same social media software. Kaplan and Haelein (2010) define social media as "a group of Internet-based applications that build on the ideological and technological foundations of Web 2.0, and that allow the creation and exchange of user-generated content" (p. 61). Social media tools have created multi-user virtual environments where students and teachers can move beyond the static desktop computer interface to a virtual environment of blogs, wikis, personal learning networks (PLNs), and multimedia collaborations. Although social media tools are used primarily by the consumer to connect and establish personal relationships, the benefit of social media software tools to education promotes the creation of knowledge through collaboration with others. The most recent evolution of Web 2.0 to cloud computing has enabled access to information, resources, and databases unencumbered by wires and drives.

Many universities support twenty-first-century learning by providing open courseware collections that include audio and video lectures as well as access to their library collections. The Massachusetts Institute of Technology (MIT) was one of the first to offer open access to its online courses, setting an example and providing a model for open access education (http://ocw.mit.edu/index.htm). MIT's website receives two-million-plus visits from interested individuals, students, and educators from around the world. Cornell University offers a selection of its library collection on a free Internet archive. University of California, Berkeley, broadcasts on its own YouTube channel, and Apple provides many institutions with a platform for disseminating educational content via iTunes U. The recent emergence of the Massive Open Online Course (MOOC) allows any individual to take a lesson from the university of his or her choice, for free, with no limit on the number of students attending. Coursera.org offers MOOCs in partnership with universities to tens of thousands of students across the globe free of charge.

This chapter will describe the use of Web 2.0 social media software tools as an adjunct to enhancing instructional practice in the context of a constructivist paradigm. Web 2.0 social software tools employ web-based technologies to promote interaction between participants to not only contribute content but also interact with the content and create content. The chapter will explore how the embedded principles of participation, collaboration, cooperation, and creativity inherent in Web 2.0 social media tools can promote the active learning principles of engagement, interaction, and self-directed learning where students take ownership and management of their learning process (Mason & Rennie, 2008). In addition, the chapter will highlight the benefits of Web 2.0 social media tools in establishing a learning environment that empowers the social construction of knowledge within a student-centered learning environment. That is, how Web 2.0 social media tools can be utilized to empower learners to contribute to the course content, develop and communicate their own insights and opinions, integrate their own understanding of knowledge with their personal experiences, and learn from others' through collaboration. Although the use of social media tools continues to gain acceptance with educators and educational institutions, there are existing barriers that inhibit institutions and educators from incorporating social media into their curriculum, as well as issues of privacy and security that need to be solved.

Web 2.0

The World Wide Web (WWW) was created by Berners-Lee in 1989 and has evolved from a virtual environment that allows users to not just read but also interact, collaborate, and create knowledge that can be published on the WWW. At its inception, the WWW, commonly referred to as Web 1.0, was read-only. It was composed of static web pages that were portals to information posted and controlled by the site owner, the webmaster. There was no interaction with the user or between users and no exchange of information or communication. Technological advances allowed users to interact with each other and contribute to the web using social media software tools. Users could now read, write, and publish to the web. This evolution of the Internet became commonly referred to as Web 2.0. Web 2.0 is often called the social web and has democratized learning and knowledge generation by providing social media software tools that connect people to content and individuals to other individuals who collaborate in the creation of new content.

The term "Web 2.0" is attributed to being introduced by O'Reilly Media in 2003 (O'Reilly, 2005), and refers to the second-generation evolution of the WWW that allows for web-based interactions, applications, and communities. O'Reilly (2005) defined Web 2.0 as "a set of economic, social, and technology trends that collectively form the basis for the next generation of the Internet—a more mature, distinctive medium characterized by user participation, openness, and network effects" (p. 4). Gillmor (2004) described Web 2.0 as the "read/write Web." What were originally static web pages became interactive, and users began to access information using social media to remix content in unique and different ways. The WWW had evolved to become virtual communities promoting social and idea networking. The evolution of the WWW into Web 2.0 is more than a reiteration of Web 1.0 with refinements to its existing programming; it is an evolution of thinking that has created a new perspective on how software can facilitate social interaction and the generation of knowledge. The term "social media" is often used interchangeably with Web 2.0 and refers to social software tools that enable users to interact in virtual relationships and to create user-generated content (Cormode & Krishnamurthy, 2008). Social media includes global social network sites such as Facebook, video-sharing sites such as YouTube, image-sharing sites such as Flickr, blogs such as Tumblr and WordPress, including the micro-blog Twitter, and social bookmarking sites that curate information and research sources such as Delicious, Evernote, and Pinterest.

Students in the twenty-first century have access to the sum total of human knowledge by accessing Web 2.0. They use social media software to make meaning of this myriad flow of information to create idea networks, exchange their views on content, create new content, and collaborate with others outside of the classroom. In the United States two-thirds (66 percent) of online adults and three-quarters (73 percent) of online teenagers (ages 12–17) use social media (Lenhart, Purcell, Smith, & Zickuhr, 2010).

Net Generation Learners

Net generation learners were born after 1982 during the advent of the personal computer (PC) and many are either in colleges and universities or are entering colleges and universities. Many are beginning their careers as educators in schools, colleges, and universities. They have coexisted with the virtual world of the Internet and have incorporated the Internet into each of their developmental stages and across their educational milestones. They are actively engaged in using Web 2.0 and social media applications to communicate and network to build relationships. Many have grown up with the WWW in their grade school and high school classrooms, and they are accustomed to accessing the Internet to enhance their learning during class and in completing homework assignments. This generation has never known life without the Internet, and they employ technology as a tool to engage in purposeful activity to gain instantaneous access to information and people. Their primary source of information about the world they experience is web-based content.

They are typically early adopters of the latest emerging technologies and are seen as using the technology in innovative ways to share their lived experience with their peers. Educators experience this generation as being focused on grades and performance and actively involved in extracurricular activities and social issues. As a generation they tend to identify with parent values and have a close ongoing relationship with their parents, often remaining at home longer than their parent's generation (Howe & Strauss, 2000).

What differentiates the Net Generation from earlier generations is their tendency to prefer hands-on experiential learning. Marc Prensky (2001) describes this generation of students as digital natives: "our students today are all native speakers of the digital language of computers, video games and the Internet" (p. 1). It is this experience of being born into the digital age that leads educators to believe, and to have had the experience, that the Net Generation conceptualize and integrate information differently from previous generations of learners. They access information quickly, remixing images, music, text, and video from multiple sources simultaneously and disseminating this information across multiple media platforms ranging from instant messages to videos on YouTube, podcasts, blogs, and personal updates on Facebook. They expect on-demand access to information and are in constant digital communication with their peer group to share the creation of their own content and their life activities. This technological competence enhances their personal lived experience and is grounded in social network relationships and entertainment. For many this competence with technology does not automatically translate to critical thinking, critical reflection, and problem solving in a learning environment.

An American study on teen content creators and consumers (Lenhard & Madden, 2005) reported that 57 percent of online teens create content and publish it on the WWW using one or more applications of social media. That is equal to half of all teens, ages 12–17, or about twelve million adolescents. Their activity on the Internet ranges from publishing their lived experience and worldview on a personal blog to creating web pages, and sharing and remixing original content in a combination of photos, stories, and/or videos online.

Their technological expertise and familiarity with the Internet do not guarantee that they can navigate the Internet to access knowledge resources to self-direct their learning. Educators should not adopt a default assumption that the Net Generation is hardwired to take responsibility for their own learning by using the Internet to enhance their existing learning environments. They may have grown up in a digital era and demonstrate technological competence, but they still require critical reflective thinking skills to discern what information out of the vast amounts of knowledge available on the Internet to integrate into their intellectual growth and development. It would be false to expect that this generation of digital natives requires or expects that their learning is dependent on technology. Hartman, Moskal, and Dziuban (2005) report that as an outcome of their research, students see technology as a means to an end; their expectation is to be involved with teachers and fellow students, overriding a desire to use technology.

A student technology survey by Oblinger and Oblinger (2005) revealed that the majority of students preferred a moderate amount of technology in their classes. Students reported that they appreciate the convenience of having access to online syllabi, class readings, and online submission of assignments. In addition, the survey highlighted that students also want face-to-face interaction. This replicates the results of many distance education studies that show students often report that the learning experience is lacking when all course interactions are maintained only in the online environment. Wegerif (1998) and Rovai (2007) have documented that learning increased when students in online courses were able to increase their interaction, communication, and community with other students.

Net Generation Learning

Net generation learning (NGL) is an evolving educational movement committed to transforming the student learning experience by providing a learning environment that enhances the ability of every student to reach his or her individual learning potential. The pedagogical foundation of NGL focuses on an active learning environment that incorporates the experimentation and exploration of concepts and problems where the teacher is no longer central to the transmission of knowledge. Students are provided personalized instruction based on need, skill, and interest and are encouraged to utilize Web 2.0 and social media technology to engage each other in the process of collaboration and problem solving.

The purpose of employing technology in the classroom is as an adjunct to increase participation in learning, to increase contribution to learning, and to bring real-world experiences into the student learning experience. Net generation teaching and learning accepts the student experience of participation and collaboration in utilizing Web 2.0 tools and understands the benefits of incorporating these tools into a student-centered learning environment where students are empowered to take responsibility for their own learning.

Research in Education

Research in education reform has revealed a move from teacher-centered and didactic learning environments to an adoption of student-centered and constructivist methods (Aldridge, Fraser, Taylor, & Chen, 2000; Healey & Jenkins, 2000; Kolb & Kolb, 2005; Lee, 2007). Constructivism has its origins in the cognitive theories of Piaget (1926), who developed the concepts of active learning, schemes, assimilation, and accommodation, and Vygotsky (1978), who developed the concepts of social constructivism, group work, and apprenticeship. The basic premise of constructivist theory is that individuals create their own meaning through experience.

The shift from an objectivist to a constructivist approach to learning and teaching is premised on the notion that "people learn best through personally meaningful experiences that enable them to connect new knowledge to what they already believe or understand" (Killen, 2007, p. 2). Education from a constructivist view focuses on learning as a "process," rather than on an objectivist view that concentrates on outcome. From a constructivist perspective, students are encouraged to learn the main ideas on their own through discovery of other viewpoints, critical thinking, and reflective discourse that emphasizes conceptual understanding rather than rote learning.

Constructivism (Piaget, 1926) is rooted in the belief that learning and knowledge occurs through mental construction and through fitting new experience and ideas into existing knowledge. Piaget (1971, 1973) emphasized the role of a learner's interaction with the environment and surrounding as critical to his or her understanding of the world and cognitive capacity. Meaningful learning is considered to occur through the construction of knowledge rather than passive receipt. Vygotsky (1978) acknowledges that knowledge is personally constructed; however, he also acknowledged that the cultural experiences and social interactions are necessary in forming an individual's construction of meaning. Glasersfeld (1995), a proponent of radical constructivism, defines knowledge construction as an adaptive activity requiring interaction with experience. Therefore, knowledge is not passively received but rather developed actively by the individual, "as our thinking, conceptualising, and our language are developed from and in the domain of our experience, we have no way of incorporating anything that lies beyond this domain" (p. 11).

More recent adaptations of constructivism further emphasize the social process of learning, and claim that learning is more effective when it occurs through interpersonal channels and in cooperative environments. Learning is believed to be collaborative, cooperative, and conversational, providing students with opportunities to interact with each other and to clarify and share ideas, to seek assistance, to negotiate problems and to discuss solutions. Taylor (1998) views constructivism within a social and cultural environment, but adds a critical dimension aimed at reforming these environments in order to improve the success of constructivism applied as a referent. McLoughlin and Lee (2007) stated that, "effective learning is conversational in nature, and that it necessitates a social dimension, including communication, dialogue and shared activity" (p. 671). Similarly,

Higgs and McCarthy (2005) claim that we learn the most through social and communal activities and that meaning is shaped and knowledge is constructed through interaction with peers and reflection. Constructivist pedagogy requires learners to construct their own meaning, and thus understanding, through problem solving.

Windschitl (1998) states that "constructivism in practice involves phenomena distributed across multiple contexts of teaching" (p. 132). Consistent to each school of constructivism is the premise that learning is an active and social experience in which learners are engaged in active dialogue with their classmates and their teachers. The goal is to establish and participate in interactive learning communities where teachers and students collaborate to solve real-world problems (Educational Broadcasting Corporation, 2004; Kearsley, 2009). Social constructivism emphasizes the importance of the learner being actively involved in the learning process, unlike other educational viewpoints where the responsibility rests with the teacher to deliver knowledge while the learner passively receives it.

Dalsgaard (2006) argues that social media software tools can support a social constructivist approach to learning by providing students with personal tools and engaging them in social networks, thus allowing learners to direct their own problem-solving process. Social media software allows students to have direct access to others' worldview, many teachers and peers in a collaborative, cooperative, and participatory experience of discovery, and development of new knowledge. Social networking sites and social media tools complement the constructivist paradigm of learning in that students are engaged through personal meaningful experiences that enable them to connect newly acquired knowledge to what they already know, believe, and understand. Web 2.0 and social media tools have promise and potential to enhance the social process of learning by utilizing cooperative, collaborative, and conversational learning.

Web 2.0 in the Classroom

Bennet et al. (2007) in a systematic review of the literature discusses the use of social media in education as a paradigm shift. The use of social media in the classroom or the incorporation of social media into one's teaching practice changes and challenges the traditional teacher-centered didactic paradigm and promotes a student-centered paradigm. Many teachers blog about their experience in incorporating Web 2.0 technology and social media tools to support teaching and learning in the classroom. They are advocates of the demonstrated potential of social media to transform the practice of teaching. This anecdotal support for the use of social media has provided numerous examples of how social media has been utilized in the classroom and the influence that social media has had on their learning environment. However, there is little research evidence about how effective social media tools are influencing education outcomes. Those who are using social media in their teaching are excited about the results. They write about increased student engagement and participation and that social media tools encourage learning communities where students and teachers learn from each other.

In a two-year investigation into the ways in which Web 2.0 technology and social media tools are being used to support teaching and learning in the classroom, Light and Polin (2010) reported that overall social media tools "show potential to transform many aspects of teaching when teachers are thoughtful about how they use the tools and they are blended with careful instructional design" (p. 3). They describe the current practice of what they refer to as "Web 2.0 teachers." They discovered that these teachers are using "the networked nature and ease of Web 2.0 to create virtual extensions of their classrooms and that the Web 2.0 tools that teachers are selecting are very easy to use, and this ease of use appears to be a key factor in the decision to use any individual tool" (p. 3). In addition, they report that "educators are using Web 2.0 tools to promote new avenues of communication among teachers, students, and the community in ways that can strengthen the community of learners" (p. 3). They note that "as the networked nature of Web 2.0 begins to blur our traditional boundaries between school/home, public/private or youth/adult culture, it presents an emerging challenge" (p. 3).

Web 2.0 is an integral part of the majority of individuals' lived experience in how they access information, communicate, and connect to relationships in the twenty-first century. It would seem to be common sense to incorporate Web 2.0 technology into schools and classrooms to promote relationships and communication in the acquisition of knowledge. Brown, Collins, and Duguid (1989) provided an argument against the perception that knowledge is separate from the real world by researching how cognition occurs in everyday activities. They conclude that "knowledge is situated, being in part a product of the activity, context, and culture in which it is developed and used" (p. 1).

Social Media Software

Blogs. A weblog or blog can be described as an online journal with one or many contributors. Besides straight text and hyperlinks, many blogs incorporate other forms of media, such as images and video. A blog is an individual's (blogger's) public commentary on news or particular subject areas or social issues. Blogs allow an individual to express his or her personal opinion and worldview to the WWW community. Blogs are used for any number of purposes determined by the blogger, for example, as a learning journal for students to reflect on learning, as well as a vehicle for social commentary or to promote professional development by providing research information of a specific field or profession.

Watrall and Ellison (2006) conducted focus groups with students who used blogs as part of their course work; they found that students liked the fact that everyone had a voice, they could write more naturally, they valued reading the view of other students, and they appreciated gaining access to new material. Research in the application of blogs to courses reported that blogs increase collaboration (Curtis & Lawson, 2001), promote a sense of community (Palloff & Pratt, 1999), and facilitate higher-order thinking (Garrison, Anderson, & Archer, 2001), interaction (Rovai, 2007), and reflection of time on task (Meyer, 2003). Farmer, Yue, and Brooks (2008) conducted a case study of blogging in an undergraduate liberal arts course. While 96 percent of the students made at least one entry, half of the students made eleven or more entries. The importance of posting was confirmed for students when early posts garnered comments from others, which kept the conversation going. In some cases, an accomplished writer would offer an idea that would "take off and spread throughout the class as a self-generating discussion" (p. 22).

By developing a blog, students not only develop critical thinking and experiment with articulating their views and opinions, they take creative risks by incorporating the use of learned sophisticated language and design elements. Students acquire creative, critical, communicative, and collaborative skills promoted by managing a blog that is beneficial to them in both scholarly and professional contexts. Rovai and Barnum (2003) argued that increased and active interaction was a significant predictor of students' perception of learning, and interaction increased when the topics of the discussion were authentic and meaningful to the students (Rovai, 2007).

Many schools are seeing the educational benefits of blogging. Teachers are mainly creating subject-specific blogs or blogs documenting a particular project. The aim is to use them to provide a more collaborative and interesting learning experience. In addition, blogging:

- Encourages higher-order skills such as reflection and analysis in addition to reading, writing, and collaboration;
- Promotes peer learning, peer assessment, and a sense of owner-ship, all of which are highly motivational;
- Involves easy-to-use technology;
- Supports video, audio, and other media and file types, creating a very dynamic learning experience and supporting various learning styles;
- Extends learning to outside of the school environment.

Social Bookmarking. Social bookmarking enables individuals to curate and contribute to a collective research and resource gathering process. As an educational tool, these links are then organized and stored for personal use, but also shared with the entire class, enabling a rich and dynamic student-generated resource library for the course (Rheingold, 2009). Social bookmarking sites such as Delicious allow users to upload their own favorite site bookmarks so that everybody else in the world can see and use those bookmarks.

Using a social bookmarking site instead of traditional bookmarking has a number of advantages:

- Bookmarks are available on any computer. Since bookmarks are stored to the web, they can be accessed and edited from anywhere.
- Social bookmarks can be searched; this helps to locate sites in large bookmark collections. Additionally, the entire network's bookmarks can be searched. Users can often find new resources from their peers.
- A note can be written for each social bookmark. This can help a user to remember what was important for a certain bookmark, especially for large websites or for specific purposes for saving a website.
- Users can share their research with the entire network.

Wikis. A wiki is a group of Web pages that allows multiple users to add content, similar to a discussion forum or blog, but also permits others to edit the content (Arreguin, 2004). What distinguishes wikis from other forms of social media is that there is no inherent structure; wiki pages can be interconnected and organized as determined by the users, and, unlike blogs, information is not presented by default in a reverse-chronological order. Wikis can also serve as platforms to collectively develop and track group projects and teamwork and is a web application designed to allow multiple authors to add, remove, and edit content (Cunningham & Leuf, 2001).

Raitman, Augar, and Zhou (2005) surveyed students in online courses that used wikis and found that 90 percent of those responding were satisfied and 10 percent were unsatisfied with the experience. Positive comments about the wikis were their convenience and accessibility anytime, their editing ability, which seemed to increase ownership over the final product, and their democratic nature, which built on opinions and research by many students.

In essence, wikis offer an online space for collaborative authorship and writing. They are available online for all web users or for members of specific communities, and they include version-control tools that allow authors to track the history of specific pages and the history of their personal contributions. A wiki also offers the ability to interact with an evolving document over time. It allows teachers and learners to see the evolution of a written task, and to continually comment on it, rather than offering comments only on the final draft. A wiki can be useful for tracking and streamlining group projects. Because students are responsible for the content they add to the wiki page, wikis can cultivate a greater sense of accountability and information-filtering skills.

YouTube. YouTube has become the second-largest search engine on the Internet and has become an enormously popular form of Web 2.0 new media. *Wired Magazine* cites an average of 65,000 uploads and a hundred million videos viewed per day on YouTube (Godwin-Jones, 2007).

Traditionally, video has been adopted by educators as a powerful educational and motivational tool. YouTube is increasingly being used by educators as a pedagogic resource to achieve curriculum outcome goals offering vignette videos on almost every subject category from science to art to language to mathematics. Khan Academy tutorial math videos hosted by YouTube have become a favorite of students and teachers as a resource and study guide.

Teachers and students alike find that video is an effective catalyst and facilitator for classroom discussions. Coupled with hands-on learning, a video-enhanced curriculum can be influential in expanding the learning experience.

Twitter. Twitter advertises itself as a service for friends, family, and coworkers to communicate and stay connected through the exchange of quick, frequent answers. It is digital communication that takes place in a network formed around a shared interest. It allows 140 characters to say what you want to say. Founded in 2006, Twitter is an information and social network with particular designed elements and user practices that distinguish it from other social media. These include its follower structure, link sharing, use of hashtags, and real-time searching (Johnson, 2009).

Twitter has been incorporated into the classroom of many educators who use it for an open discussion in class that can be continued out of class. It has been used to engage students in creating a community of learners. Many educators use Twitter to provide instant feedback to students on homework assignments, additional resources, and follow-up comments on classroom discussions.

Greenhow and Gleason (2012) present a number of ways in which Twitter can be used in support of higher education. They consider Twitter to be a mechanism to:

- Increase student motivation and engagement with course content. Students can be engaged in short-term activities that help keep them progressing toward small, manageable goals that are more tangible than long-term, abstract objectives.
- Increase student-to-student interactions, which can help to build and maintain a learning community whose influence can stretch beyond the confines of the classroom or even the duration of the course.
- Increase student-instructor interactions. Some teachers use Twitter to increase their availability and provide a quick and informal way for students to ask questions or stay linked in to the course content.

- Promote collaborative meaning-making process with each other and their teacher. Twitter allows information to be quickly shared, considered, and re-shared in a process that can rapidly lead to new insights and understandings.
- Allow students to develop twenty-first-century skills. The very act of engaging in digitally mediated communications helps to develop useful skills that will be needed in the work world. The collaboration and teamwork skills that Twitter can support are also valuable in a hyper-connected work world where much of the daily communication may happen virtually.

Provide a low barrier to publishing and self-expression. The informal writing necessitated by working within the constraints of Twitter helps to remove many of the barriers to contributing to academic discussions that may make many students feel excluded. This does not represent a dumbing down of the content, but rather a way to make students think efficiently and express themselves clearly while still feeling that they understand the requirements of participation in a conversation.

Encourage academic risk taking. The informal nature of the medium and the seemingly temporary nature of it encourages students to share freely and to express themselves more candidly than may happen in a face-to-face classroom environment where all eyes are on them should they choose to speak (Greenhow & Gleason, 2012).

Twitter has become for many educators a primary source of professional development where they join (follow) other educators in sharing resources, experiences, and ideas on teaching in the twenty-first century and the evolution of social media as a teaching tool.

Benefits to Web 2.0 to Learning

Students and educators now have equal access to a virtual learning environment where it is possible to search for, locate, and quickly access a myriad of information resources anytime in any place to address immediate real-time learning needs. Woolfolk and Margetts (2010) state that one of the primary goals of education is to provide students with the skills and knowledge to successfully participate in society. In the twenty-first century most jobs and the majority of organizations use social media. Therefore, many educators believe that it is their responsibility to integrate social media into their teaching practice in order to meet that goal.

Web 2.0 technology enables students and educators to collaborate and participate in a creative learning experience, constructing and generating knowledge personalized to their own unique learning style. Social media has the potential to transform learning and teaching processes by offering innovative ways to learn by supporting learner-centered approaches; group work and inquiry projects; interactive forms that lead to reflective, deeper, and participative learning; learning by doing; inquiry learning; problem solving; and creativity (European Commission, 2008).

It is believed that members of the Net Generation have experienced a change in cognitive processes and learning patterns due to having grown up in the digital age of information and communication technology and that their familiarity with social media and technological competence can be utilized in facilitating knowledge acquisition. Attwell (2007) notes that use of social media tools reflect current communication and working patterns in the world outside the classroom and therefore incorporating social media into the classroom is better fitted to preparing learners for the demands of society and equipping them with the necessary skills for a successful professional career. For the educator, social media enhances teaching style, offering a familiar way for students to engage in learning and with the educator facilitating the discovery of knowledge.

Advocates of incorporating social media into their teaching practice espouse a number of benefits to the process of learning and the acquisition of knowledge. For them, social media facilitates pedagogical innovation by enhancing traditional learning and teaching patterns and generating new and innovative ways of acquiring and managing knowledge. In addition, they utilize social media tools to recognize the diversity of users and to develop personalized educational experiences, offering opportunities for flexible, distributed learning, which could provide learners with more varied opportunities to engage with learning and develop their own creative skills (Rudd, Colligan, & Naik, 2006). Educators currently incorporating social media into the classroom curriculum employ it as vehicle to promote autonomous, independent, and self-directed learners and to facilitate the development of twenty-first-century skills that enable them to connect, interact, and collaborate successfully with a variety of people on different tasks and in diverse environments.

Brock (2005) identifies a number of potential benefits for learners by incorporating social media into the learning process. He considers that social media:

- Promotes critical and analytical thinking;
- Promotes creative, intuitive, and associational thinking;
- Promotes analogical thinking;
- Has the potential for increasing access and exposure to quality information.

The decision of which tools should or shouldn't be used by learners and teachers should depend on the specific pedagogical needs of a teaching situation as determined by the teacher. Social media tools and Web 2.0 technologies are congruent with the understanding of learning as socially constructed, which has been a cornerstone of twenty-first-century pedagogical theory. Blogs, YouTube, and wikis provide a means to encourage and make visible the social construction of knowledge as defined by a constructivist theory.

Social media software tools promote twenty-first-century thinking about educational practice. In particular it provides learners with new opportunities to be self-directed in their learning and to engage in collaborative and cooperative research. Incorporating social media into teaching and learning can facilitate collaborative ways of working with peers, teachers, and expert in the field, which promotes the development of new knowledge. Social media can promote the development of the twenty-first-century skills of collaboration, critical thinking, and digital citizenship, which equips students well for the world of work.

However, there is limited research evidence to confirm how widely online forums, wikis, blogs, podcasts, and so on are being used in virtual learning environments and if the use of social software increases learning outcomes. Cook, Holley, and Andrew (2007) describe one of the primary challenges to integrating social media into the classroom as one between welcoming a diversity of resources that the WWW has to offer while acknowledging the need to facilitate the students' ability to navigate the WWW using digital competence and critical thinking. Adopting social software tools in education as a default because students are already using it may abdicate responsibility of thoughtfully incorporating the tool into the curriculum to enhance classroom discourse and reflection and to engage students in the exploration of critical thinking.

Incorporating social media only to digitize lectures, texts, and journals without the interaction of reflection and discourse fails to recognize the ability of students to learn how to harness the web as a tool as opposed to a toy.

Pedagogical Challenge

Why use social media software in education? One popular argument for the use of social media is that students have incorporated social software tools into every aspect of their lifestyles. It is for them integral to how they interact, communicate with each other, and participate in society. Incorporating Web 2.0 technology into education is congruent with a student-centered approach to learning. It allows students to communicate with other students, with experts in the field, and to expand their networks to include many worldviews. The Web 2.0 technology allows and encourages individuals to learn from each other while retaining individual control over their time, space, activity, and learning relationship.

There continues to be a significant debate over what constitutes the advantages and disadvantages of incorporating social software into mainstream education. The debate is fueled by the lack of reliable, original pedagogical research and evaluation evidence to support incorporating social media/Web 2.0 into the classroom. To date, much of the actual experimentation using technology within higher education has focused on particular specialist subject areas or research domains (Fountain, 2005).

Research on utilizing social media tools in education has emphasized that students will engage in the use of social media in the classroom in collaborative, inquiry-based learning environments with teachers who are willing to facilitate access to Web 2.0 to assist them in transforming knowledge and skills into product, solutions, and new information. However, some members of the teaching community have been hesitant to use social media tools in the classroom because it competes with their traditional educational paradigm that is more hierarchical and instructional and less student-centered (where students contribute to the educational experience and participate in peer-to-peer learning).

Despite the fact that the majority of higher educational institutions utilize Learning Management Systems (LMS) and the LMS offer social media tools in some capacity, the tools are underutilized by instructors. A study by Hanson and Robson (2004) demonstrated that 95 percent of LMS usage involved the minimal use of the available content management and communication tools. Educators posted the course syllabus, made announcements, and used assessments that are congruent with a teacher-centered paradigm and merely replicated the traditional course model online. The tools that encourage participation, collaboration, and a more student-centered paradigm such as wiki, blogs, and discussion boards/forums were not used to their potential.

Savery and Duffy (1995) state that learner motivation increases when responsibility for the solution of a given problem as well as the process of inquiry rests with the learner. Motivation also expands as student ownership for learning increases (Savery, 1998, 1999). An integral component in the design of student-centered learning is a declaration by learners of what they know combined with the recognition of that which they need to learn more about. Student-centered learning is collaborative learning wherein the learners accept responsibility for acquiring information and resources and bringing that back to the learning group to help inform the development of a solution to a problem.

The debate about the effectiveness of incorporating social media into the classroom learning environment needs to evolve from being critical of or advocating for to a more evidence-based discussion. Tools are understood only through their use and uses, rather than through some abstract conceptualization of their characteristics. This means that social media tools are best understood by evaluating what students learn through their use in education and whether there is a measurable influence on education outcomes. The challenge for educators in the twenty-first century is pedagogical change as their role evolves from one of delivering content to one of assisting students to discover content on their own.

Anecdotal evidence of an individual educators' experience of why incorporating technology into the classroom is an advantage or disadvantage is more often grounded in pedagogical bias rather than how the technology might advantage students. Embracing the benefits of incorporating technology into the classroom requires a pedagogical shift from an objectivist paradigm, where learning is external to human experience, to a constructivist paradigm, where learners construct their own reality and an individual's knowledge is a function of one's prior experience (Jonassen, 1991). The use of social media/Web 2.0 tools from a constructivist theory enhances instructional practice in which expertise is distributed, knowledge is shared, and work is collaborative. The learning process of making connections is constructive as opposed to instructive. The pedagogical challenge is not whether technology aligns with a constructivist paradigm and is not aligned with an objectivist paradigm; the challenge in teaching in the twenty-first century is understanding and meeting the needs of today's learners. Technology should always be at the service of pedagogy.

Conclusions

Prensky (2001) suggested that the Net Generation learners are digital natives taught by "digital immigrant instructors, who speak an outdated language" (p. 2). While this may have been the case a decade ago, as the Net Generation brought technology to school and teachers struggled to comprehend its place in the classroom, many educators have embraced the potential of Web 2.0 tools in engaging students and have become assimilated into the digital age. These educators fully comprehend that technology skills have become an essential component of student success and future employment. Net Generation teachers not only employ the use of technology to facilitate the learning process but also provide the learner with critical skills in collaboration and communication to be successful in acquiring the evolving occupations of the digital age.

The Internet has evolved into a participative medium from just a mere source of information. There is less of a divide between digital natives and digital immigrants as each has become a citizen of a community, the global village, where technology serves the purpose of providing access to the WWW and the ability to tailor information to meet one's specific needs.

The Net Generation demonstrates the technical competence to navigate the web to access specific information of personal interest and utilizes social media primarily for socializing and entertainment. However, educators experience that they lack the information technology literacy required to meet the needs of the twenty-first-century workforce and often struggle to transfer their technological competence into an academic setting that requires critical thinking and reflection on knowledge. As Lippincott (2006) notes, an emerging area of literacy is needed for students to increase their fluency with representing their knowledge in the digital world.

The reality is that the Net Generation are digital natives fluent in the language of technology and adaptable to the evolving technology of the digital world; however, teachers are no longer digital immigrants struggling to integrate into a digital culture. In a 2012 social media survey by

Pearson Publishing on faculty use of social media, they revealed that most faculty use social media, the majority (64%) using it for personal reasons rather than professional or for teaching. Also, 44.7 percent of the faculty surveyed disclosed that they use social media professionally and 33.8 percent of faculty surveyed disclosed that they use social media in their teaching practice (Moran, Seaman, & Tinti-Kane, 2012). The advancing wave of new technologies and the gravitation to cloud computing challenges both twenty-first-century learners and teachers to find new ways of incorporating technology rather than employing new technology in old ways. Social media and Web 2.0 tools enable students and teachers to not only collaborate and cooperate but also navigate the classroom of the global village.

Net Generation teachers incorporate social media tools in a learning environment of exploration where students learn to use Web 2.0 technology to acquire the twenty-first-century skills of thinking critically about concepts and issues and understanding the process of inquiry and critical analysis in order to make meaning of the overwhelming amount of information through cooperation and collaboration in the creation of knowledge. Successful and effective use of social media in one's teaching practice is about the pedagogy, not the technology. The purpose is to incorporate social media tools in such a way that promotes engagement, participation in the learning process as well as collaboration in the building of new knowledge. The challenge is to facilitate innovative ways to stimulate students to learn, collaborate, and create, and not just adopt Web 2.0 technology as an electronic version of storing read-only content and maintaining traditional assumptions about learning and knowledge (Bryant, 2007).

Web 2.0 levels the playing field between the Net Generation and educators. Each has equal access to the WWW where they can collaborate, create, and share information. This virtual learning environment can be connected directly to the classroom to engage students and teachers in becoming interactive participants in building knowledge via blogs, wikis, social bookmarking, and social network sites. The social media tools are intrinsically user-centered interactive and participatory and therefore congruent with a student-centered teaching and learning environment.

Despite being a decade into the twenty-first century, there is minimal empirical research on the effectiveness of social media in learning compared to the growing anecdotal evidence that social media is a benefit to the learning process in that it promotes engagement, participation, and collaboration. Adopting social media in the classroom because of one's own comfort and familiarity for personal use or taking a default position that the students are already using it, so there is no choice, ignores the barriers to effective use of social media in education. Careful analyses of the use of social media and its effect on learners involves considering the following barriers and seeking solutions (Wood, Mueller, Willoughby, Specht, & Deyoung, 2005):

- Concerns about the integrity of online student submissions
- Concerns about privacy
- Lack of integration with learning management systems
- Takes too much time to learn or use
- Lack of support at institution

In addition, there are a number of potential consequences in digitally engaging students or implementing new curriculum that requires students to participate in online activities. Not only is there a need for continued research into the benefits of social media to learning, educators and education administrators need to create appropriate technology policies and curriculum that evolves with legislation, privacy, and appropriate online conduct.

Educators need to participate in ongoing professional development on privacy and security as much as they participate in professional development on the innovative uses of social media to enhance learning. Finding solutions to the barriers will require continued research into the effectiveness of social media in improving the actual outcomes of education.

Although the debate over the place of social media in education needs to continue in order to fully comprehend the potential and effectiveness of social media in education, there is a consensus in education. The Internet will continue to evolve, and the WWW will continue to mature, changing and enhancing the way society interacts and communicates. John Culkin (1967) summed up Marshall McLuhan's position on the influence of technology on society with the quote: "we shape our tools and therefore they shape us" (p. 3).

References

Aldridge, J. M., Fraser, B. J., Taylor, P. C., & Chen, C. C. (2000). Constructivist learning environments in a cross-national study in Taiwan and Australia. *International Journal of Science Education, 22*(1), 37–55.

Arreguin, C. (2004). Wikis. In B. Hoffman (Ed.), *Encyclopedia of educational technology*. Retrieved from http://coe.sdsu.edu/eet/Articles/wikis/start.htm

Attwell, G. (2007). Personal learning environments—the future of eLearning? *eLearning Papers*, 2. Retrieved from http://www.elearningeuropa.info/out/?doc_id=9758&rsr_id=11561

Aviv, R. (2000). Educational performance of ALN via content analysis. *Journal of Asynchronous Learning Networks, 4*(2), 53–72.

Bandura, A. (1977). *Social learning theory*. New York, NY: General Learning Press.

Bennett, S., Maton, K., & Kervin, L. (2008). The digital natives debate: A critical review of the evidence. *British Journal of Educational Technology, 39*(5), 775-786.

Berners-Lee, T. (2000). *Weaving the Web*. New York, NY: HarperCollins.

Berners-Lee, T. (1989). *Information management: A proposal*. Retrieved from http://www.w3.org/History/1989/proposal.html

Brock, E. (2005). Brain of the blogger. *Eide Neurolearning Blog*. Retrieved from http://eideneurolearningblog.blogspot.com/2005/03/brain-of-blogger.html

Brown, J. S., Collins, A., & Duguid, P. (1989). Situated cognition and the culture of learning. *Educational Researcher, 18*(1), 32–42.

Bryant, L. (2007). Emerging trends in social software for education. *Emerging Technologies for Learning, 2*, 9–22. Retrieved from http://partners.becta.org.uk/page_documents/research/emerging_technologies07_chapter1.pdf

Conway, C. (2006) *YouTube and the cultural studies classroom*. Retrieved from http://www.insidehighered.com/views/2006/11/13/conway.

Cook, J., Holley, D., Andrew, D. (2007). A stakeholder approach to implementing e-learning in a university. *British Journal of Educational Technology, 38*(5), 784–794.

Cormode, G., & Krishnamurthy, B. (2008). Key differences between Web 1.0 and Web 2.0. *First Monday, 13*(6).

Culkin, J. (1967). Each culture develops its own sense ratio to meet the demands of the environment. In G. Stearn (Ed.), *McLuhan: Hot and cool* (pp. 49–57). New York, NY: New American Library.

Cunningham, W., & Leuf, B. (2001). *The Wiki way: Quick collaboration on the Web.* Boston: Addison-Wesley.

Curtis, D. D., & Lawson, M. J. (2001). Exploring online collaborative learning. *Journal of Asynchronous Learning Networks, 5*(1), 21–34.

Dalsgaard, C. (2006). Social software: E-learning beyond learning management systems. *European Journal of Open, Distance & E-Learning.* Retrieved from http://www.eurodl.org/materials/contrib/2006/ Christian_Dalsgaard.htm

Educational Broadcasting Corporation. (2004). *Constructivism as a paradigm for teaching and learning.* Retrieved from http://www.thirteen.org/ edonline/concept2class/constructivism/index_sub4.html

Educause Learning Initiative. (2006). *7 things you should know about YouTube.* Retrieved from http://www.educause.edu/content. asp?page_id=7495&bhcp=1

European Commission (2008). *Commission staff working document. The use of ICT to support innovation and lifelong learning for all—A report on progress.* SEC (2008) 2629 final. Retrieved from http://ec.europa.eu/ education/lifelong-learning-programme/doc/sec2629.pdf

Farmer, B., Yue, A., & Brooks, C. (2008). Using blogging for higher order learning in large cohort university teaching: A case study. *Australasian Journal of Educational Technology, 24*(2), 123–136.

Fountain, R. (2005). Wiki pedagogy. *Dossiers Technopedagogiques*. Retrieved from http://profetic.org/dossiers/article.php3?id_article=969

Garrison, D. R., Anderson, T., & Archer, W. (2001). Critical thinking, cognitive presence and computer conferencing in distance education. *The American Journal of Distance Education, 15*(1), 7–23.

Gillmor, D. (2004). We the media: The rise of citizen journalism. *National Civic Review, 93*(3), 58–63.

Glasersfeld, E. (1995). A constructivist approach to teaching. In L. Steffe & J. Gale (Eds.), *Constructivism in education* (pp. 3–16). Mahwah, New Jersey: Lawrence Erlbaum Associates, Inc.

Glasersfeld, E. (1984). An introduction to radical constructivism. In P. Watzlawick, *The Invented Reality* (pp. 17–40). New York, NY: W. W. Norton & Company.

Godwin-Jones, R. (2007). *Digital video update: YouTube, flash, high-definition*. Retrieved from http://www.allbusiness.com/technology/4051526-1.html

Greenhow, C., & Gleason, B. (2012). Twitteracy: Tweeting as a new literacy practice. *The Educational Forum, 76*(4).

Hanson, P., & Robson, R. (2004). Evaluating course management technology: pilot study. *Educause Center for Applied Research Research Bulletin*, (24), Boulder, CO. Retrieved from http://www.educause.edu/library/ERB0424

Hartman, J., Moskal, P., & Dziuban, C. (2005). Preparing the academy of today for the learner of tomorrow. In D. G. Oblinger & L. Oblinger (Eds.), *Educating the Net Generation*. Washington, DC: Educause.

Healey, M., & Jenkins, A. (2000). Kolb's experiential learning theory and its application in geography in higher education. *Journal of Geography, 99*(5), 185–195.

Higgs, B., & McCarthy, M. (2005). Active learning—from lecture theatre to field-work. In S. Moore, G. O'Neill, and B. McMullin (Eds.), *Emerging issues in the practice of university learning and teaching*. Dublin, Ireland: AISHE.

Howe, N., & Strauss, W. (2000). *Millennials rising: The next greatest generation*. New York, NY: Vintage Books.

Jenkins, H. (2007). From YouTube to YoUniversity. *Chronicle of Higher Education: Chronicle Review, 53*(24), B9–B10.

Johnson, S. (2009, June 5). How Twitter will change the way we live. *Time*. Retrieved from http://www.time.com/time/magazine/article/0,9171,1902818,00.html

Jonassen, D. H. (1992). Objectivism versus constructivism: Do we need a new philosophical paradigm? *Educational Technology Research and Development, 39*(3), 5–14.

Kaplan, A. M., & Haelein, M. (2010). Users of the world, unite! The challenges and opportunities of social media. *Business Horizons, 53*, 59–68.

Kearsley, G. (2009). Constructivist theory. Retrieved from http://tip.psychology.org/bruner.html

Killen, R. (2007). *Effective teaching strategies: Lessons from research and practice*. South Melbourne, Australia: Thomson Social Science Press.

Kolb, A. Y., & Kolb, D. A. (2005). Learning styles and learning spaces: Enhancing experiential learning in higher education. *Academy of Management Learning & Education, 1*(2), 193–212.

Kvavik, R. B., Caruso, J. B., & Morgan, G. (2004). *ECAR study of students and information technology, 2004: Convenience, connection, and control, 5*, 43. Boulder, CO: EDUCAUSE Center for Applied Research Study. Retrieved from http://www.educause.edu/ers0405/

Lee, L. M. (2007). *The construction of a constructivist: Learning how to teach without teaching*, Malaysia: Penerbit USM.

Lenhart, A., Purcell, K., Smith, A., & Zickuhr, K. (2010). *Social medial and mobile Internet use among teens and young adults*. Washington, DC: Pew Internet & American Life Project.

Lenhart, A., & Madden, M. (2005). *Reports. Family, friends & community*: *Teen content creators and consumers*. Pew Internet & American Life Project. Retrieved from http://www.pewInternet.org/pdfs/PIP_Teens_Content_Creation.pdf

Light, D., & Polin, K. (2010). *Integrating Web 2.0 tools into the classroom: Changing the culture of learning*. New York, NY: EDC Center for Children and Technology.

Lippincott, J. K. (2006). Learning, engagement and technology (preprint version). In Craig Gibson (Ed.), *Student engagement and information literacy*. Chicago: Association of College and Research Libraries.

Marzano, R. J. (2006). *A different kind of classroom: Teaching with dimensions of learning*. Retrieved from http://pdonline.ascd.org/pd_online/dol02/1992marzano_chapter1.html

Mason ,R., & Rennie, F. (2008). *E-learning and social networking handbook*. New York, NY: Routledge.

McLoughlin, C. & Lee, M. (2007). Social software and participatory learning: Pedagogical choices with technology affordances in the Web2.0 era. *Current, 664–675*. Retrieved from http://www.ascilite.org.au/conferences/singapore07/procs/mcloughlin.pdf

McLuhan, M., & Powers, B. R. (1999). *The global village: Transformations in world life and media in the 21st century*. New York, NY: Oxford University Press.

McLuhan, M. (1964). *Understanding media*. New York, NY: Mentor.

Miers, J. (2004). *BELTS or braces? Technology school of the future*. Retrieved from http://www.tsof.edu.au/research/Reports04/miers.asp

Misanchuk, E., Schwier, R., & Boling, E. (1996). *Visual design for instructional multimedia.* [CD-ROM]. Saskatoon: University of Saskatchewan.

MIT. (2007, April). Open courseware: 6 years later, bigger than ever. *ZDNet.* Retrieved from http://education.zdnet.com/?p=957

Meyer, K. A. (2003). Face-to-face versus threaded discussions: The role of time and higher-order thinking. *Journal of Asynchronous Learning Networks, 7*(3).

Moran, M., Seaman, J., & Tinti-Kane, H. (2012). *Teaching, learning, and sharing: How today's higher education faculty use social media.* Boston, MA: Pearson Learning Solutions and Babson Survey Research Group.

Oblinger, D., & Oblinger, J. (2005). *Educating the Net Generation.* Washington, DC: Educause. Retrieved from http//www.educause.edu/educatingthenetgen

Oblinger, D. (2003) Boomers, Gen-Xers, and Millennials: Understanding the "new students." *EDUCAUSE Review, 38*(4), 36–40.

Olsen, S. (2005). *The "millennials" usher in a new era.* Retrieved from http://news.com.com/2009-1025_3-5944666.html

O'Reilly, T. (2005). *What Is Web 2.0—Design patterns and business models for the next generation of software.* Retrieved from O'Reilly blog: http://oreilly.com/web2/archive/what-is-web-20.html

Palloff, R. M., & Pratt, K. (1999). *Building learning communities in cyberspace.* San Francisco, CA: Jossey-Bass.

Papert, S. (1980). *Mindstorms: Children, computers and powerful ideas.* New York, NY: Basic Books.

Piaget, J. (1973). *Memory and intelligence.* New York, NY: Basic Books.

Piaget, J. (1971). *Biology and knowledge.* Chicago, IL: University of Chicago Press.

Piaget, J. (1926). *The language and thought of the child*. London, UK: Routledge and Keagan Paul.

Prensky, M. (2001). Digital natives, digital immigrants, part 1. *On the Horizon, 9*(5), 1–6. Retrieved from http://dx.doi.org/10.1108/10748120110424816

Raitman, R., Augar, N., & Zhou, W. (2005). *Employing wikis for online collaboration in the e-learning environment: Case study*. Proceedings of the Third International Conference on Information Technology and Applications.

Rheingold, H. (2009). *The social media classroom* [Weblog comment]. Retrieved from http://dmlcentral.net/blog/howard-rheingold/social-media-classroom

Rovai, A. P. (2007). Facilitating online discussions effectively. *Internet and Higher Education, 10*, 77–88.

Rovai, A. P., & Barnum, K. T. (2003). On-line course effectiveness: An analysis of student interactions and perceptions of learning. *Journal of Distance Education, 18*(1), 57–73.

Rudd, T., Colligan, F., & Naik, R. (2006). Learner voice. *Futurelab*. Retrieved from www.futurelab.org.uk/resources/documents/handbooks/learner_voice.pdf

Savery, J. R. (1999). Enhancing motivation and learning through collaboration and the use of problems. In S. Fellows & K. Ahmet (Eds.), *Inspiring students: Case studies in motivating the learner* (pp. 33–42). London, UK: Kogan Page.

Savery, J. R. (1998). Fostering ownership with computer supported collaborative writing in higher education. In C. J. Bonk & K. S. King (Eds.), *Electronic collaborators: Learner-centered technologies for literacy, apprenticeship, and discourse* (pp. 103–127). Mahwah, NJ: Lawrence Erlbaum.

Savery, J. R., & Duffy, T. M. (1995). Problem-based learning: An instructional model and its constructivist framework. In B. Wilson (Ed.),

Constructivist learning environments: Case studies in instructional design (pp. 135–148). Englewood Cliffs, NJ: Educational Technology Publications.

Skiba, D. (2007). Nursing education 2.0: YouTube. *Nursing Education Perspectives, 28*(2), 100–102. Retrieved from http://nln.allenpress. com/nlnonline/?request=get-document&issn=15365026&volume =028&issue=02&page=0100#s5

Tapscott, D. (1997). *Growing up digital: The rise of the Net Generation.* New York, NY: McGraw-Hill.

Taylor, E. W. (1998). *The theory and practice of transformative learning: A critical review* (Information Series No. 374). Columbus, OH: ERIC Clearinghouse on Adult, Career & Vocational Education, Center on Education and Training for Employment, College of Education, the Ohio State University.

Vygotsky, L. S. (1978). *Mind and society: The development of higher mental processes.* Cambridge, MA: Harvard University Press.

Watrall, E., & Ellison, N. (2006). *Blogs for learning: A case study.* Retrieved from http://www.higheredblogcon.com/teaching/watrall/blogs-for-learning2/player.html

Wegerif, R. (1998). The social dimension of asynchronous learning networks. *Journal of Asynchronous Learning Networks, 2*(1).

Windschitl, M. (1998). The WWW and classroom research: What path should we take? *Educational Researcher, 27*(1), 28–33.

Wood, E., Mueller, J., Willoughby, T., Specht, J., & Deyoung, T. (2005). Teachers' perceptions: Barriers and supports to using technology in the classroom. *Education, Communication & Information, 5*(2).

Woolfolk, A., & Margetts, K. (2010). *Educational Psychology.* Frenchs Forest: Pearson Education.

11

Promoting Authentic Learning by Engaging in "Real-World" Research

Ellen K. Carruth, PhD, *LMHC*
Laura Schmuldt, PhD, *NCC*
Division of Arts and Sciences

Abstract

In this chapter, the authors describe the benefits of engaging in action research in a counselor education program. Action research is defined, and the concepts are illustrated with examples from one such project (i.e., "Finding Their Voice"). Additionally, the process of "learning by doing" (Dewey, 1897) is illustrated throughout the chapter with examples from the current project. The authors advocate for implementing action research in education as a means of increasing authenticity in learning. The authors discuss the benefits of action research in counselor education, and the authors describe ways in which members of other academic disciplines might infuse this collection of activities into their own curriculum.

Introduction

In the field of mental health counseling, some researchers have highlighted a lack of congruence between research and practice (e.g., Guiffrida, Douthit, Lynch, & Mackie, 2011). For many practitioners, research is not a primary professional responsibility, and as a result, counselors may not have had opportunities to engage in research investigations that could be potentially beneficial to their client populations. Interestingly, the current standards proposed by the Council for Accreditation of Counseling and Related Educational Programs (CACREP) stipulate that counselors be made aware of "the importance of research in advancing the counseling profession" (CACREP, 2009, Standard G.8.a). Aside from counselor education programs, scholars have discussed the culture of research across institutions of higher education and have described a similar disconnect between research and practice. Schön (1995) described this as a quandary of "rigor and relevance," and called upon scholars to pay attention to the problems of the "swampy lowlands," which are "of greatest human concern" (p. 28). Traditional research methods may not be amenable to the inherently complex and "messy" problems often faced by mental health clinicians. Guiffrida and colleagues (2011) highlighted this important work and made the case for counselors and counselor educators to delve into the complexities of real-world problems through action-research. Given these disparate views regarding the importance of research as a professional behavior and the reported lack of relevant research in the counseling field, the current discussion will offer one possible solution for educators in counselor education programs. The following discussion is twofold: first, the authors describe a real-world action-research project designed to explore the perceived impact of budget cuts in community mental health; and second, the authors outline student/faculty learning experiences that occurred alongside the research.

Finding Their Voice

This chapter will include information regarding the process of promoting authentic learning by engaging in "real-world" research by describing an action-research project, entitled "Finding Their Voice." This project will be described next, in an effort to provide contextual relevance for the reader.

Project Description

This particular project ("Finding Their Voice") was developed by one author (Ellen) after her experience working as a case manager in the mental health system. Ellen was working with approximately 110 clients, all of whom were chronically mentally ill, and were recipients of state assistance, usually in the form of Medicaid vouchers. During this time, the state of Washington experienced significant funding cuts that targeted many of the programs that provide services to individuals with disabilities (Gregoire, 2010). These clients experienced severe hardships on a daily basis: many were homeless, many had multiple disabilities that affected their ability to live successfully in their community, and many had severely limited incomes that prohibited participation in growth-fostering activities. Ellen witnessed clients losing their housing, losing their cash assistance, losing their food assistance, and losing prescription and medical benefits. Given her place in the lives of these clients (i.e., as a case manager), Ellen was aware of the impacts of these cuts from a unique perspective.

Because of this firsthand knowledge, Ellen decided to develop an exploratory investigation in which other clinicians could discuss their own perceptions of the ways in which budget cuts have affected their clients. To accomplish this objective, Ellen designed a research proposal in which focus group interviews (Morgan, 1988) would be the primary method of data collection. Focus groups as qualitative research combine elements of individual interviews and participant observation. The main benefit of the focus group is the "opportunity to observe a large amount of interaction on a topic in a limited period of time" (Morgan, 1988, p. 15). Additionally, focus groups are especially suited for research questions that are exploratory in nature (Morgan, 1988).

Getting Started

As the project began to take shape, Ellen decided that the topic would be quite relevant for students in the master's program in counseling. Ellen was aware that some were interested in conducting research; in fact, some were interested in conducting research specific to community mental health issues. Ellen decided to invite these students to participate in the project, based on their expressed interests.

Ellen submitted the original Institutional Review Board (IRB) proposal in June, and scheduled the first team meeting in July, shortly thereafter. At this meeting, Ellen introduced the team members to the project, discussed the qualitative research paradigm, and discussed the initial steps of the project (i.e., IRB approval, recruiting strategies, and informed consent). During this meeting, Ellen encouraged team members to start thinking about keeping a reflective journal of their experiences through the process. Reflective journaling is a process through which individuals have the opportunity to practice self-awareness, and the activity might serve as a lens through which individuals may view their experiences, either in retrospect or in vivo (Raelin, 2000).

After the protocol was initially approved, Ellen became aware of an unexpected requirement for recruiting participants: the IRB had an existing policy, stating that "organizational consent" should be obtained from any agencies that agreed to participate in the study. Accordingly, after receiving the initial approval, Ellen began to prepare information packets that could then be submitted to potential agency directors in order to obtain their consent before recruiting individual participants. Unbeknownst to Ellen and to the team, this particular issue (i.e., organizational consent) was to become a significant challenge in the forward momentum of the project.

Bracketing

As the team waited to hear back from agencies, a bracketing interview was scheduled. Bracketing, in qualitative research, is one way to mitigate potential negative effects of personal preconceptions regarding the research question (Tufford & Newman, 2012). This particular strategy is often seen in phenomenological investigations, which is one method of qualitative inquiry. Creswell (2013) asserted that "phenomenology provides a deep understanding of a phenomenon as experienced by several individuals" (p. 82). In phenomenological research, researchers are called on to identify their own personal assumptions about the phenomenon in question through bracketing. In this particular case, Ellen had firsthand experience with this phenomenon (as a case manager). In order to strengthen the "rigor" of this particular investigation, the bracketing interview was to be the time for team members to express our own assumptions about the research questions so that these assumptions could be "suspended" during data collection and analysis. Additionally, the bracketing process was an opportunity to "experience" one aspect of the process of qualitative inquiry in a personally meaningful way.

Certain members of the research team were unable to attend the scheduled bracketing interview. Consequently, the team was faced with a challenge: How can we move forward given that not all members of the team had an opportunity to participate in bracketing? For Ellen, this was beyond her current knowledge and understanding of the concept of bracketing. She decided that it would be necessary to reach out to the professional community and seek guidance. Ellen accomplished this by positing a question to a well-known electronic mailing list that many counselor educators used as a discussion forum. The question was presented as follows (Carruth, 2012):

Hello, esteemed colleagues,

I am a new faculty member, and have recently received IRB approval to begin my first post-dissertation research study. I've designed the study, recruited students for membership on the research team, briefed the students about the process, etc.

I have stumbled into an unexpected event, however. I have a group of four students, and we are beginning an exploration of the perceived impacts of budget cuts on consumers of community mental health in Washington State, from the perspective of service providers.

I established a time (the team agreed) for our "bracketing" interview. I arranged for a colleague to facilitate the interview, and then two of the four students on my team didn't show up. Because I had made arrangements with my colleague, we went ahead and "bracketed" the rest of us. I am a bit lost as to what I should do next, though.

I don't know if I should:
a) bracket the other members separately,
b) scrap that interview and reschedule for the whole team,
c) prohibit those team members from the data collection,
d) "drop" those members from the team, or
e) ????

I am keenly aware of the perceptions of the team members that were present and how this turn of events may impact group cohesion. I'm at a loss here, and would sincerely appreciate input/suggestions/insights based on your experiences.

Thank you in advance for your time and consideration.

Ellen K. Carruth, PhD, LMHC

From this query, Ellen received a number of responses, One, in particular, was extraordinarily helpful in reminding her that bracketing, from a phenomenological perspective, is a process, not a discrete event. In fact, bracketing is amorphous, by its very nature (Tufford & Newman, 2012). The team discussed the issue and made a plan for continuing the process of bracketing. This particular activity was a unique opportunity for Ellen to teach the members of the team about a specific strategy used in qualitative research to ensure the trustworthiness of data that are collected throughout the project (Creswell, 2013). Additionally, it was an opportunity for Ellen to model her own process of learning.

Making Contacts

As the team waited to hear back from individual agencies that had been solicited, one serendipitous event took place. A fellow faculty member at the university was a member of a local council that advocated for agencies that serve people of color in the local community. This colleague was gracious enough to inform the executive director (ED) of this group about the research study.

This ED contacted Ellen, and expressed interest in learning more and possibly partnering on the project. Ellen went to meet with another member of this group, who was also an ED of a local counseling agency that serves a minority group. During this meeting, initial plans were made to coordinate a focus group interview with identified agencies that serve people of color. As Ellen brought this news back to the university and the research team, the energy was palpable, as this was the team's first real "taste" of the broader impact that this study could make.

Ellen approached the provost of the university, explaining the study and the recent interaction with key stakeholders in the community. The provost graciously offered money to provide lunches for this focus group. Up until this point, no monies had been involved in the study. As this could be seen as an inducement for participation, it was necessary for the team to revise the original IRB protocol, to reflect this new development. Ellen enlisted the assistance of her team in revising the protocol. This activity provided an opportunity for team members to move through the process of revising a research protocol in a way (in vivo, as the project took shape) that is different from most traditional classroom activities.

The team worked diligently to update the protocol and submit it to the IRB so that an expedited review might occur, and the team could meet the deadline. However, the IRB's review schedule was already established, and, consequently, the team was not able to meet the deadline. Ellen did remain in contact with these professionals, and eventually was invited to attend a board meeting during which the ED of the council allowed Ellen, and one research team member, to present the project to this group of professionals.

Following this meeting, Ellen and the team member were able to speak individually with several professionals. From these contacts, the two were introduced to another key stakeholder in the community: the director of the local human services coalition. They went to meet with this individual a few weeks later, and through this contact, were introduced to the county's Director of Mental Health and Chemical Dependency Treatment. This contact offered the researchers the opportunity to leave flyers at the regional directors' meeting, whose attendees were directors and managers of community mental health and substance abuse treatment centers in the local area.

Throughout the process of making professional contacts, Ellen and the research team members were learning about (a) the process of conducting research, (b) the time and effort required to "launch" relevant research in the community, and (c) the importance of collaboration (between universities and communities) that Schön (1995) described. Additionally, opportunities for learning were apparent throughout the actual process of gaining IRB consent for this study. These opportunities proved to be meaningful because of the "position" in the success of the current project. Team members were motivated to learn based on their investment in the "real-world relevance" of this project.

Challenges

In spite of the contacts being made, the research team had only received two responses from the agencies that had been solicited, and both of these responses were negative. Without agency consent, the research team was unable to query individual participants by word of mouth. Almost six months had passed by this time, and the motivation level of individual team members was fluctuating. In fact, Ellen was becoming discouraged with the lack of progress in recruiting. Because of her frustrations, she began to reach out to other colleagues regarding the notion of obtaining "organizational consent" prior to recruiting participants. The consensus among Ellen's professional colleagues was that this policy was not relevant in this context because the identified population of participants was not a "vulnerable" population (clinicians working in professional roles with consumers of CMHSA treatment). So Ellen and the team decided to query the university's IRB regarding this policy in the context of the proposed project.

This was a pivotal point for Ellen, as a faculty member, and for the team. First, Ellen viewed the opportunity to address the IRB as a moment of significant professional development, as a first-year faculty member. Second, Ellen perceived that this particular step in the process would be a learning opportunity for team members. The team was frustrated. There was a desire to collect data, but, after six months, no opportunity. The sentiment was that we were all "in this together" now, and team members expressed interest in addressing the problem while maintaining the integrity of the project. The process of experiencing this frustration was important in the team's development. Bandura (1986) discussed the influence of *affective arousal* as it relates to an individual's learning. This same concept of *affective arousal* has been explored in the counselor education literature (e.g., Carruth & Woodside, 2010; Larson, 1998; Leach & Stoltenberg, 1997). In the current context, *affective arousal* (i.e., frustration) served to motivate the team: the shared experience of frustration allowed the team to investigate the problem collaboratively.

First, Ellen tasked individual team members with reviewing the Belmont Report (1979), which is the U.S. Department of Health and Human Services' report on the ethical conduct of research involving human subjects. This activity provided the team with an opportunity to co-construct a rationale for querying the policy of "organization consent" in the context of the current study (i.e., "Finding Their Voice"). Team members discussed their interpretations of the document, and the general consensus was that this particular university policy may have been set in place to protect "vulnerable participants," such as individuals under the age of eighteen, or individuals with a mental illness. In the current study, the identified population of participants was not inherently vulnerable. Team members were able to conceptualize the ethical duty of respecting the autonomy of participants as coming into conflict with this particular policy. That is, by seeking organizational consent prior to individual participant consent, were we not *causing* participants to become vulnerable, in the sense that their anonymity would not be protected from their employer? According to the Belmont Report (1979), "even if individual researchers are treating their research subjects fairly, and even if IRBs are taking care to assure that subjects are selected fairly within a particular institution, unjust social patterns may nevertheless appear in the overall distribution of burdens and benefits of research" (p. 9). During discussions with the team, Ellen found opportunities to provide specific instruction regarding ethics in human subjects' research that may not have occurred in the context of the traditional classroom.

With information from these discussions in hand, Ellen approached the IRB. In querying the policy, Ellen learned that it was, in fact, in place to protect vulnerable participants. In working through discussions with the co-chair of the IRB, Ellen discovered that the language in the original IRB protocol was not clear regarding the intended recruiting strategies. After this discussion, Ellen was encouraged by the co-chair to resubmit the protocol to the IRB, and clarify the intent with recruiting. The IRB reviewed this draft of the protocol, and approved a "word of mouth" recruiting strategy. While the apparent "frustrations" of the team members were related to the inability to successfully gain agency consent, the lesson learned here for Ellen and for her team was about the importance of clarity in describing the research to the IRB. John Dewey (1897) described the necessity for the instructor to become a collaborative partner in the learning process so that students can *independently discover* meaning. Dewey's notion of "learning by doing" still holds true in higher education today.

Current Status

At the time of this writing, the research team has scheduled its first interview, and members of the team have recently presented at a national professional conference on the lessons learned during an action-research project. The project has taken on a life of its own. While there have been a number of frustrations throughout, the learning has been significant. Having the opportunity to explore a problem that is relevant to the profession and the local community is immeasurably beneficial for all involved. Some of the benefits are discussed below.

What Is "Real-World" Research?

"I hear and I forget; I see and I remember; I do and I understand" (Chinese proverb)

For Ellen and her team, moving through the "messy" process of exploring a real-world problem (the impact of budget cuts on client recovery) provided opportunities to engage in "spontaneous" learning. The team was composed of students and recent graduates in the counseling psychology program; they were studying to become mental health counselors. For this group, this particular "problem" was highly relevant, as it represented the professional context into which they were moving.

Scholars have explained the need for relevance in research (e.g., Schön, 1995), and others have encouraged researchers to use action-research methods to bridge the "research-practitioner gap" in the counseling profession (Guiffrida et al, 2011). These scholars make the case that "real-world" research is, in effect, a shift away from the theoretical, toward the practical. "Real-world" research indicates investigation of problems that exist in communities; its very essence implies social action. The notion of *social action* is strongly correlated with the work of Lewin (1946, 1951). Snyder (2009) described social action as a set of activities that individuals can use to address the problems of society; one such activity being action research.

Action Research

In addition to the concept of *social action*, action research (AR) as a method of investigation was first described by Kurt Lewin in the 1940s. One of the primary tenets of his work was that it is possible for theory and practice to be in symbiotic relationship, where one informs the other

(Snyder, 2009). AR has been implemented in numerous disciplines since its original inception. As the method has increased in popularity, scholars have defined the approach differently, depending on the nature of their discipline. Consequently, Bradbury and Reason (2003) believed that AR may be best understood as a collection of research approaches.

To illustrate the variety of iterations in the conception of AR, four dominant varieties of AR have been identified by O'Brien (1988). These include traditional action research, contextual action research, radical action research, and educational action research. Traditional action research has roots in organizational psychology and generally encompasses the use of T-groups to solicit information from stakeholders. This is often specific to business settings. Contextual action research is also referred to as "action learning" and is intended to minimize power differentials and emphasize ownership among all participants. In this viewpoint, participants are encouraged to view themselves as co-creators of research (rather than simply as respondents). Radical action research is a subset of action research. It has the stated goal of working toward social transformation and engaging participants in self-advocacy. Finally, educational action research is a method that is specific to educational reform. It often consists of university-based researchers working directly with teachers in primary and secondary educational settings. Tools implemented in action research include surveys, journaling about research activities, structured and unstructured interviews, reviewing autobiographies, debriefing research participants, and conducting focus groups (O'Brien, 1988; Jordi, 2011).

While numerous iterations of AR have been described in various disciplines, for the purposes of this discussion and this project, Lewin's model of AR was implemented (Lewin, 1946). He defined AR as "a comparative research on the conditions and effects of various forms of social action, and research leading to social action" (Lewin, 1946, p. 34). Extending this original work, Bargal (2008) outlined the principles of AR based on Lewin's work as follows:

1. Action research combines a systematic study, sometimes experimental, of a social problem as well as the endeavors to solve it.
2. Action research includes a spiral process of data collection to determine goals, action to implement goals, and assessment of the results of the intervention.
3. Action research requires feedback of the results of intervention to all parties involved in the research.

4. Action research implies continuous cooperation between researchers and practitioners.
5. Action research relies on the principles of group dynamics and is anchored in its change phases. The phases are unfreezing, moving, and refreezing. Decision making is mutual and is carried out in a public way.
6. Action research takes into account issues of values, objectives, and power needs of the parties involved.
7. Action research serves to create knowledge, to formulate principles of intervention, and to develop instruments for selection, intervention, and training.
8. Within the framework of action research, there is an emphasis on the recruitment, training, and support of the change agents (p. 19).

Several of these principles are relevant to the current discussion. First, this study (i.e., "Finding Their Voice") requires "continuous cooperation between researchers and practitioners" (Bargal, 2008, p. 19). Members of the research team have different levels of involvement with practitioners. Some have personal relationships with professionals in the field, and are using their knowledge of professionals to recruit participants for the focus groups. Other members are employed in the field presently and have unique knowledge of current issues that affect practitioners. Second, the current study is also in keeping with Lewin's conception of AR in that this project is exploratory in nature, and one of the possible outcomes will be the creation of new knowledge (i.e., the impact of budget cuts on consumers of mental health counseling). Additionally, the results of this initial exploration may lead to the creation of survey instruments designed to target a broader audience of practitioners. The expected outcome of this phase of the research will be to provide statistical data to key stakeholders and decision makers regarding the effect of budget cuts on consumers of community mental health.

Why Should We Use AR in Counselor Education Programs?

Early leaders in educational and social thought (e.g., Dewey, 1897; Lewin, 1946) espoused the benefits of learning in vivo. Specific to this discussion, AR is one method of learning in vivo and it is particularly well suited to counselor education programs, given that this process encourages collaboration among professionals in an attempt to address the problems that directly affect them. Additionally, McLeod (1999; as cited in Guiffrida et al., 2011) encouraged the use of AR in counseling because of the emphasis on skills that are inherent in the counseling process (e.g., reflection, collaboration, and meaning making). In thinking about the need for AR in counselor education programs, two important considerations are (a) the current curriculum standards, as defined by CACREP (2009), and (b) the value of experiential learning in counselor education programs (Paisley & Hayes, 2000).

Curriculum Standards

As mentioned previously, CACREP is the nationally recognized accreditation body for graduate counseling programs. Several CACREP standards are relevant to the inclusion of action research in counselor education programs. First, according to the 2009 standards, programs are to instruct students in research methods that include "qualitative, quantitative, single-case designs, action research and outcomes-based research" (CACREP Standard II.8.b, 2009). If AR is viewed as a "collection of research activities" (Bradbury & Reason, 2003), then it seems to address this particular standard well, as the inclusion of qualitative activities, quantitative activities, single-case design, and outcomes-based activities could all fall under the banner of AR activities.

Furthermore, CACREP standards specify that an individual entering the field of professional mental health counseling "understands effective strategies to support client advocacy and influence public policy and government relations on local, state and national levels to enhance equity, increase funding, and promote programs that affect the practice of clinical mental health counseling" (CACREP, 2009, CMHC, E.4). By Lewin's (1946) original description, AR is situated in social action. The current project has provided opportunities for the research team to become aware of and involved in local advocacy efforts. The inclusion of AR into counselor education programs may provide opportunities for program faculty to bridge a needed gap between community outreach and academic work. For example, in the current study, the research team had an opportunity to meet with the executive director of a local human services coalition.

This meeting served multiple purposes. First, it allowed the research team to discuss the project with an important member of the professional community. Second, it allowed the researcher to introduce the director to the counseling program at her university, and to offer options for possible future collaborations. One example of the potential for collaboration was that this executive director had knowledge of a number of community health agencies in the area nearby the university. As the university had recently relocated, a new counseling center had opened in conjunction with the university. The researcher wrote letters to these community health agencies, inviting them to refer clients for counseling who had little ability to pay for services at more traditional mental health centers. Hence, the program and the community both stand to benefit from this initial collaboration.

Lastly, CACREP standards include a number of mandates regarding the importance of advocacy and social justice. These standards state that the counseling professional "knows public policies on the local, state and national levels that affect the quality and accessibility of mental health services" (CACREP, 2009, CMHC, E.6) and "advocates for policies programs, and services that are equitable and responsive to the unique needs of clients" (CACREP, 2009, CMHC, F.2). Through implementing action research in counselor education, faculty members ensure that multiple standards are addressed, and more importantly, they model for students the spirit of the language of the standards: to engage in social justice within the field of counseling.

Experiential Learning

Paisley and Hayes (2000) described the significance of experiential learning in their discussion of constructivist counselor education. These scholars asserted that "people are able to reason in increasingly complex and abstract ways and that their understanding of experience is embedded in a social context" (p. 82). It stands to reason that social learning is likely to influence the development of cognitive complexity, which has been mentioned as a desirable trait among counseling professionals (e.g., Holloway & Wolleat, 1980; Spengler & Strohmer, 1994; Walker & Spengler, 1995). Cognitively complex counselors possess the ability to hold multiple, sometimes disparate, points of view simultaneously, in order to reach conclusions in conceptualizations about their clients. If situating students in a "real-world" learning context promotes cognitive complexity, then the potential benefits of engaging in AR can be corroborated further.

The idea of learning in a social context has a long history in developmental psychology. Notably, Bandura postulated a theory of social learning in 1977. In this work, he introduced the notion of *self-efficacy*, which has been cited frequently as a desired trait for counselors (e.g., Leach & Stoltenberg, 1997; Lent, Hill, & Hoffman, 2003; Lent, Hoffman, Hill, Treistman, Mount, & Singley, 2006; O'Brien & Heppner, 1996).

Self-efficacy, or the ability to believe that you are capable of performing in a certain situation, is influenced by four factors: (1) mastery, (2) modeling, (3) social persuasion, and (4) affective arousal (Bandura, 1977, 1986). Of these factors, Bandura named *mastery*, or performing an action repeatedly until the behavior becomes automatic, as the most influential factor. Second to this was the notion of *modeling*; watching another, more skilled person, complete the behavior. Third, Bandura described the notion of *social persuasion* as influential on the development of self-efficacy. This speaks to the importance of situating learning experiences in social contexts, as is the case in the current discussion. Finally, Bandura asserted that *affective arousal* was influential in the development of self-efficacy. That is, the degree to which a person experiences anxiety associated with performing a new behavior will influence that person's self-efficacy (Larson, 1998).

For the research team, Bandura's theory was evident on multiple levels. For Ellen, there was an awareness of her position as a leader in regards to her research team members, and an awareness of their "eyes" on her during this process. Meaning, Ellen was embarking upon a new role; one that she had not assumed prior to this project. With this new role came a level of *affective arousal*. Ellen recognized that her team was dependent on her to assume a position of authority. Ellen was also aware of the influence of *social persuasion* on her own learning. This was especially relevant as the team members collectively decided to challenge the IRB's policy regarding organizational consent. Because Ellen was aware of the frustrations of her team members, she learned an important lesson. In order to effectively facilitate a meaningful learning environment, there were times in which she needed to assume a position of authority, and there were other times in which she needed to step down from that position, so to speak. bel hooks (1994) reminded readers that "seeing the classroom as a communal place enhances the likelihood of collective effort in creating and sustaining a learning community" (p. 8). Regarding the IRB issue, Ellen enlisted the assistance of all of her team members. She asked each to review the Belmont Report, and to provide their interpretations of the report in the current context. Members of the team discovered nuances in the Belmont Report that Ellen had missed. This particular point in the overall process was quite significant for members of the team, as each individual had an opportunity to share his or her views on the topic. This process allowed the team to learn about institution review in a meaningful way, based on the frustrations and motivations experienced by members of the team.

In their journals, members of the research team discussed their own frustrations with the IRB issue, and they also reported appreciation for Ellen's willingness to persist in finding a solution to this particular predicament. *Modeling* (Bandura, 1986) became relevant during this process, as Ellen was in a position to teach—through actions—the appropriate way to handle a policy disagreement in a professional and ethical manner.

In sum, different factors (mastery, modeling, social persuasion, and affective arousal) affected different team members in different ways at different points. Ellen was motivated by affective arousal; team members were motivated by modeling. What's important here is to remember that creating a space in which learning can occur is at the essence of learning in a social context. In her discussion of *Communities of Practice*, Wenger (1998) challenged readers by asking:

> What if we adopted a different perspective, one that placed learning in the context of our lived experience of participation in the world? . . . What if, in addition, we assumed that learning is, in its essence, a fundamentally social phenomenon, reflecting our own deeply social nature as human beings capable of knowing? (p. 3)

How Do We Promote Authentic Learning?

Situating learning outside of the classroom (Wenger, 1998) in order to meet the call to become "agents of social change" (Lee & Hipolito-Degado, 2007) may seem to be a daunting task for educators. However, many scholars have espoused the benefits of community engagement and service learning (e.g., DePrince, Priebe, & Taylor-Newton, 2011; Soslau & Yost, 2007; Woodside, Carruth, Clapp, & Robertson, 2006) as a means of promoting authentic learning.

Service Learning

Service learning is one strategy for promoting authentic learning. Service learning involves infusing curriculum with community engagement. Students engage in real-world learning outside of the theoretical confines of the traditional classroom. Instead of studying about problems, students are encouraged to immerse themselves in the social context of the problem. This immersion promotes a number of skills for students who will

- learn to translate theory into practice,
- explore the possibilities of their profession (Woodside et al., 2006),
- have opportunities to increase their learning and contribute to their community,
- have opportunities to make real-life connections to the subject matter (Soslau & Yost, 2007), and
- likely improve their critical thinking skills in relation to their peers (DePrince et al., 2011).

Given these benefits, and the importance of AR in counseling programs, it seems apropos to consider the inclusion of AR activities as strategies for service learning and social action. As mentioned earlier, scholars have defined AR in numerous ways, and as a result, many different iterations of the ways in which AR might be included in a curriculum could be inferred. Service learning projects might be one way that educators could implement AR into counselor education programs.

In the current study, members of the research team discussed several of the benefits of this project. Members found involvement in the process of research to be personally and professionally relevant, and their responses support the importance of learning in a social environment. For example, when asked how being involved in this project has informed the way they were thinking about being counselors and working in the field, members reported the following:

- "I learned about all of the possible directions I could focus my efforts postgraduation."
- "The potential for exploring human behavior is exciting."
- "I appreciate the opportunity to participate in work that might make positive social change."
- "I understand the relevance of research to practice."
- "I am hopeful that this work might inform legislature."
- "Being on this team validates the work I do with clients."

Team members also discussed the particular benefits that they saw from involvement in this project. Members reported the following:

- "The opportunity allows me to explore my own personal interests [in research] in a safe, supportive, and encouraging environment."
- "I love learning from other people."
- "Understanding how much work is involved in the research process is enlightening as I prepare for my doctoral studies."
- "Being a part of a group of people who have the same interests is a great feeling."
- "This research directly looks at client needs and offers hope and direction for the mental health system."

In this project, promoting authentic learning through action research was dependent, in part, on the commitment and motivation of the instructor (Ellen). The students involved in the process reflected on their appreciation for Ellen and her commitment to this work, and Ellen reflected similarly in her journal:

The benefits for me are immeasurable. First, I have found my "sea legs," so to speak, as far as facilitating a research group. I have learned valuable lessons regarding the times when my own personal insecurities held me back from pushing through and being appropriately assertive. I've learned more and more about research methods through the need to communicate these things to my team. I've learned to embrace the role of "leader" even though I strive to maintain a collaborative environment. I've enjoyed knowing my students and team members on a different level. I've enjoyed the co-construc-tion of knowledge that we've experienced—the Belmont Report, for example. I've been able to have firsthand experience in community involvement, and I am learning to respect the position of my work in the larger community. In fact, I've learned that my work has a place in the larger community. This work has provided purpose for me. I am motivated to do this.

In reflection, Ellen's learning during this process was centered on her perceived ethical duty. For Ellen, modeling (Bandura, 1986) ethically responsible conduct was of paramount importance throughout the process. As such, several ethical considerations come to mind that are relevant to this discussion of promoting authentic learning.

Ethical Considerations

In the current study, a number of ethical issues have been encountered. For example, as is the case with all research, the primary ethical duty of the research team has been to ensure the safety, confidentiality, and anonymity of the research participants. In this particular study, the method of data collection is the focus group interview. According to Morgan (1988), the very nature of the focus group impairs the researchers' ability to protect the anonymity of participants. Teaching members of the research team the importance of protecting human subjects, ensuring confidentiality, and adhering to specific methods of recruiting and communicating with participants allowed the students to comprehend the essence of these ethical guidelines in a unique way.

Also, the process of bracketing the research team (described above) provided significant opportunities for Ellen to offer instruction regarding ethical considerations during the collection of data and the reporting of results. Framing the importance of the bracketing interview early in the process allowed for team members to enter into each further step from a position of awareness of the potential for bias to enter into the discussion.

"Finding Their Voice" provided opportunities for learning that have been situated in a contextually relevant environment. As the authors have described above, the potential benefits for counselor education are significant. Other disciplines have also espoused the benefits of AR; these are mentioned briefly, below.

Application beyond Counselor Education

Action research has been utilized in a variety of disciplines ranging from business to education and health care. The advantages consistently noted by researchers include the inherent empowerment of shifting the focus to inclusivity, respect for stakeholders, and the "real-world" applications generated by the process.

Marketing, product development, manufacturing, organizational change, information systems, accounting, small business, and management have all implemented action research to address issues ranging from productivity to employee compliance (Puhakainen & Siponen, 2010). Emerging data documenting action-research projects in developing nations suggest its adaptability across cultures. For example, Gedeon (2011) described the use of action research in teaching business ethics in Sub-Saharan Africa, and Erdener (2011) conducted similar research in Central Asia. Molina, Aguirre, Breceda, and Cambero (2011) investigated developing technology parks in Mexico also using action research. Action research is attractive to managers in the business sector as it encourages ownership of ideas for both researchers and stakeholders. Action research collapses variables of specific business practices and provides flexibility for data collection (Baskerville, 1999).

The field of education has generated considerable action research. Through action research, educators, students, parents, and academic faculty have identified and fleshed out solutions to a myriad of issues including inequality and the effects of high-stakes testing. A review of the literature indicates that action research might be (a) utilized to examine parents' pedagogical expectations (Lam & Kwong, 2012) and (b) implemented to transform physical education (Enright, 2012).

Action research has also been used in health-care settings to involve both practitioners and patients in the process of evaluating and changing services. Collaboration in health care has generated action-research data ranging from understanding the experiences of Somali women in the American health-care system (Pavlish, Noor, & Brandt, 2010) to health education in England (MacFarlane, Singleton, & Green, 2009) and provisions for health care with indigenous communities (Kendall, Sunderland, Barnett, Nalder, & Matthews, 2011).

Conclusion

Using action research as a way to promote authentic learning has a long history in education (e.g., Kurt Lewin, 1946). In this chapter, the authors have described action research as a collection of activities that is beneficial for higher education programs, including counselor education. The educational benefits of this type of research include (a) meeting curriculum standards (e.g., CACREP) in a creative way, (b) providing opportunities for real-world learning, (c) teaching research methods that can influence professional practice, (d) engaging in social action, (e) fostering collaborative relationships between universities and communities, and (f) infusing advocacy and social justice into the curriculum. Students involved in the current project have had the opportunity to learn about possible directions to pursue postgraduation and have had the opportunity to participate in a project that they find to be meaningful and relevant to their future work. The research team, which includes students, alumni (new professionals), and faculty have commented on the benefits of the collaborative nature of the current project, and how being involved with a group of like-minded individuals is enjoyable and motivating. As faculty members are continuously tasked with promoting educational opportunities that provide relevance to the workplace, action research can occupy a position of encouraging relevant learning experiences for students regardless of the discipline.

References

Bandura, A. (1977). *Social learning theory*. Englewood Cliffs, NJ: Prentice Hall.

Bandura, A. (1986). *Social foundations of thought and action*. Englewood Cliffs, NJ: Prentice Hall.

Bargal, D. (2008). Action research: A paradigm for achieving social change. *Small Group Research, 39*(1), 17–27. doi: 10.1177/104649640731

Baskerville, R. (1999). Investigating information systems with action research. *Communications of the Association for Information Systems, 2,* 19.

Belmont Report. (1979). *The Belmont Report: Ethical principles and guidelines for the protection of human subjects of research.* Retrieved January 5, 2013, from hhs.gov/ohrp/humansubjects/guidance/belmont.html

Bradbury, H., & Reason, P. (2003). Action research: An opportunity for revitalizing research purpose and practice. *Qualitative Social Work, 2*(2), 155–175.

Carruth, E. K. (2012, September 28). Seeking advice regarding a bracketing interview gone awry [Electronic mailing list message]. Retrieved from https://listserv.kent.edu/wa.exe?A0=CESNET-L

Carruth, E. K., & Woodside, M. (2010). The development of counseling self-efficacy: A case study. *North Carolina Counseling Association Journal, 3,* 4–17.

Council for Accreditation of Counseling and Related Educational Programs (CACREP). (2009). *2009 CACREP accreditation manual.* Alexandria, VA: Author.

Creswell, J. W. (2013). *Qualitative inquiry and research design: Choosing among five approaches* (3rd ed.). Los Angeles, CA: Sage.

DePrince, A. P., Priebe, S. J., & Taylor-Newton, A. (2011). Learning about violence against women in research methods: A comparison to traditional pedagogy. *Psychological Trauma: Theory, Research, Practice, and Policy, 3*(3), 215–222.

Dewey, J. (1897). My pedagogic creed. *School Journal, 54,* 77–80.

Enright, E. (2012). Physical education in all sorts of corners: Student activists transgressing formal physical education curricular boundaries. *Research Quarterly for Exercise and Sport, 83,* 255–267.

Erdener, C. (2011). Business ethics as a field of teaching, training and research in Central Asia. *Journal of Business Ethics, 104,* 7–18.

Gedeon, R. (2011). Business ethics as a field of teaching, training and research in Sub-Saharan Africa. *Journal of Business Ethics, 104,* 83–92.

Gregoire, C. (2010). *Proposed 2011–13 budget and policy highlights: Transforming Washington's budget.* Retrieved June 19, 2011, from http://www.ofm.wa.gov/budget11/highlights/highlights.pdf

Guiffrida, D. A., Douthit, K. Z., Lynch, M. F., & Mackie, K. L. (2011). Publishing action research in counseling journals. *Journal of Counseling and Development, 89,* 282–287.

Holloway, E. L., & Wolleat, P. L. (1980). Relationship of counselor conceptual level to clinical hypothesis formation. *Journal of Counseling Psychology, 27,* 539–545.

hooks, b. (1994). *Teaching to transgress: Education as the practice of freedom.* New York, NY: Routledge.

Jordi, R. (2011). Reframing the concept of reflection: Consciousness, experiential learning, and reflective learning practices. *Adult Education Quarterly, 61,* 181–197.

Kendall, E., Sunderland, N., Barnett, L., Naldler, G., & Matthews, C. (2011). Beyond the rhetoric of participatory research in indigenous communities. *Qualitative Health Research, 21,* 1719–1728.

Lam, C., & Kwong, W. (2012). The "Paradox of Empowerment" in parent education: A reflexive examination of parents' pedagogical expectations. *Family Relations, 61,* 65–74.

Larson, L. M. (1998). The social cognitive model of counselor training. *The Counseling Psychologist, 26,* 219–273.

Leach, M. M., & Stoltenberg, C. D. (1997). Self-efficacy and counselor development: Testing the integrated developmental model. *Counselor Education and Supervision, 37*(2), 115–124.

Lee, C., & Hipolito-Delgado, C. (2007). Introduction: Counselors as agents of social justice. In C. Lee, *Counseling for social justice* (2nd ed.) Alexandria, VA: American Counseling Association.

Lent, R. W., Hill, C. E., & Hoffman, M. A. (2003). Development and validation of the Counselor Activity Self-Efficacy Scales. *Journal of Counseling Psychology, 50*, 97–108.

Lent, R. W., Hoffman, M. A., Hill, C. E., Treistman, D., Mount, M., & Singley, D. (2006). Client-specific counselor self-efficacy in novice counselors: Relation to perceptions of session quality. *Journal of Counseling Psychology, 53*, 453–463.

Lewin, K. (1946), Action research and minority problems. *Journal of Social Issues, 2*, 34–46. doi: 10.1111/j.1540-4560.1946.tb02295.x

Lewin, K. (1951). *Field theory in social science: Selected theoretical papers* [Original work published 1944]. D. Cartwright (Ed.). New York, NY: Harper and Row.

MacFarlane, A., Singleton, C., & Green, E. (2009). Language barriers in health and social care consultations in the community: A comparative study of responses in Ireland and England. *Health Policy, 92*, 203–210.

Molina, A., Aguirre, J., Breceda, M., & Cambero, C. (2011). Technology parks and knowledge-based development in Mexico: Tecnologico de Monterrey CIT2 experience. *International Journal of Entrepreneurship and Innovation Management, 13*, 199–224.

Morgan, D. (1988). Focus groups as qualitative research. *Sage University Paper Series on Qualitative Research Methods, 16*. Newbury Park, CA: Sage.

O'Brien, K. M., & Heppner, M. J. (1996). Applying social cognitive career theory to training career counselors. *Career Development Quarterly, 44,* 367–377.

O'Brien, R. (1998). *An overview of the methodological approach of action research.* Retrieved March, 17, 2013, from http://www.web.net/~robrien/papers/arfinal.html

Paisley, P. O., & Hayes, R. L. (2000). Counselor under construction: Implications for constructivist-developmental program design. In G. McAuliffe & K. Eriksen (2000), *Preparing counselors and therapists: Creating constructivist and developmental programs.* Association for Counselor Education and Supervision. Virginia Beach, VA: The Donning Company.

Pavilsh, C, Noor, S., & Brandt, J. (2010). Somali immigrant women and the American health care system: Discordant beliefs, divergent expectations, and silent worries. *Social Science and Medicine, 71,* 353–361.

Puhakainen, P., & Siponen, M. (2010). Improving employees' compliance through information systems security training: An action research study. *MIS Quarterly, 34,* 757–778.

Raelin, J. A. (2000). *Work-based learning: The new frontier of management development.* Upper Saddle River, New Jersey: Prentice Hall.

Schön, D. (1995). Knowing-in-action: The new scholarship requires a new epistemology. *Change* (Nov.-Dec.), 27–34.

Snyder, M. (2009). In the footsteps of Kurt Lewin: Practical theorizing, action research, and the psychology of social action. *Journal of Social Issues, 65*(1), 225–245.

Soslau, E. G., & Yost, D. S. (2007). Urban service-learning: An authentic teaching strategy to deliver a standards-driven curriculum. *Journal of Experiential Education, 30*(1), 36–53.

Spengler, P. M., & Strohmer, D. C. (1994). Clinical judgment biases: The moderating roles of counselor cognitive complexity and counselor client preferences. *Journal of Counseling Psychology, 41,* 8–17.

Tufford, L., & Newman, P. (2012). Bracketing in qualitative research. *Qualitative Social Work, 11*(80). doi: 10.1177/1473325010368316

Walker, B. S., & Spengler, P. M. (1995). Clinical judgment of major depression in AIDS patients: The effects of clinician complexity and stereotyping. *Professional Psychology: Research and Practice, 26,* 269–273.

Wenger, E. (1998). *Communities of practice: Learning, meaning, and identity.* New York, NY: Cambridge University Press.

Woodside, M., Carruth, E. K., Clapp, S., & Robertson, J. (2006). "I could not have been more wrong in my preconceived ideas": The experience of service learning. *Human Service Education, 26*(1), 5–24.

Legitimate Peripheral Participation: Learning Reconceived as a Transformation of Social Identity

Arden Henley, EdD, *School of Arts and Sciences*

Abstract

This chapter responds to a critical and often overlooked dimension of the graduate education of professionals. It presents an approach to teaching and learning that is fully compatible with performance-based ideas and a focus on outcomes, while incorporating the perspective of the profession as a social entity.

Introduction

To belong in a profession or any other definable community of practice entails more than familiarity with a particular domain of knowledge or even the mastery of a set of competencies. Belonging to a profession also entails a transformation of social identity. An *initiation* into a community of practice is required. In the case of education, for example, the person is not only learning about pedagogy, he or she is *becoming* a teacher. From this perspective, learning is fundamentally a sociocultural phenomenon and cannot be separated from participation in the social world of practice.

The concept of *legitimate peripheral participation* addresses *how* this transformation is typically carried out by communities of practice and by implication, *how* such a transformation can most effectively be refined and contributed to by postsecondary educational institutions (Lave & Wenger, 1991; Wenger, 1998; Lave & Wenger, 2002).

Situated Learning

Legitimate peripheral participation in action was first described by Wenger and Lave based on their work with claims adjusters in a large insurance corporation (Wenger, 1998). Like many organizations, the insurance company had a training department made up of specialists in education and training. Despite the evident expertise of the trainers, the company had been finding that its training programs were notably unsuccessful, as well as less than valued by participants. Wenger and his colleague, Lave, asked the question, "If adjusters are not learning in the courses and workshops provided, how are they learning, if at all?"

A social anthropologist, Jean Lave's earlier research on apprenticeship sensitized her to the participatory and social dimensions of learning. Informed by this lens, Wenger and Lave found an ongoing, on-the-ground, highly *situated* process of learning and a complex network of informal instructional resources (Lave & Wenger, 1991; Wenger, McDermott, & Snyder, 2002). Adjusters were learning, but not in the way the organization had imagined. Learning was primarily taking place through adjusters' participation in their work guided by more experienced adjusters and by *informal* experts in this community of practice who were themselves adjusters and could be reliably turned to as sources of information, practice, and encouragement.

As it initiated new members, the community of practice demonstrated an awareness of a gradual and incremental learning process taking place through engagement in the work itself. New adjusters were understood to be capable of responding to certain claims and not others. As in apprenticeship, work was assigned to new adjusters that enabled their engagement in the practice at a level commensurate with their competency. Over time the ante was raised and more complex claims assigned. It was this graduated inclusion and associated mastery over time that resulted in Wenger and Lave's use of the term "legitimate peripheral participation" (Lave & Wenger, 1998). It points to a journey that resembles apprenticeship (Lave & Wenger, 1998) because it entails higher levels of participation in the work of a community of practice over time. Intellectual, linguistic, and ethical refinements take place as a person moves from neophyte or prospective practitioner to full membership in a community of practice through successive elevations in status. This kind of learning does not lend itself solely to the dissemination of abstract frameworks, but also to conversation, storytelling, coaching, and "learning by example."

Wenger and Lave also noticed another kind of learning that was taking place as new adjusters became more and more a part of the scene and moved from *novice* to *ordained* status. They were clearly picking up on a whole spectrum of, what has become known as, *tacit knowledge* (Polanyi, 1966). This knowledge ranged from the colloquial terminology used to categorize claims to correct behavior in the lunchroom. There was a transmission of lore from experienced practitioners to new learners that was enabling successive degrees of inclusion in the community of practice. The new practitioners moved from outsider to insider and from a conditional kind of acceptance to recognized membership in the community. In the context of their working lives, they *became* claims adjusters.

This is a different version of learning than one in which viable knowledge is assumed to be cognitive and expressible primarily in academic terms. The view of learning as fundamentally a transformation of identity through participation in a community of practice is more social and less individualistic and more performance-focused and less intellectual, though the effect on the individual and the significance of intellectual development is by no means diminished. In this view, cognitive frameworks play a mediating and enabling rather than formative role. This socially *trans-formative* view emphasizes the importance of *epistemological correctness*. Epistemological correctness, as Wenger and Lave employ the term, implies that learning should be organized in a way that is congruent with how people learn in the context of a given community of practice (Wenger, 1998, p. 100).

At the Interface

The critical interface in relation to counselor knowledge and practice, for example, takes place when the counselor meets with an individual, group, or family in need of assistance. Can you imagine being a beginning therapist and facing your first family? The following scenario about this experience reflects the relevance of the ideas discussed in this article at that interface:

> David and Nila, Nila's mother Raminder, and their two sons Ujal and Suk are waiting in the family therapy room as you arrive. They are twenty minutes early for their first appointment. David is Caucasian, and Nila and Raminder are from the Punjab area of India. Ujal, thirteen years old, peers intently at his iPhone, and Suk, eleven, is talking in a loud voice in Punjabi to his mother. Raminder tries to no avail to interrupt what is very quickly becoming an argument between mother and son. David looks tense and angry, but does nothing.

Who are you going speak to, and what are you going to say? Family therapy theories dance around in your head. Initially based on cybernetics and increasingly incorporating postmodern ideas, family therapy theories are complex and elegant, and there are a lot of them. If you haven't learned family therapy as performance and if you don't experience some sense of yourself as a bona fide therapist, you will not know what to do. Your polite but ineffectual responses will be swept up in the well-rehearsed family drama that is already playing out.

Suk doesn't want to be here and he doesn't see why he has to. Ujal is the problem. He has been refusing to go to school for weeks. David and Nila don't know how to collaborate in handling the situation, not to speak of dealing with Raminder's constant interference.

Yes, you know a lot about family therapy. You have read the latest research about families with problems, as well as being able to sketch out in some detail the parameters of several theories about family therapy, but what to do?

It is never going to be easy to face the complex, dynamic, and often multicultural realities presented by contemporary families, but it does help to have participated in a performance-based learning process with experienced practitioners. You have some feeling for what to do and experience some confidence that you can step in, forestall the drama that is beginning to unfold, and lead the conversation in a productive direction. The family has enacted this drama many times; it is not going to help them to do it another time.

An Epistemologically Correct Way to Educate Practitioners

Since the education of practitioners should address how practitioners "learn" the practice, practitioner programs must include all of a mastery of a practice, acquisition of a body of knowledge, and a high level of integration of theory and practice. They should also incorporate the transmission of tacit knowledge and a means of affecting increasing identification as a professional. Epistemologically correct programs should be organized in ways that reflect successively greater opportunities to engage in practice, and experienced practitioners should be engaged in instruction. Graduates should not be put in the position of *beginning to learn the practice* after graduation.

In relation to successively greater opportunities to engage in practice, the inclusion of case studies, practice-related experiential exercises, and simulations in course work followed by supervised internships should be emphasized. The inclusion of internships also imposes an ethical constraint that relates to how practitioner education should be organized. Educators have to be sure that interns have achieved sufficient levels of competence and ethical sensitivity to do no harm to clients. Accordingly, practitioner-focused programs should require that students pass practice-focused comprehensive exams or comparable competency-based assessments prior to their engagement in internships. Further assurance is provided by high levels of oversight from field supervisors.

In postsecondary education, the concept of instruction by practitioners or *scholar/practitioners* is known, but very much limited to professional schools in fields such as medicine and law and, in some instances, arts education. The conventional view, particularly in regulatory contexts, is that the use of practitioners, as instructors, risks depriving students of up-to-date academic knowledge and research-based findings. The status of research-based scholarly and academic knowledge is epistemologically privileged in this view. Though it is perhaps a valid priority in the context of preparing academicians and researchers, it is at odds with how people learn practices such as counseling and educational leadership. It is a limiting view in environments in which the primary goal is the preparation of practitioners because it fails to address the imperative to equip graduates with the competencies, knowledge, and ethical sensitivities to engage in professional practice, as well as a feeling of membership in the community of practice.

From the perspective of a situated understanding of learning and the critical phenomenon of legitimate peripheral participation, the conventional view promotes *practice distant instruction,* which leaves graduates in the position of having to begin to master the practice and join the community of practice at the point of graduation. New graduates have to be trained by those who employ their services. Adding internships at the end of a program taught largely by academics and not practitioners does not fully compensate for the process of systematically developing the performance of practice throughout the program. The conventional approach also inadvertently promotes instruction by recent doctoral graduates with little experience or by faculty whose preference is to engage in research and publication rather than teaching and practice. The conventional view typically underestimates the engagement of preeminent practitioners in learning emerging theory, research, and practice on an ongoing basis and their wide-ranging contributions to knowledge development. It assumes that source of significant knowledge is primarily academic and risks depriving significant fields of endeavor such as counseling and educational leadership of *practice-informed knowledge* and ironically, impels a schism between practice and scholarly activity that in the end undermines the relevance and importance of scholarly activity. A reflection of this schism is an almost unilateral disregard of scholarly activity and publication by practitioners. This disregard further highlights the potential significance of scholar/practitioners as bridge builders between the otherwise partitioned communities of the academy and practitioners.

The engagement of scholar/practitioners in postsecondary education enhances the relevance of instruction, adds a greater awareness of the safety of clients and the community, and contributes to the employability of graduates. Scholar/practitioners are members of a community of practice who have intellectual and research-attuned interests and want to create a context to share these interests with students and with one another. The concepts of situated learning and legitimate peripheral participation help to understand and further refine instruction by scholar/practitioners and programs that are designed for practitioners.

The Role of the University

A view of education that incorporates transforming social identity through sequential inclusion in practice changes a number of dimensions of education. Students are seen as colleagues from the outset, and their status as present or future members of a community of practice is explicitly recognized. For example, initial contact with a new cohort of students is considered as much a welcoming of new members of a community as it is an orientation. Community development, as well as academic points of view, inform program management. Creating a harmonious community is a significant part of program delivery, and, consistent with the findings of situated learning, the program supports the many ways in which students learn from one another and the ways faculty learn from students. The program provides multiple opportunities for students to work together on projects and assignments.

A sensitivity to the inclusion of students in a community of practice results in a different understanding of curriculum. Curriculum is a contract between the university and the community of practice, and between the university and the society that it seeks to serve. As such, the curriculum is essentially situated and cannot be "considered in isolation, manipulated in arbitrary didactic terms, or analyzed apart from the social relations that shape legitimate peripheral participation" (Lave & Wenger, 1991, p. 97). Program and course outcomes are expressly directed at equipping students for the performance of specific competencies and membership in the community of practice. And ultimately, it invites thinking of universities anew—it invites seeing the university from community development, as well as academic and research points of view. How can the university become a valued center of dialogue and lifelong learning for specific communities of practice and its community and environment as a whole?

The concepts of situated learning and legitimate peripheral participation help in formulating the ways in which the university can more effectively serve communities of professional practice and incorporate scholar/practitioners as instructors. Situated learning and legitimate peripheral participation represent an understanding of learning that is congruent with acquiring the competencies and ethical sensibilities required of professional practice as an essential aspect of postsecondary education and provide a means of introducing the integration of theory and practice by including participation in practitioner-informed practice from the outset of and throughout the program. These concepts also lead to an integration of learning and community that invites a seamless continuation of learning from degree-focused programs to lifelong learning via continuing education.

While recognizing the value and legitimacy of other forms of postsecondary education, the role of the postsecondary institution in the context of the graduate education of practitioners is to become a "good host" for the mutual learning of aspiring members and seasoned practitioners and the evolution of particular communities of practice. The institution's objective is to serve its constituent communities of practice well so that they, in turn, can contribute to the well-being of individuals, families, and communities. The "engaged university" provides a supportive and hospitable environment in which accomplished practitioners can teach, perform research, and share their realization with aspiring practitioners and the community of practice. The objective of the "engaged university" is to create a robust intellectual commons for the professions and shape this commons in a way that consciously serves the community. It listens to the community in which it is situated and responds to the community in terms of what it has heard. How can we eliminate homelessness in our community? How can we face increasing health-care costs as our population demographics continue to shift dramatically? How do we help people make sense of life in the twenty-first century and contribute to the shaping of a better world?

References

Henley, A. (2011). *Social architecture: Notes & essays*. Vancouver, BC: WriteRoom Press.

Lave, J., & Wenger, E. (1991). *Situated learning: Legitimate peripheral participation*. Cambridge, UK: Cambridge University Press.

Lave, J., & Wenger, E. (2002). Legitimate peripheral participation in communities of practice. In M. R. Lea & K. Nicoll (Eds.), *Distributed learning: Social and cultural approaches to practice* (pp. 56–63). New York, NY: Routledge Falmer.

Polanyi, M. (1966). *The tacit dimension*. University of Chicago Press.

Wenger, E. (1998). *Communities of practice: Learning, meaning and identity*. New York, NY: Cambridge University Press.

Wenger, E., McDermott, R., & Snyder, W. M. (2002). *Cultivating communities of practice: A guide to managing knowledge*. Boston, MA: Harvard Business School Press.

13

Overcoming Self-Inflicted Traits Encountered by Adult Learners

Paul D. Shuler, PhD, *School of Management*

Abstract

Four major self-inflicting traits that prevent adult students from succeeding in the classroom include apathy, fear of failure, anxiety, and fear of change. By merging Herrmann's (1996) brain dominance theory and Bandura's (1997) concept of high and low self-efficacy, eight student types emerge. By understanding these student types, instructors can be more equipped to identify and combat the four self-inflicting traits in the classroom. This chapter provides specific examples and tables—based on two decades of university teaching and administration experience—to aid instructors and administrators in helping students prevent or overcome apathy, fear of failure, anxiety, and fear of change.

Introduction

When Susan leaned her head inside my office door, I was glad to see her. She was clearly one of the school's best students, but she needed a frank discussion about missing too much class time. Intelligent and full of energy, she should not be wasting so much potential. I waved her to come into my office and have a seat while my mind prepared its best sermon regarding the woes of missing too much class. I was taken by surprise as she laid a piece of paper on my desk, sat down clutching her purse and a book to her chest, and declared, "Hi Dr. Shuler, I'm dropping, and I need you to sign this paper."

As school director, I had to sign all student drop forms. I admit my first response was simply a gut reaction, "Is everything OK?"

"Yep," she said, with no further explanation.

"Are you changing schools or majors?"

"Nope," again she spoke without explanation, only this time she began squirming in her seat. Perhaps I could save her, I thought. Asking more questions, I learned that she had decided to stay at home and raise children. While I view motherhood as the noblest of all professions, her reasoning made me cringe. She feared that once she graduated she might "fail in the real world" (her words), so now she was in my office wanting to drop out of school—after accumulating thousands of dollars in tuition, but no college degree.

It amazes me when perfectly capable students find reasons not to succeed. Usually it does not appear to be a conscious effort, but a subconscious mental trigger activated when these students come too close to academic success.

After class one evening, Charles, a young man nearly twice my size who often sat in the back row, approached me and hesitantly said, "Dr. Shuler, I really enjoy school, but I have a problem."

I curiously replied, "OK, perhaps I can help. What is on your mind?" Looking at the floor, he began telling me how his wife and friends are worried that after he graduates and gets a good job, he will change and want a new wife and friends.

Susan was experiencing fear of failure, and Charles fear of change. These are two of four common self-inflicting traits that prevent adult students from succeeding in the classroom: apathy, fear of failure, anxiety, and fear of change (Shuler, 2013). How should instructors and administrators respond to such student revelations? Is it possible to identify or even prevent such discouraging sentiments felt by adult students and their inner circle of influence? What follows is an effort to aid instructors and administrators in understanding, identifying, and combating student apathy, fear of failure, anxiety, and fear of change.

Eight Types of Students

Even when two situations appear to be the same, students are not (the same). For example, two students may experience anxiety but react differently. To help classify potentially helpful responses that allow for student differences, I synthesized two models (Herrmann, 1996; Bandura, 1997) to create eight types of students.

Four Student Types

First, I drew from Herrmann's (1996) work on thinking preferences related to brain dominance and combined this with my two decades of experience in higher education and administration to define the following four student types: Analyzers, Feelers, Visualizers, and Organizers.

Analyzers. Facts and logic are important to analyzers, who often overlook emotions and feelings, though not always intentionally. Analyzers can focus on solving problems to the point of ignoring their surroundings, including others. Their inner power comes from patience and determination. Analyzers gather facts and think reflectively. "What?" questions (e.g., "what are the facts?") are typical question starters for analyzers. In the classroom, analyzers may get lost in their contemplations regarding a topic mentioned. These students are likely to spend considerable time analyzing topics, syllabi, presentation components, etc., and frequently tell the instructor how to improve these items.

Feelers. Emotions and feelings of others are important to feelers, who tend to stay in the background waiting to provide support to someone in need. Feelers are typically good at expressing what they are thinking and feeling because they use animated body language, articulate their emotions, and sometimes think aloud. Classroom learning is an exciting activity for feelers when there is an "everybody-wins" classroom environment. To feelers, "who?" questions are the most important. In the classroom, feelers will follow the instructor's lead, regardless of how the syllabus or class outline reads. At any given time, an instructor can ask feelers about a specific situation within the classroom, and they are likely to know what emotions and feelings classmates have been experiencing.

Visualizers. The present and future are important to visualizers who tend to focus on the big picture and possibilities. Full of energy, visualizers do not recognize some human and worldly boundaries. Considering human and natural rules as guidelines (versus hard-and-fast rules), visualizers will attempt to create their own rules. Good at generating ideas, visualizers will not be kept "inside the box" and tend to thrive on change. Visualizers tend to go with their intuition, which can lead to quick decision making. "Why?" and "why not?" questions are the most important questions for visualizers, although they will also speak of possibilities, asking "what if?" questions. In the classroom, visualizers have trouble sitting still and will sometimes ask questions because they feel uncomfortable sitting still and are looking for a reason to physically move (e.g., raise a hand).

Organizers. Maintaining structure is important to organizers, who will often focus on rules, guidelines, procedures, and ethics. Organizers think about matters concerning the here and now of the physical world. The future is uncertain, so organizers give little thought to it. "How?" questions (e.g., "how should it be done?") take precedent over "what if?" or "why?" questions. Organizers' critical thinking and decision-making skills are likely to involve both discipline and established criteria (rules, guidelines, procedures). Classroom learning is a comfortable activity for organizers, as long as the instructor and assignments follow relevant rules and guidelines. Organizers are uncomfortable if the syllabus or class outline is not followed, assignments do not exactly match instructions, or class does not start and end on time. Organizers will likely look closely at instructor credentials.

Influences of Self-Efficacy

Second, I drew from Bandura's (1997) work on self-efficacy to create both high and low efficacy examples for each of the four types of students. Bandura defined self-efficacy as people's beliefs in their own competence or power to produce a desired and intended effect (make things happen).

In general, regardless of student type, students with high self-efficacy will study harder and more often when the subject appears difficult. However, students with low self-efficacy would simply feel overwhelmed or hopeless and not study or study inadequately. This second attitude and resulting action create self-induced failure, further supporting the person's low self-efficacy. Students' internal, subconscious view of their self-efficacy plays an external, conscious role in how motivated they are toward a task (Snyder & Wright, 2002). The amount of effort a person exerts is in accordance with the effects they are expecting from their actions. The more reward or self-satisfaction they expect from a task, the more effort they will put into it.

According to Bandura, self-efficacy is influenced by four major sources: personal experience, vicarious experience, social persuasion, and physiological/emotional factors. Recognizing these influences will help instructors understand how students reach high and low self-efficacy levels.

Personal experiences. Personal experiences are the most important factor deciding a person's self-efficacy level (Bandura, 1977). The successful completion of a task raises one's belief that he or she will be successful at a similar task in the future. Conversely, failure at a task in the past lowers self-efficacy for similar tasks in the future.

Vicarious experiences. Vicarious experiences, also called "modeling" by Bandura (1977), involve watching others and noting outcomes versus consequences (good or bad). Bandura proposed that when a person sees someone else succeed, self-efficacy levels will increase for both parties, assuming there are notable similarities between them and their perceived skill levels. The other way is also true; when a person sees someone else fail, self-efficacy levels will decrease.

Social persuasions. Social persuasions are the encouragements or discouragements we receive from others. Social persuasions can have a strong influence, significantly altering our confidence (Bandura, 1997). Positive persuasions increase self-efficacy levels; negative persuasions decrease self-efficacy levels. For example, when a teacher provides specific feedback to a student on what he or she did well, the student's confidence, or self-efficacy level, increases. Interestingly, Bandura found it takes less effort to decrease someone's self-efficacy level than to increase it through social persuasion.

Physiological and emotional factors. When placed in stressful situations, people commonly exhibit physical signs of distress such as dry mouth, aches and pains, fatigue, fear, hives, or nausea. According to Bandura (1990), our perceptions of these responses will increase or decrease our self-efficacy levels. For example, if a student gets "butterflies" and starts sweating before making a speech in front of the class, he or she might perceive this as a sign of inability, thus lowering self-efficacy. On the other hand, a student with high self-efficacy is likely to ignore these stress signs and consider them as normal, or even welcome them as a sign of adrenaline that helps in staying alert and focused.

Merging High and Low Self-Efficacy with the Four Student Types

Students with high and low self-efficacy exist within each of the four student types. This division of each type establishes eight student types. All eight types exist within most classrooms.

Table 1 shows possible traits and actions that might be associated with each of the eight different student types. While these categories are not yet grounded in formal research, I have defined these descriptions based on my understanding of the above-mentioned theoretical frameworks and my twenty years of experience in education circles. This table provides a quick guide to understanding the needs of each of the eight personality types, based on my observations.

Table 1. *How to Recognize Students by Thinking Type and Self-Efficacy*

Student Type	Self-Efficacy Level	Description
Analyzers	High	Analyzers with higher self-efficacy levels • speak in terms of facts and details. • consider feelings and policies, but speak of them as facts and details. • display confidence in making decisions. • look for clear expectations and take steps to meet them.
	Low	Analyzers with lower self-efficacy levels • are tied to facts and details. • believe that facts equal critical thinking. • are perceived as indecisive. • use gathering more facts as a reason to not make a decision.
Feelers	High	Feelers with higher self-efficacy levels • consider feelings when thinking critically. • understand that sometimes tough decisions need to be made for the good of the whole. • tend to focus more on the positive than the negative emotions of a situation. • tend to be good negotiators and mediators.
	Low	Feelers with lower self-efficacy levels • allow feelings to overtake critical thinking. • become mired in negative feelings. • frequently lose desire to make decisions. • tend to be high or low emotionally.

Visualizers	High	Visualizers with higher self-efficacy levels • envision all possibilities when thinking critically. • take action without hesitation. • create strategies to achieve an objective. • often feel equal with the instructor.
	Low	Visualizers with lower self-efficacy levels • tend to believe positive possibilities will not likely come true. • tend to focus on negative possibilities. • prefer to complain versus taking action. • sometimes become "class clowns."
Organizers	High	Organizers with higher self-efficacy levels • are often considered experts on rules but are also open to other factors. • may not like change but tend to understand that change is sometimes necessary. • keep everyone (including the instructor) honest in following procedures and guidelines through constructive criticism.
	Low	Organizers with lower self-efficacy levels • can sometimes be confined to rules. • may refuse to look at other factors. • can become upset if any decisions or actions are not within the rules. • sometimes allow guidelines to become rules. • sometimes fail to consider or accept change.

Combating the Four Self-Inflicting Traits

Using the eight student types described in Table 1, I will now share how I have helped these different types of students when they are struggling with the four self-inflicting traits: apathy, fear of failure, anxiety, and fear of change.

Apathy

Apathy involves having an indifferent attitude toward a subject or object (Blase, 1986). Apathy can occur in the classroom when students believe they have no control over their situation. Apathetic students will often remain passive, even when faced with failure or dropping a class. Apathy is not caused by an *actual* lack of control, but rather by the *perception* of having a lack of control (Rotter, 1990). If students believe they do not control their own environment, they will often lack a sense of commitment. This belief may cause students to become discouraged and apathetic, attempting to withdraw from any difficult decision making or action.

People with positive self-efficacy are more likely to persevere and complete a difficult task than people with negative self-efficacy (Bandura, 1990). Even when students with high self-efficacy fail, they tend to believe that they simply have "not succeeded, yet." Apathetic students would leave off the "yet" and just say, "I have not succeeded." This one word explains a big difference in attitude and effort.

The self-defense mechanism of an apathetic mind often places blame of failure on something external, such as the instructor, the environment, a fellow student, or the child who kept him or her awake the night before. By helping apathetic students understand how much they control their environment and what actions they can take to effect changes in their environment, instructors influence attitude and behavior versus causing students to shut down. I have discussed each of the student types in more detail below, again based on my experiences and observations.

Analyzers. When analyzers experience apathy, they will either move on or spend their time gathering facts about the situation. Information is comforting to analyzers. By gaining more information (facts), they attempt to understand the situation better. However, apathetic analyzers need to be nudged, and sometimes pushed, to make a decision or take action.

I knew a student, Michael, who always talked about going to Italy as if it were going to happen next week. He eagerly spoke in detail about his yet-to-be-taken trip to Italy to anyone who would listen. He would produce brochures and pictures of the places he planned to visit. When someone asked him when he was going, he would answer, "I don't know, but soon!" This continued for three years. One day, he was in my office showing me some new brochures for his trip to Italy and I asked him what was keeping him from going. He replied, "I never seem to have enough money. I doubt I ever will." He dejectedly sat down, and it was obvious I had deflated his ideal-trip balloon by asking a simple, but practical, question. "How much does it cost?" I asked. With miserable tone, he gave me a figure of several thousand dollars. It was obvious he had done his research; the figure he gave was very exact. It was also obvious that he felt helpless in achieving such a large figure.

I proceeded to help him break down that cost by dividing it by 156 weeks (the number of weeks in the three years I had known him). This new figure was relatively small. I then explained to him that if he had saved that small amount each week since I had known him, then he would be in Italy right now instead of in my office. In the process, I explained how interest would also accumulate, adding to his savings. His eyes brightened and he became excited. He was full of new energy now that he realized he had control over making this dream come true. He left my office thanking me. Just over two years later, I received a postcard from Italy from Michael.

Feelers. Apathy in feelers is difficult to overcome. True to their title, feelers feel emotions deeply. To get apathetic feelers to take action, they must be convinced their actions will benefit others in a positive way (Herrmann, 1996). An instructor can explain in vivid detail what others will feel and specifically how they will be helped by the student's action(s). Another effective tool is modeling. Provide students with specific details of other students taking the same actions and the positive effects they had on those around them.

As part of a group in charge of hiring speakers for a medical technology postsecondary school, I searched for the best speakers. It soon became evident to me that the speakers who students paid more attention to were not necessarily the best speakers in my view. In a field (medical) dominated by feelers, these students were most moved by speakers who had faced the same issues they were facing and succeeded, but not necessarily the first time or in the most successful fashion. They also wanted to hear about the speakers' relationships and how those relationships were affected by the struggles and subsequent success of the speakers. For students with low self-efficacy, I found that we could not stop at just the speaker series.

These students needed encouragement and outward recognition of the positive effect their actions were having on others, along with constant reminders of the speakers' experiences.

Visualizers. Fun and spontaneity are behaviors many visualizers value. However, apathy often triggers the opposite of these behaviors, which can create conflict within visualizers. Based on my observations, it appears the most common cause of turning visualizers apathetic are their visions of a negative future, even when that future is unlikely. An instructor can help visualizers by painting a clear and detailed picture of a positive future. The objective is to make the positive future more clear than the negative future. I have instructed visualizer students with high self-efficacy in apathetic moods to cut out pictures of goals, such as homes, diplomas, and cars, and post the pictures on their refrigerator or bathroom mirror.

I had one visualizer student with low self-efficacy that was apathetic toward career options after finishing school. Through indirect questioning over a period of several weeks, I found this student's passions included anything to do with American Indians and reading. By the time the student graduated, she had decided to organize and spearhead the building of a library dedicated to American Indian literature. Perhaps my line of questioning about her passions had something to do with the newfound entrepreneurial endeavor.

Organizers. Billy was an organizer with low self-efficacy. If something happened that was not according to written school policy, he argued about it, even if it had nothing to do with him or his class. His father died the week of semester finals. Billy came to my office to tell me of his father's death and as he started to leave, he commented, "Thank you for all you have done. I will be dropping out of school." Stunned for a moment, I asked him what he meant. He replied, "Since I will be missing finals, I will be flunking out of school and cannot afford to retake this semester." I asked him to sit down and I explained that we could arrange for him to take the finals the following week. He explained that he had read the school handbook and class syllabi and there was nothing that allowed for his exact situation and it would not be fair to the other students. This was classic organizer thinking, so I told him I understood and that I would look further into it for him. He left and I looked. Billy was right that we had nothing for his exact situation in the school handbook that allowed him to take the finals later. Therefore, I wrote an exception letter and received emergency board approval. When I produced the approved letter to Billy, his eyes became watery and he simply said, "Thank you, sir."

I realize not everyone can provide an approved exception letter, but my point in telling Billy's story is that as an organizer, he felt helpless and that attending school was out of his control because there was no rule in place for his situation. He was willing to walk away from his potential future because of it. Recognizing that verbal approval would not be enough, I took the extra steps to gain written approval and followed through by getting back to Billy as I promised. Had Billy held high self-efficacy views, we could have worked out something in writing between us, but instead he needed to see high-level authority approval.

Fear of Failure

Fear of failure can inhibit critical thinking skills, cause students to feel out of control, and perpetuate a lack of motivation (Kember, Wong, & Leung, 1999). As the potential devastation of failure looms in students' minds, the price of success may seem too high, so some students may stop trying. Unfortunately, giving up only encourages failure, so the vicious downward cycle continues. If students give up too many times, they are likely to stop trying altogether. Fear of failure keeps people from taking action or following through on intentions. As a result, students often get distracted and hinder their chances to achieve their goals.

Fear of failure involving test taking is common. One strategy I have used to help students overcome test-taking anxieties is to have students take all the tests they can on topics that do not matter, until they are comfortable with the anxiety of the test-taking process. A similar strategy is to have students take practice tests in the exact chair and room as they will take the "real" test. While I do not have scientific evidence, I believe students are less fearful because they are able to visualize a non-stressful test-taking experience in their classroom environment. While the fear does not go away completely, these strategies help students manage their fear so that it does not inhibit critical thinking and decision-making skills.

Analyzers. The best approach for analyzers dealing with fear of failure is to help them analyze the facts. They will recognize the benefit of determining what the facts "say." Analyzers with high self-efficacy will likely rate each of their successes with more importance than each of their failures. Analyzers with low self-efficacy will likely rate each of their failures with more importance than each of their successes. As instructors, we can suggest that these students put their T-accounts (see Figure 1) in writing. Often students exaggerate the number of negative items in their mind while minimizing the number of positive items. By putting the supporting examples in black and white, students can objectively analyze them. Instructors can also help students focus on the positive column and how to get more items into the positive column. Another helpful component is to add an importance or weighted value to each item. In Figure 1, the positive column is the "YES."

Fig. 1. *"Am I a Good Person?"*

YES	NO
• I never committed a serious crime.	• I tell an occasional lie.
• I give occasional donations to charity.	• I stole Mrs. Smith's dollar when I was seventeen years old.
• I volunteer once a month for the elderly.	• I said hurtful things to Jack when I shouldn't have.
• I have never yelled at my child.	• I borrowed Nate's movie and never returned it.
• I helped John wash his car just to be nice.	• I could have helped Ryan move, but didn't.
• I did not go to Jennifer's wild party.	• I was grumpy with David one day last week.
• I gave Amy my red shirt since she liked it so much.	
• I always wave when I see a friend.	
• I try to smile at others even when I feel down.	

Low self-efficacy analyzers will focus on this column

High self-efficacy analyzers will focus on this column

Feelers. Strong emotions accompany each failure for feelers. What feelers must avoid is falling deeper into the failure trap caused by their deeply felt emotions. The sadness, anger, or helplessness that can accompany failing is typically felt stronger by feelers than other personality types. Feelers must find activities that bring positive feelings soon after a failure to offset and limit the negative feelings. Surrounding themselves with positive people will help a feeler avoid the negative fear-of-failure spiral.

Remember Susan, mentioned in the introduction? Susan appeared to have high self-efficacy, was people-oriented and typically expressive, yet fearful of hurting others. Susan was a feeler and was struggling mightily with fear of failure. She had failed early in her life and now feared she would again, despite her current success and hard work in school. As a feeler, her underlying fear was how her family would react if she failed again. We looked at two things: experiences of others like her (a form of vicarious experience) and how her family would feel about her if she found success or failed. She decided to stay in school after seeing that others similar to her had gone on to succeed, and acknowledging that her family would love her regardless if she failed or succeeded.

Another student, Mary, was returning to school after thirty years of working as a stay-at-home mother. A wonderfully sweet woman, she was a feeler who had devoted her life to helping others. With no children at home and a recently disabled husband, Mary enrolled in our medical assistant program. Feeling very unsure, insecure, and vulnerable in this new academic world, her self-efficacy levels were very low. Almost daily, I made it a point to check in with Mary to measure the "temperature" of her attitude. Almost always, she would speak of her likelihood to fail. "I am just too old for this, Dr. Shuler. I want to do this, but I don't know; I think I am just too old." I made it my goal to show Mary that age had nothing to do with her success in the medical assisting program, but I needed to do this from a relationship viewpoint, not by using facts or policies or reports.

I asked Mary if she would bring her husband to school with her one day and let me show him around while she was in class. She agreed and later that week I had the pleasure of meeting and spending some time with "Mr. Mary." During our visit, we toured the school and I made sure we observed Mary's class in session. Mary's husband was soft-spoken, a man of few words; he seemed genuinely interested in everything I shared with him.

After Mary's class ended, the three of us gathered in my office and I asked some questions about what it meant to Mary's husband to have Mary pursuing her medical assisting degree. What followed was a strong combination of emotions from both Mary and her husband. He felt inadequate as a newly disabled worker. She had a strong desire to help him shoulder the household financial responsibility. He felt proud of Mary for enrolling. She felt scared entering an academic and work world new to her. He admired her for trying something new—he doubted he could do that himself. They both shed tears at different points.

Those are just a few of the emotions that came out that day, but the amazing thing to me was that none of these feelings had been verbalized between Mary and her husband prior to that day. As they tenderly hugged each other and left my office with red eyes and smiles on their faces, it became obvious that Mary now knew—without assuming—how grateful and proud her husband was of her pursuing this difficult journey. In addition, he now knew that Mary would need his outward support and encouragement. From that point forward, a smiling and positive Mary would greet me each day in the hallways.

Visualizers. Visualizers will envision the future. Visualizers with high self-efficacy will see past the failures and think, "If I could just . . . then I will be fine." Visualizers with low self-efficacy often see glasses as half-empty, versus half-full, and often let a failure generate an image of a failure-filled future. Visualizers' intellectual vision focuses on the big picture and long-term outcomes. It is best to help students with this personality see details and short-term actions that can lead to the desired big-picture and long-term outcomes. Creating a specific action plan can be effective in getting them out of their current situation.

The following real-life anecdote is more about success after college, but it provides a true example of helping a visualizer overcome fear of failure. Larry was smart and energetic. Full of self-confidence, Larry often spoke of starting his own business when he graduated. Near his graduation date, I asked Larry in private about his plans after school. He spoke of finding a job and "workin' for the man." I nonchalantly asked him what happened to starting his own business and he started telling me about a friend of his that tried to start a business, "He failed miserably and he is smarter than I am, so I guess I will skip over that dream," he said with a nervous laugh.

I asked him if he still wanted to start a business. He emphatically told me yes, so I sat him down and we outlined step-by-step what he would need to do to safeguard his success. In the process, we discussed and identified where his friend had likely gone wrong in his entrepreneurial attempt. Larry had high self-efficacy, but his visualizer thinking only allowed him to see the big picture. He needed help in identifying the details. If he had low self-efficacy, I would have done the same thing, but in addition I would have placed him in contact with a mentor or stayed in contact with him, checking on his status, celebrating small successes, and answering any questions on a regular basis.

Organizers. Organizers will attempt to stay within the policies and rules of a situation, even if it means continued failure. Cautious and prudent, organizers caught in a downward spiral of fearing failure may blame others for their downfall and become withdrawn. We can help organizers withdraw from the situation long enough to organize their thoughts regarding what went wrong and then develop a detailed, written plan for getting out of the downward spiral.

Ned was former military and manager of a health clinic. Starting a second career, Ned had decided to earn a degree in computer software. About halfway through his second computer software course, he came to me, and with a sigh, he began telling me that he was considering dropping out of school. When asked why, he spoke of how he would never make it through this class. He then went on to explain about each assignment in his current class, and how he believed too many were theoretical assignments. "I came here to learn computer software, not the theory behind it. Employers don't give a crap about theory."

I asked him if he still wanted to be a computer software engineer, and without hesitation he stated, "Yes, sir!" Then I asked him if he needed this degree to do that. He said, "Yes, sir, I suppose so."

"Do you need this class to earn that degree to get that job?" I prodded some more.

"Yes, sir I do," he said.

I replied, "Then you better start learning some theory. The teachers are the experts and they have a reason for you needing to know theory. You will need it on the job more than you realize." He acknowledged that I was probably right and had a much-improved attitude as he left my office. As a high-self-efficacy organizer, Ned needed to see the big picture that this class and degree were necessary to get where he wanted from a career standpoint. He also needed to hear that those in charge of the classroom knew what they were doing. Had Ned been a low-self-efficacy organizer, I would have also discussed consequences of dropping out of school and organized follow-up meetings to monitor his progress.

Anxiety

Some anxiety or stress is good (Bandura, 1990). Ask any professional athlete when he or she performs best, and the answer will likely be when he or she is somewhat anxious. For decades, I have played tournament tennis. When I am calm and relaxed before a tournament match, I tend to come out flat—not aggressive, energetic, or focused enough. When I am a little anxious, I tend to be aggressive, energetic, and focused. When I am very anxious right before a match, I tend to be too aggressive and my attention is easily drawn to anything that moves or makes a sound, on or off the tennis court. The same can be true of students in a classroom. Having some anxiety heightens students' awareness and keeps them sharp. However, anxiety becomes disruptive or even dangerous when it overwhelms students and causes memory loss or physical change (such as sweating or dizziness). Too much anxiety can interfere with critical thinking and taking action (Gelman, 2004). Any of the thinking types can suffer from anxiety. However, what causes anxiety and how each student type attempts to prevail over it are different.

Analyzers. One reason analyzers often experience anxiety is their strong desire to achieve perfection. Realizing and acknowledging this is a big step in overcoming anxiety for analyzers. An instructor can help students realize there are many tasks where perfection seldom occurs; therefore, expecting perfection every time is impractical. Attempting perfection in a compliant and realistic manner is an indication of "positive striving" (Bieling, Israeli, & Antony, 2004). However, unrealistic expectation of perfection to the point of causing depression, stress, general anxiety, and test-taking anxiety results in emotional distress (Bieling, Israeli, & Antony, 2004). Instructors must help analyzers keep a practical, positive-striving perspective.

I have an analyzer daughter with high self-efficacy. She is deflated for a week anytime she earns below 100 percent on any test or assignment. At least once per semester, I have a sit-down discussion with her regarding expectations and instructors striving to make her stretch. She does fine after each session until the following semester. If she had low self-efficacy, I would need to also show specifically how small of an effect this one lower grade had on her class, semester, and degree grade-point averages.

Feelers. Feelers experience anxiety if feelings are hurt. Helping feeling students not absorb the feelings of others will limit the anxiety felt by feelers. Of course, this is often easier said than done. These students absorb anxiety from other students and may bring to the classroom anxiety absorbed from their non-school environment. A legitimate method to help feeler students overcome this trait is remembering and employing the difference between empathy and sympathy. A person with sympathy for another joins them in the "ditch of despair," feeling the same feelings and despair An empathetic person, however, keeps planted in reality to help the other person out of their rut (Stephens Ministry, 2000).

Steven was a very bright student who had earned high A grades in one of my prior classes. During the first few weeks of my current class, he continued to earn As. Then I noticed two Cs in a row. I asked him to speak with me after class one day. After some small talk about family members (classical feeler conversation), I asked Steven about his dip in grades. He described to me in great depth about his grandmother's illness and how it was affecting his concentration and studies. During the discussion he expressed that it was his grandmother who had encouraged him the most to earn his degree. I asked him what are some of the things that make his grandmother the happiest. His success in school was high on that list. This would have been enough for a high-self-efficacy feeler to take action and do what they could to make their relative happy—in this case, to do well in school. However, Steven was a low-self-efficacy feeler; therefore, I continued to ask him what he had control over when it came to making his grandmother happy. We concluded he had no control over the illness and many other things, but he did have control over something important to his grandmother—his success in school.

Visualizers. Visualizers will feel anxiety if they are hemmed in by many rules and policies. While rules and policies can make decision making less of a challenge, they can make visualizers feel valueless and claustrophobic. Helping visualizers find ways to be creative and spontaneous within the rules and policies can prevent these feelings. When appropriate and justified, visualizers can find ways to challenge the status quo (current rules and policies) to feel valuable, challenged, and energized. It requires successful critical thinking to determine what is appropriate and justified, and to determine what actions to take, so I encourage instructors to be proactive in discussing this with classes and individual students.

I recently had a student wanting to turn in an assignment that was far beyond the minimal requirements, but to do so he would have to include an interview with a particular someone in another country. He knew what he wanted, but the time difference was causing issues in getting the interview completed. It was going to cause the student to turn his assignment in a day late. Given the student's proactive nature in obtaining the interview and in coming to me with his situation, I believed him to have high self-efficacy. I explained that I could not change the due date, but his choices were to turn in an average assignment on time or a great assignment a day late. Then we discussed which would be better for him, grade-wise and knowledge-wise. He cheerfully finished the expanded assignment and expressed gratitude for pushing him beyond his comfort zone. In reality, he had pushed himself and I had simply allowed it by minimizing the anxiety.

Organizers. Organizers experience anxiety when things are out of order. When an event does not follow the planned agenda or takes more than its allotted time, organizers will feel anxious. An instructor simply acknowledging that "events involving people often do not go as planned" will aid organizers. Part of this process is to encourage the creation of "what if?" scenarios. Organizers will limit anxiety in their critical thinking, problem solving, and decision making by having documented alternative action plans for each situation (Herrmann, 1996).

The forming of student teams is a common anxiety producer for organizers. Organizers with high self-efficacy will either perform on the team and not say anything or will voice to me his or her displeasure in having to rely on other people to earn a grade. For these organizers, I explain the importance the Advisory Board has placed on teaming and how beneficial teaming is in the social society in which we live. This provides to organizers an authority figure (Advisory Board) and provides some practical explanation. Organizers with low self-efficacy will simply not participate in the teaming assignment or complain about the assignment, but not explain what it is they do not like about it. For these students, I reiterate the rules and policies established by the school and syllabus, along with consequences of action and nonaction.

Fear of Change

As people age, the youthful mode of taking risks begins to disappear (Wood, Busemeyer, Koling, Cox, & Davis, 2005). Facing the unknown may become troubling, as many people fear the unfamiliar. Yet, in an ironic twist, instructors aspire to change students. Instructors strive to change students' mindsets, abilities, potential, knowledge, and more. Along with these changes, expectations and views of the world may also change unexpectedly. Unforeseen changes can be unsettling.

Analyzers. Most analyzers do not fear change as long as they can analyze the facts and reflect on the change before or during the change. Let analyzers know about potential changes, along with the facts concerning why the change is necessary. This can be as simple as discussing expected changes with the entire class during the first week. Individually, help analyzers sort through the facts and separate these from opinions and assumptions:

- A fact is a truth. The War of 1812 was fought in 1812 (plus several other years). That is a fact.
- An opinion is someone's belief or viewpoint, such as "The War of 1812 was a worthy cause."
- An assumption is when someone thinks that something is probably true, usually based on a fact or opinion. "Since the War of 1812 is just named for one year, it must have only lasted one year" is an assumption.

Charles, from the introduction, is an analyzer struggling with fear of change. His introspection of his family's views and analytical approach to this (and other situations I had witnessed) indicate that he is an analyzer. Based on class interactions, I felt certain his self-efficacy was on the high end. We sat down together and wrote down what were the facts, opinions, and assumptions regarding his situation. Then we briefly discussed Herrmann's four thinking-preference types. This was all he needed to realize how to approach family and friends regarding their fear of change. Had Charles's self-efficacy been low, we would have discussed the same topics, but I would have emphasized how he could address his and others' opinions and assumptions.

Feelers. Feelers are okay with change as long as others are okay with the change. Show feelers examples of other students who have dealt with the same changes successfully and how they did it. Vicarious experience and social persuasions work well with feelers. Also, help feelers see where those around them—family, friends, fellow students, or workers—benefit from the change.

Amy came to my office one day very distraught over a change in an assignment I had made earlier in the week. I asked her why it was a concern. She voiced that the changes were "inconveniences" to the students. I probed what made the changes inconvenient and her resistance began to break down. The more details I asked for, the more defensive she became and finally she blurted out, "OK, I don't see a problem with the changes myself, but Monroe and Susie both feel that . . ." A feeler, Amy was truly distressed by the discomfort I had caused the other students. As a feeler with high self-efficacy, she had taken it upon herself to come to me to mediate a solution that would make everyone happy. Realizing this, I was able to discuss with Amy the best way for Monroe and Susie (and anyone else) to incorporate the changes with minimal disruption.

If Amy had been a low-self-efficacy feeler, she likely would not have come to me and I would have been responsible for noticing her distress and approaching her with questions concerning the root of her distress. Then I would have approached Monroe, Amy, and Susie together to explain incorporating the changes.

Visualizers. Visualizers welcome change and are typically instigators of change (Herrmann, 1996). What they need help with is how to handle those around them dealing with the changes. Help the visualizer understand the four personality types so that they can speak in their "languages." For example, an analyzer wants to "analyze" the change, while a feeler is trying to talk through emotions felt during change, and an organizer is trying to stabilize the insecurity that comes with change.

Jacob was a computer software major with high self-efficacy who openly exhibited his excitement for his new career. For Jacob this was great, but for those close to him the change was unsettling. When his wife moved out, he came to me in tears, considering leaving school. Through his overwhelming excitement, Jacob had been oblivious to his wife's fear of change. I asked him a few questions about his wife to get a feel for her thinking type and it appeared she was an organizer—someone who values stability and security. Then I asked Jacob if they had discussed details of what would happen after he graduated. They had not. Soon after, Jacob sat down calmly with his wife and worked out detailed plans for the future. She moved back in and was happier and satisfied instead of scared and worried.

Had Jacob been a low-self-efficacy visualizer, I would have set a meeting for Jacob and his wife, in which someone would have mediated. As a visualizer with high self-efficacy, Jacob knew what he wanted and went after it. In this case, it was his wife back. A visualizer with low self-efficacy will know what he or she wants, but will fail to take the necessary action or walk away if there is conflict. This is why visualizers need someone to help push them into action and make sure they do not walk away when it gets tough.

Organizers. Organizers do not like change and will typically fight against it, but will adapt if required. Stability and security are among the traits organizers value most. Provide an organizer with exact expectations that come with the change and do so preferably in writing. Having it in writing helps make it "true" in the eyes of organizers. Explaining to a class the types of changes you expect to occur during the semester will help organizers mentally prepare and accept these changes. For unexpected changes, explain why they are necessary and how they will bring stability to the situation.

Because it was decided that only a teacher with a master's degree or higher could teach Organizational Politics, I was tasked with teaching organizational politics to Heating, Ventilation, and Air Conditioning (HVAC) students. The HVAC field is dominated by organizers (high and low self-efficacy). These students were very agitated because they would no longer be taught this class, which they felt was a waste of time anyway, by an HVAC instructor. I had heard that the HVAC instructor spent most of the class time discussing HVAC, not organizational politics, which suited the students just fine. During the first class meeting, I took role and then asked them what specific goals they wanted to achieve by earning their degree in HVAC. I wrote everything they said on the marker boards. Then I handed out the syllabus and class outline, and we discussed each. As we did this, I made sure to point out exactly where on the syllabus or class outline each of their goals would be addressed. For example, job security I tied to formal and informal organizational communications, and financial security I tied to business structure checks and balances. Often I connected a class-mentioned goal to multiple places on the syllabus and class outline. Included in the syllabus and in our discussion were specific consequences for misbehavior, tardiness, and absences, for which I made sure to point out and follow to the letter throughout the class. No significant attitude problem existed with the students after that first class.

A Quick Guide for Combating the Four Self-Inflicting Traits

Table 2 provides a framework allowing instructors to identify and combat these four self-inflicting traits in an organized, practical approach. It serves as a quick reference guide based on my own experiences and observations for helping students of each personality type and self-efficacy with each of the four self-inflicted traits. I also encourage you to keep a diary of what has worked and not worked in each new situation, while noting which student type and self-inflicting difficulty types are involved.

Table 2. *How to Help Students by Thinking Type and Self-Efficacy: A Quick Guide*

		Four Self-Inflicting Traits			
Student	Self-Efficacy Level	Apathy	Fear of Failure	Anxiety	Fear of Change
Analyzers	High	Use facts to show actions that can positively affect.	Put facts, opinions, and assumptions in writing.	Make expectations realistic.	Provide the facts and allow them to voice their thoughts.
	Low	Help determine when to go from "gathering facts" to taking action.	Bring focus on the positive and provide positive activities.	Show cause and effect of specific actions and be supportive.	Provide the facts and address any opinions or assumptions.
Feelers	High	Show actions will improve relationships and others' feelings.	Provide examples of positive actions and encourage.	Provide assurance of relationships and feelings.	Show how event will or has helped others.
	Low	Provide vicarious experiences and support.	Tell them how it makes you feel.	Train them to be empathetic versus sympathetic.	Show how event will or has helped others just like them or those close to them.

Visualizers	High	Explain positive meanings of physical attributes.	Suggest actions they can take to find success.	Show them where they can be creative.	Help them communicate with others.
	Low	Create a positive building experience.	Co-create action plan and celebrate small successes.	Show them that you value their input and involvement in class.	Help them communicate with others.
Organizers	High	Explain organizational and societal expectations.	Help them see the "big picture."	Provide structure and explain reason for departures.	Provide expectations in writing.
	Low	Set rules and consequences and follow through.	Put facts in writing and determine a written plan of action.	Provide order and structure.	Provide exact expectations in writing and potential consequences.

Conclusion

Helping students overcome apathy, fear of failure, anxiety, and fear of change is not a simple task. However, instructors can help students prevent and overcome each of the four major self-inflicting traits that prevent adult students from succeeding in the classroom. The first step is understanding the different student types. The second step is understanding the four common self-inflicting traits. Finally, the third step is merging these concepts to create strategies to help move students from thinking "I have not succeeded" to "I have not succeeded, yet" to "I have succeeded!"

References

Bandura, A. (1977). Self-efficacy: Toward a unifying theory of behavioral change. *Psychological Review, 84*(2), 191–215.

Bandura, A. (1990). Perceived self-efficacy in the exercise of personal agency. *Journal of Applied Sport Psychology, 2*(2), 128–163.

Bandura, A. (1997). *Self-efficacy: The exercise of control.* New York: Freeman and Sons.

Bieling, P. J., Israeli, A. L., & Antony, M. M. (2004). Is perfectionism good, bad, or both? Examining models of the perfectionism construct. *Personality and Individual Differences, 36*(6), 1373–1385.

Blase, J. J. (1986). A qualitative analysis of sources of teacher stress: Consequences for performance. *American Educational Research Journal, 23*(1), 13–40.

Gelman, C. R. (2004). Anxiety experienced by foundation-year MSW students entering field placement: Implications for admissions, curriculum, and field education. *Journal of Social Work Education,* 39–54.

Herrmann, N. (1996). *The whole brain business book.* New York, NY: McGraw-Hill.

Kember, D., Wong, A., & Leung, D. Y. (1999). Reconsidering the dimensions of approaches to learning. *British Journal of Educational Psychology, 69*(3), 323–343.

Rotter, J. (1990). Internal versus external control of reinforcement: A case history of a variable. *American Psychologist, 45*(4), 489–93. doi:10.1037/0003-066X.45.4.489

Shuler, P. (2013). *Critical thinking: A career choice.* [Manuscript submitted for publication.]

Snyder, C. R., & Wright, E. (2002). *Handbook of positive psychology.* Oxford, NY: Oxford University Press.

Stephens Ministry. (2000). *Stephens Ministry training manual.* St. Louis, MO: Stephens Ministry.

Wood, S., Busemeyer, J., Koling, A., Cox, C. R., & Davis, H. (2005). Older adults as adaptive decision makers: evidence from the Iowa Gambling Task. *Psychology and Aging, 20*(2), 220.

A Model to Create a More Prepared and Effective Workforce through Essential Skills Training

Carla Weaver, MA, MSc, and Lovey Sidhu, MEd,
School of Management

Abstract

This chapter defines Essential Skills (reading, writing, numeracy, document use, computer skills, working with others, teamwork, oral communication and thinking skills), describes an employer training model and pilot project, and then offers recommendations for applying lessons learned to incorporate Essential Skills into the academic environment to better prepare students for the workplace. A principle faculty member from City University of Seattle was hired independently to work on the pilot project to develop a model for small businesses to embed essential workplace skills into workplace training. The project was supported by the Canadian federal government. The result of the project was a training model that can be adopted by any size business or organization to incorporate Essential Skills into training. The model was successful in the three organizations where it was piloted and the deliverables from the project included a website (found at www.westproject.ca), which is still live and contains training resources for small businesses and a printed resource guide. A link to the resource guide can be found at the same website.

Introduction to Essentials Skills

"Approximately 14 percent of U.S. adults can't read. In 2003, the U.S. government tested 19,000 adults on their literacy skills in three areas—the ability to gather information from an article, understand a document, and do arithmetic using information from a document. In the first category—prose literacy—the percentage of adults lacking basic literacy was 14.5 percent" (NBC News, Education Nation, 2011, NAAL section, para. 1.) Similarly, "in Canada, 42 percent of Canadian adults between the ages of sixteen and sixty-five have low literacy skills" (Canadian Literacy Network, n.d., para. 1). The statistics are staggering and the low literacy skills affect the productivity in our workplaces and the ability of our adults to learn new skills, whether in the workplace or the classroom.

Through extensive research, the Government of Canada, along with other national and international agencies, identified and validated key literacy and Essential Skills. Earlier work in Canada, the United States, Australia, and Great Britain identified a set of skills that were used in virtually all occupations. These "Essential Skills" are used in nearly every job and throughout daily life in different ways and at varying levels of complexity. They provide the foundation for learning all other skills and enable people to evolve with their jobs and adapt to workplace change (HRSDC, 2013).

Essential Skills are not the technical skills required to competently perform a particular occupation; rather, they are the skills *applied* in all occupations. Essential Skills are **enabling skills** that help people perform the tasks required by their occupation and other activities of daily life (HSRDC, 2007).

The nine Essential Skills are used in different forms, at varying degrees of complexity, and are needed for learning, work, and life. Below is a description of each Essential Skill (as defined by HRSDC):

- **Reading:** understanding materials written in sentences or paragraphs;
- **Document Use:** finding, understanding, or entering information in various types of documents;
- **Numeracy:** using numbers and thinking in quantitative terms to complete tasks;
- **Writing:** communicating by arranging words, numbers, or symbols on paper or a computer screen;
- **Oral Communication:** using speech to exchange thoughts and information;
- **Working with Others:** interacting with others to complete tasks;
- **Thinking:** finding and evaluating information to make rational decisions or to organize work;
- **Computer Use:** using computers and other forms of technology; and
- **Continuous Learning:** participating in an ongoing process of improving skills and knowledge.

Employers invest in training when there is a hard business reason to do so, and because Essential Skills help workers to innovate and adapt to workplace change, organizations are becoming increasingly aware that they need to maximize the skills of their workforces, in order to compete and grow (HRSDC, 2011). Companies including Syncrude Canada Ltd, BHP Billiton Diamonds Inc., and Canada Bread Atlantic each participated in the Essential Skills initiatives to support employee skill development in an effort to improve business practices and implement solutions to address their business issues (Sidhu & Weaver, 2013).

- The kinds of outcomes that employers who invest in Essential Skills training tend to measure and manage include the following:
- Skill gains (Essential Skills, or firm-specific, job-specific or technical skills);
- Attitude change—for example, increased commitment to achieving individual, team, and organizational goals;

- Increased engagement in the workplace; and
- Knowledge acquisition and application—for example, enhanced employee understanding of the workplace.

Essential Skills Gaps:

The Relationship between Training and Employee Development

Deficits in Essential Skills limit the employees' ability to effectively complete their job tasks and their ability to effectively acquire new knowledge. "Too many people lack the required level of Essential Skills to fully participate and succeed in today's increasingly knowledge- and service-based economy. Investing in machinery and education is critical. Investing in Canadians' Essential Skills for living, learning and working is just as important but much less recognized or understood" (Lane & Hirsch, 2012, September 6, para. 4). When employees lack the skills needed to do the job, it affects the employers' abilities to meet customers' expectations and to achieve their business goals.

In recent years, there was greater emphasis on technical skills and a move away from valuing or investing in soft skills, such as communicating, working with others, thinking, and continuous learning. Although many employers continued to recognize the value of developing employees with these skills, the recession caused employers to cut expenses, and one of the first places to be cut is training and most often, soft skills training.

While delivering training is a powerful and effective way to increase employee commitment and loyalty, training must be directly related to an organization's goals and be specific to the workers' tasks to be successful. Employees need to believe that the skills gained from training will help them to accomplish their jobs. When this is achieved, a culture is created where employees develop their knowledge to benefit the organization and contribute to achieving the company's goals (Sidhu & Weaver, 2013).

216

Employee Training and Development Applied to Small Business

Due to the recent recession, new demographics in the workforce and rapidly changing technology, skills and creativity are extremely important to help companies grow and succeed. This reinforces the idea that workers need well-developed skills that are specific to their organization's needs and goals in order to do their jobs well, and a business faces the risk of not achieving its goals without a well-trained and qualified workforce. Larger organizations may be better equipped to attract the best workers because they are able to offer more comprehensive benefits programs and greater opportunities for career advancement, yet all organizations need to train and develop their workforces in order to meet their company goals. Small businesses may even have a greater need for training than larger organizations to mitigate this risk.

To a small business, its workforce is one of its most valuable assets. However, often, a small business has limited resources to invest in Human Resources programs, especially training, and they may even consider that training is dispensable in a situation where resources are tight. Companies with fewer than five hundred employees spend more per employee on training, but dedicate less time per employee than do larger organizations because it's more difficult for small companies to make use of training that's been developed for larger organizations due to applicability (Stillwagon, 2010). Further, the effect of a workforce lacking the Essential Skills may be more detrimental to a small business with limited resources than to a larger organization with ample resources.

While employee-training programs can be expensive for a small business, training should not be looked at as a cost; rather, it is a long-term investment toward the success and growth of the business. Investing in training develops a competent workforce with the Essential Skills required for productivity and innovation. It's important for small-business owners to foster and encourage skills development through an environment that supports career growth (Sidhu & Weaver, 2013).

> *A well-trained workforce is essential for the success of a small business.*

Essential Skills and Academic Success

As an educator in the postsecondary sector, you may be asking yourself, "I don't have any illiterate students in my classroom, do I?" Literacy gaps are often perceived as an inability to read or write and attributed to language barriers, socioeconomic status, or marginalized learners. Essentials Skills include literacy skills such as reading, writing, and numeracy and are a complex mix of skills that an individual can use at work, at home, or in the community. These skills require maintenance and upgrading over the course of a career, regardless of the profession. Less than 40 percent of adults who have some secondary school education, but who have not graduated, have adequate literacy levels. Even some college and university graduates lack adequate literacy skills (Canadian Manufacturers & Exporters Ontario, 2008).

Engaging in Essential Skills development in the postsecondary classroom will not only better equip the graduate for employment but also will assist in the development of class-based skills designed to support and enhance learning and knowledge acquisition. Students need to have the nine Essential Skills: reading, writing, numeracy, oral communication, document use, computer skills, working with others, thinking, and continuous learning, to handle the demands of their chosen professions and complete the tasks expected in the academic environment. These are broad subject areas, and it can be insulting to suggest to a student that he or she isn't able to read or do math, but the requirements can be reframed into areas of the skill that are specific and applicable to the tasks that each learner must perform (Sidhu & Weaver, 2013). For example, if students are expected to complete group presentations or create and present research, "working with others" and "oral communication" skills are an essential component to successfully complete the tasks expected. If nursing students are expected to learn medication administration practices, but are unable to compute accurate dosages, they may have "numeracy" gaps or have an inability to "use documents" effectively.

Each of the Essential Skills becomes vital to technical competence and acquisition of knowledge, skills, and abilities of their program of study. Effective Essential Skills training and development programs must focus on the needs of the learners. *What additional skills do learners need to be more effective to complete their tasks? What specific skills are the learners expected to gain? What is the best way the students learn?* Education is designed to develop and enhance students. Through strategic, well-planned Essential Skills initiatives, educators create a culture of development and lifelong learning. A culture of student development also ensures that the acquired knowledge and skills are put to use in the most productive way, which enables students to achieve their targeted learning and career goals.

Essential Skills Development in the Workplace—The Pilot Project:

Why is the Model Applicable to City University and Teaching in a University Environment?

While this pilot project was concerned with developing a training model that would assist small businesses to embed Essential Skills training into their workplace training, there are deficits in Essential Skills in the college and university classroom also. By adapting the W.E.S.T. training model to the classroom, we believe that improvements can be made in the level of soft skills and Essential Skills of our graduates, so they are more ready and capable for their careers.

Introduction to the Workplace Essential Skills Training (W.E.S.T.) Program

The Communities for Literacy project was established to address the need for sustainable, employment-based support for literacy and Essential Skills from a community perspective. The approach was designed to address both workforce shortages and skill deficiencies by supporting employers to incorporate Essential Skills development into the workplace so that individual employees could gain or maintain employment while simultaneously upgrading their literacy and Essential Skills (LES) (Sidhu, 2013).

Sources BC, in partnership with two local Chambers of Commerce and Kwantlen Polytechnic University in British Columbia, acquired funding from the government of Canada to work with local employers to help foster success with their business and human resources goals. The W.E.S.T. project provided free services including assessment and training support to selected employers in Cloverdale, South Surrey, and White Rock, British Columbia. Three small-business employers and over fifty-five employees participated in the project, and the objective of the program was to develop and test a training model to embed literacy and Essential Skills into workplace training (Sidhu & Weaver, 2013). The three small businesses included a computer consulting, support, and sales organization with multiple locations; a storage company with multiple locations; and a women's resources center with one location. These three businesses provided a broad spectrum of employees that included highly educated technical professionals, middle managers and clerical workers, warehouse staff, sales professionals, and some disadvantaged minorities with limited work skills. The Sources BC project team consisted of Dan Scott, Director of Community and Employment Services; Lovey Sidhu, an independent education and training consultant and W.E.S.T. Project Coordinator; and Carla Weaver, principal faculty at City University and an independent education and training consultant, who acted as a W.E.S.T. Training Facilitator.

The W.E.S.T. program evolved as an innovative Human Resources (HR) practice that was designed to provide focused training to employees to enhance workplace skills. The W.E.S.T. mission was to create new models for local businesses to embed Workplace Essential Skills into their training and development plans, models that not only trained and developed employees, but also empowered them to be more self-sufficient and productive. The program developed and adapted a number of resources for training employees and also for training the trainers to make clients self-sufficient. Resources were also created to assess the effectiveness of the training. All resources were made available to the community via a website and resource guide so that anyone could benefit from them.

Overview of the Model: Train-Develop-Empower

Fig. 1. *The Training Model*
(Source: Sidhu & Weaver, 2013)

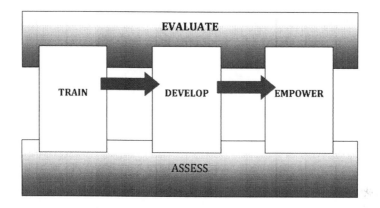

Developing a Training Program That Delivers Results

Companies must consider what additional skills their employees need to be more effective in their jobs, what specific skills they will need in order for the organization to meet future goals, and the best methods for employees to learn the required skills. Each employee brings a different skill set and experience level, so his/her learning needs are specific and therefore, it is not effective to design training that is too broad (Sidhu & Weaver, 2013).

Framework Implemented for Training and Workplace Skill Development

The framework of the W.E.S.T. Training Model includes the following: (Sidhu & Weaver, 2013):

1. Conducting ongoing **ASSESS**ments
Determining needs related to identifying core workplace skills that require attention, defining the purpose of training, ensuring that training helps the company and department to achieve their goals, deciding

on how many and which employees will need training, deciding how to implement the training into daily workplace activities, and assessing employees' current skills levels in job-specific tasks and Essential Skills.

2. Creating job-related focused and specific **TRAIN**ing

Based on the assessment, confirming which core workplace skills require training, defining objectives and desired outcomes for the training, determining measures for how learners will demonstrate change, and developing training specific to the job.

3. **DEVELOP** employees to meet their future goals and **EVALUATE** training

Training should help to develop skills that will be helpful to employees to meet long-term organizational goals. Additionally, the training should include methods showing how to use the skills and help to increase the self-sufficiency and independence of workers by developing decision-making skills.

From a management point of view, training programs must be evaluated in order to measure their effectiveness and whether they produce the desired results from both employers' and employees' perspectives.

4. Developing a culture of **EMPOWER**ment

When employees feel empowered, they actively participate in training and work effectively with each other to mentor and support each other. They also become more open to change, which includes adapting better to new policies, technology, and organizational changes, and employee retention rates improve.

> *A culture of lifelong learning and empowerment depends on strategic, well-planned training programs leading to empowerment.*

Each step is described in more detail in the sections to follow. While the model is general in its description as it relates to content, this project was concerned with embedding Essential Skills into training, so at each step, we were concerned with both meeting training needs for specific work tasks and also determining needs to target Essential Skills mastery within any training that was developed and delivered.

Step 1: Assess

Because small businesses are often understaffed or don't have HR departments to carry on employee assessments, training is implemented based on *assumptions* about what is needed, and thus, it may not meet the needs of the employee or lead to the achievement of the company's strategic goals. Without first assessing training needs, training may result in little or no change in employee behavior and may lead to employee complaints about training being "useless" or a "waste of time." A thorough assessment *before* training plans are developed and implemented is imperative for successful training and outcomes (Sidhu & Weaver, 2013).

A **needs analysis**, an assessment method to determine the *need* for training, assists in identifying the main reasons for training, and identifies specific training goals. A comprehensive needs analysis requires time, energy, and resources to gather information, but the data collected is invaluable. By investing time before training begins, an organization can ensure that any training developed will be focused on specifically meeting the goals of the company and needs of the employees (Sidhu & Weaver, 2013).

Information collected in a needs analysis also provides an organization with data that can be used to:

- develop policies and procedures;
- measure employee satisfaction;
- identify gaps within the organization (in communication, information sharing, etc.);
- create or change job descriptions; and
- measure the success of training programs (Sidhu & Weaver, 2013).

The steps in a needs analysis are illustrated below:

Fig. 2. *Steps to Conduct a Needs Analysis*
(Source: Sidhu & Weaver, 2013)

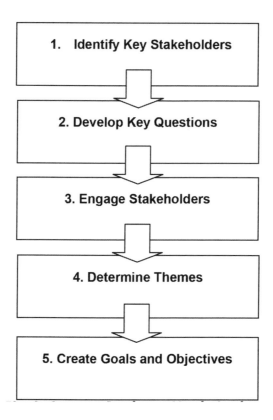

1. Identify Key Stakeholders

A stakeholder is a "person, group, or organization that has a direct or indirect stake in an organization because it can affect or be affected by the organization's actions, objectives and policies" (BusinessDictionary.com, 2012). A needs analysis involves all levels of the organization including frontline staff, managers, directors, and customers. By identifying two to three members from each stakeholder group, the needs analysis will provide the most comprehensive data.

This is an essential first step to ensure that training goals and objectives are aligned at all levels. Training programs that are developed on the basis of one stakeholder often miss key needs of the other parties resulting in poor training results (Sidhu & Weaver, 2013).

2. Develop Key Questions

The needs analysis involves asking a series of questions of the stakeholders to identify training needs. If the problem is not clear, then start by asking broad questions and narrowing in on more specific questions. Following are some examples of questions to start a needs assessment:

- What are the goals of the company/department?
- What does a well-organized department look like?
- Describe challenges, issues, and barriers surrounding the attainment of company/department goals.
- Describe specific job-related tasks for the various positions within the organization (Job Task Analysis). What are your responsibilities? What is your manager responsible for? What are the responsibilities of your coworkers and members in other departments?
- Describe specific areas of desired improvements within each department.
- What are the core workplace Essential Skills required to meet the goals? (Sidhu & Weaver, 2013, p. 24)

3. Engage Stakeholders

It can be challenging to find time to engage with stakeholders to obtain the needed information, but it is an important step because the data gathered will ensure that training contributes to achieving the goals of the organization.

Strategies to access stakeholders include:

- Creating small work groups to interview a few people at a time;
- Creating written surveys that people can complete on their own time;
- Contacting stakeholders by email or telephone;
- Being considerate of the time when stakeholders are most available to spend time providing the needed information;
- Offering incentives for participating; and
- Keeping meetings short and specific (Sidhu & Weaver, 2013).

4. Determine Themes

After meeting with the identified stakeholders, training designers can begin to identify themes that emerge from the information gathering, and then review the data and identify patterns, commonalities, things that are surprising, or new information. It is effective to focus on two to three key areas that were identified by most of the stakeholders.

5. Create Training Goals and Objectives

A crucial step in the development process is determining training goals and then communicating them throughout the organization. Goals should be specific and measureable. Training goals, objectives, and learning outcomes are all important elements of the training design process, and are also important in the evaluation phase of the training program.

Step 2: Train

Through strategic, well-planned training programs, the W.E.S.T. approach was to create a culture of development and lifelong learning that contributes to achievement of strategic goals.

The following diagram illustrates the cornerstones of the W.E.S.T. training model. The needs analysis, which has already been discussed in detail, is followed by developing objectives and then identifying learning outcomes, which are used to create a delivery plan including the final lesson plan, which then serves as the design document for developing the training and selecting the delivery method. All of these elements are tied in to the company's organizational goals, and this is critical to creating training that aligns with a company's strategic plan (Sidhu & Weaver, 2013).

Fig. 3. *Workshop Development*
(Source: Sidhu & Weaver, 2013)

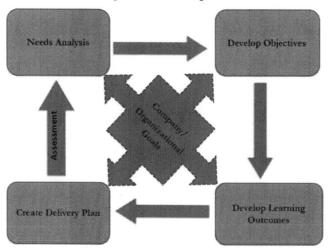

1. Connecting to the Needs Analysis

After a strategic effort has been made to assess needs before training, the next step is to create training programs that are job-related and specific with measurable outcomes that will change productivity and effectiveness for both employees and the organization as a whole.

Developing effective training is much easier when a needs assessment has been conducted. After interviewing employees and managers about what they believe will add to effectiveness and productivity, common threads can be identified, as well as the specific needs of each individual to determine how to address them through more targeted one-on-one or on-the-job training.

During the project, we always ensured that we described to our participants which Essential Skills were being addressed within the training by including this information in the learning objectives, learning outcomes, a special slide, note, or comment (e.g., document use, computer skills, etc.).

2. Developing Objectives

An objective is a statement of the intended general outcome of a unit or program, which describes a more global learning outcome.

Learning objectives describe the goals of the training, the main topics, and content. These objectives are closely tied to the company's goals, mission statements, and strategic initiatives, and in the W.E.S.T. model, they also address specific Essential Skills (Sidhu & Weaver, 2013).

3. Developing Learning Outcomes

Learning outcomes clearly articulate the knowledge, skills, and attitudes that learners will gain from the workshop or class by specifying new behaviors that learners will acquire or develop. They begin with an action verb and describe something observable or measurable.

Learning outcomes should specify what learners should be able to do on the job as a result of the training. These things fall into three possible categories (domains):

- Thinking, knowledge (cognitive domain);
- Doing, skills (psychomotor domain);
- Feeling, attitudes (affective domain) (Bloom, Engelhart, Furst, Hill, & Krathwohl, 1956).

4. Creating the Lesson Plan

While the lesson plan serves as a guide for the lesson developer, it is also a road map for the instructor who will deliver the training. The key components of a lesson plan (title, duration, required materials, objectives, outcomes) ensure that the developed training meets the needs of the learners and fulfills the required objectives for the organization.

The lesson plan includes some basic information about the topic of the training and who it's for (learner profile, the Essential Skills that will be addressed in the training, and the specific objectives of the lesson). It should contain a note about any resources that will be required by both instructor and learners, and provide guidance for instructors, such as showing pictures or models, asking leading questions, or providing reviews of previous lessons that are relevant to continuing instruction on the topic. Lesson plans also include a detailed outline of the planned content and the time allotted for each section, as well as applied activities so that learners can practice their skills. A summary of the outcomes and related session questions concludes the lesson plan.

Prior to developing a lesson plan, it is important to establish the method used to deliver the lesson. Table 1 lists different types of delivery methods commonly used to conduct training. Each offers strengths and weaknesses; therefore, it is important to evaluate and identify the method that meets both the needs of the organization and the learners.

Table 1. *Delivery Methods*

Delivery Method	Description	Strengths	Weaknesses
Classroom/ Instructor-Led Training	An instructor teaches training in a classroom to a group of learners.	• The instructor is present to answer questions and offer alternative explanations when learners don't understand the material. • It is interactive—learners and instructors can have interactive discussions and take part in group or individual activities to enhance learning. • The instructor may be an expert on the content of the material, and therefore provide greater opportunities for learning.	• Hiring an instructor and procuring a training facility can be costly. • Taking a group of workers away from their jobs all at the same time may negatively impact business. • Not all learners learn at the same pace, so modulating the pace of the training can be challenging to engage those who learn quickly while not leaving behind those who take longer to assimilate the content.

Mentoring/ On-the-Job Training	An experienced coworker or supervisor coaches and provides on-the-job hands-on training to learners.	• This is generally conducted in a one-on-one situation or in small groups, so it can take place at a pace that is suited for the learner(s). • It is specific and on-the-job, so the training is targeted at the specific tasks that must be performed by workers on the job. • The mentor is experienced in the work tasks covered, so he/she can explain how the tasks should be completed, and then supervise the learners as they complete the tasks and offer immediate feedback.	• Mentoring is more time-consuming and if there are many learners, it can take a long time to complete the training.
E-Learning— Facilitated	An instructor oversees a classroom of learners as they work through a computer-based learning program.	• Learners can ask questions of the instructor or each other, while completing hands-on training on the computer. • Less costly and resource intensive than pure instructor-led learning because there may be less development time on the part of the instructor if the e-learning is purchased from an outside vendor.	• If the e-learning is not specifically developed for the learners' needs and work tasks, then it may not be as effective as customized training that targets the specific needs of the learners. • May be more challenging for learners who are not computer-literate.

E-Learning—Self-Paced	Learners independently work through a self-paced computer-based training session without supervision. There may be an online help facility to assist learners.	• Learners can complete training on their own schedule at their own pace.	• May be more challenging for workers who are less experienced with the computer or who do not learn well on their own.
Blended Learning	A combination of instructor-led training in a classroom and self-paced e-learning, or one-on-one instructor guidance combined with e-learning.	• Combines the advantages of instructor-led training, facilitated e-learning and self-paced e-learning.	It also combines many of the disadvantages.
Self-Paced Independent Learning	Learners have a self-paced training program, such as a workbook or self-study guide and they complete it on their own without instruction. It is not computer-based.	• Learners can complete training on their own schedule at their own pace.	• May be more challenging for learners who do not learn well on their own. • It may be more difficult to monitor if and when learners have completed the training and/or they may procrastinate and not complete it in a timely manner.

(Source: Sidhu & Weaver, 2013, p. 32)

While each mode of training delivery has its pros and cons, each one is best suited for certain types of content and learner requirements, so it cannot be concluded that one mode is superior to others. Choosing the right training delivery method to meet the needs of the organization and the employees is critical.

Consider learner needs and expectations. Workers may have expectations about training methods, desired activities and topics, which should be considered when developing a training plan. If employees' expectations are not met, then the training may not meet an organization's objectives (Bacal & Associates, n.d.). For example, an older workforce, or workers who do not usually use a computer, may learn better from instructor-led training, as opposed to computer-based training. Alternatively, in a technology-based business, workers are highly computer-literate, and thus online delivery or other self-paced computer-based training may be the most effective mode of training. Skills such as typing or using software programs may be more effectively learned by hands-on-training than a lecture.

When training is specifically linked to organizational goals and learners' work tasks, learners are more engaged and the training yields better results to both the organization and the employees. Additionally, when workers are able to learn by performing the specific tasks that they need to perform on the job, they become more empowered to be self-sufficient. Skills learned in training programs must be easily transferred back to the real world by ensuring that the training is delivered when it's needed so that learners immediately apply their new skills (Brown, 2008).

Knowing how learners learn the best helps to build training that is more engaging. By considering whether they are visual learners, auditory learners, kinesthetic learners, or multimodal learners, training can be developed to suit the learning styles of the students. "For example, when learning a different language, some learners must see the words written and spelled in order to better assimilate the information (visual learners), whereas some learners must hear them spoken for the pronunciation to better learn the words (auditory learners). Some learners assimilate information better when they are able to have hands-on experience (kinesthetic learners), while some learners are multimodal, preferring to see the information presented in a number of different modes for more effective learning. Do they need to practice with guidance? What is their current skill level? All of these factors should be considered while developing the training to ensure that employees will be most engaged in the sessions" (Sidhu & Weaver, 2013, p. 34).

Variety in the delivery modes also helps learners to stay more engaged in the training, so even within a single lesson, a combination of lecture, multimedia, and hands-on delivery will help learners to remain more interested. Variety will also increase chances of meeting the needs of learners with different learning styles (Bacal & Associates, n.d.).

Training Sustainability

A continuous learning plan ensures that learning outcomes are reinforced and new skills and concepts are introduced when appropriate, either for the same workers, for new workers, or for workers in other areas of the business (Brown, 2008). Developing sustainability plans is a critical component of ensuring that workplace training initiatives continue to provide learning opportunities beyond the initial training programs. Creating mentors and developing trainers are two methods that will support the momentum of training initiatives, and these are the approaches used in the W.E.S.T.

1. Mentorship:

Mentorship is a learning relationship between an experienced person, who is adept at the work skills that must be transferred, and a learner. A mentor takes on the responsibility of transferring skills to a learner by instructing, providing feedback, coaching, and encouraging the learner on the job (Canadian Construction Sector Council, 2009).

W.E.S.T. adopted the Six Steps to Mentorship, as outlined by the Canadian Construction Sector Council (2009):

1. **Identify the point of the lesson**—the mentor sets the tone for the training and describes the context in which the skill or task is completed;
2. **Link the lesson**—the mentor demonstrates how the skill or behavior is connected to the overall process in which it takes place;
3. **Demonstrate the skill**—the mentor demonstrates the skill or task so that the learner observes how it is done correctly;
4. **Provide opportunity for practice**—the mentor gives the learner an opportunity to practice the skill;
5. **Give feedback**—the mentor offers feedback to the learner after he or she practices the skill so that the learner knows how to improve. The feedback offers encouragement and makes suggestions to correct errors or improve performance; and
6. **Assess progress**—the mentor monitors the learner's progress and decides when the learner is prepared to move on to the next task (Canadian Construction Sector Council, 2009).

2. Train the Trainers

One of the primary intentions of developing trainers in the organization is to ensure consistency and quality in training. The goal is to ultimately benefit both workers and the organization by offering consistent and effective training that is linked to the strategy of the organization leading to improved performance and a happier, more qualified workforce.

Transferring training skills to team leaders and more experienced workers also reduces training costs because workers within the organization develop their skills to train those with less experience, thus reducing the need to invest in external training.

Step 3: Evaluate

Fig. 4. *Evaluate for Program Success*
(Source: Sidhu & Weaver, 2013, p. 39)

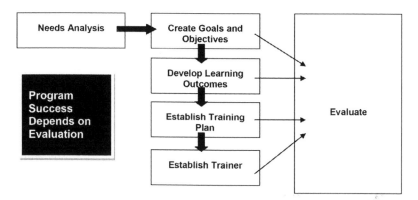

Evaluation of the training plays a vital role and is important at all stages of training to ensure ongoing program success. Information for evaluating the effectiveness of training is collected both formally and informally by talking to employees directly about their experience or by running focus groups to talk to several employees at once. Surveys with a series of specific questions about the training can also be conducted by email or telephone interviews. Evaluation is done to measure the success of training and its outcomes and to identify areas that may need further development (Sidhu & Weaver, 2013).

Evaluation should start at the needs analysis stage when organizations identify training goals and objectives, which are then measured during the evaluation stage.

Stages of Evaluations

Regardless of the stage of development, the one basic question to ask is:

> *Did we accomplish what we set out to do?*

The W.E.S.T. approach to evaluation consisted of two parts:

1. Accurately identifying factor(s) to be measured, and
2. Determining the method to be used to measure the factor(s).

It is best to initiate the evaluation process at the training stage to gather the most specific information.

Evaluate the Training Experience

While all aspects of training should be evaluated, a great way to begin the evaluation process is to collect data from participants about their training experience to learn about what worked, what didn't work, or how participants felt about the training. This information relates to the experience during the training session. It's also important to evaluate the trainer because the trainer needs to be skilled at both delivery and identifying the key outcomes of the session.

To effectively evaluate learning outcomes, the specific outcomes to be measured need to be identified. Learning outcomes describe learners' new behaviors after a learning experience by stating how the knowledge, skills, and attitudes that the learners will develop through the training will be demonstrated after training. It is important to identify the specific behavior that will be acquired as a result of training, as only the behavior we can see can be measured. Often outcomes are not explicitly stated, which limits the ability to accurately evaluate the effectiveness of the training. Keep this in mind: if you can't see it, you can't measure it!

Sometimes, a pre-assessment survey, a survey that participants complete before they begin the training, can also be implemented to invite learners to assess their skills and knowledge about both the subject matter and their Essential Skills before beginning training. After the training, they can determine whether they have improved knowledge on the topic. The instructor can also use this tool to initiate discussions with learners about progress or goals, and comment on areas that the learner should continue to develop (Sidhu & Weaver, 2013).

After the training is completed, educators can review the feedback collected and measure the outcomes to determine the effectiveness of training goals and objectives. Statements related to goals and objectives are often broad and address the overall targets.

Step 4: Develop and Empower

Successful employee development programs consider both the needs of the employees and the organization's goals. Empowerment is a process that enables employees to think, take action, take control, and make decisions in an autonomous way. The role of an employer is to remove barriers that prevent staff from acting empowered.

Creating a culture of lifelong learning and people development can result in a workforce that is eager to learn, easily adapts when presented with change and increases business flexibility. Research showed that empowerment enables employee behaviors and attitudes, and empowered employees are more satisfied and committed at work, more loyal and less stressed. The most critical behaviors affected by empowerment are performance, innovation, and organizational citizenship (Simmons, 2011). An effective method for attracting and retaining skilled workers is to consider adopting a culture of learning as a long-term commitment.

Employee empowerment is a strategy that fosters an environment in which people are dynamic, happy, and produce real results. A culture of empowerment reinforces accomplishments, employee contribution, and places value on the people who work within an organization. Leaders share organizational goals, company direction, and encourage staff to contribute to the company's vision. Staff empowerment creates an environment of trust; one in which the employees' intentions are trusted and where employers trust that staff will make the right decisions.

Empowered employees who embrace continuous learning are the foundation of a successful organization. Employers must truly recognize the power and benefits of employee empowerment. It's essential that employers take the time to learn about employee empowerment, and the principles and the practices that encourage empowerment. The next step is to trust employees; employers should believe that they will make the right decisions and provide opportunities for them to be involved in decision making, especially regarding their own jobs and careers. Employers provide the information and tools to ensure that employees are well equipped to make informed decisions and provide feedback, before, during, and after training. Communication is essential, and employers need to listen, learn, and provide leadership when employees need it. Finally, employees should be rewarded and recognized for engaging in empowered behaviors. Empowering employees has dramatic results.

W.E.S.T. Project Challenges and Outcomes

The goals of the W.E.S.T. project were:

- To increase community awareness and access to workplace training that embedded literacy and Essential Skills (Sidhu, 2013); and
- To increase capacity for workplace training that embeds literacy and Essential Skills within three communities in the region of Surrey, BC (Sidhu, 2013).

The project objectives were met by providing training with embedded Essential Skills to over fifty-five employees. While the overall project was considered to be highly successful and the developed model to have achieved its objectives, there were two main challenges that were encountered during the project:

1. The most unexpected challenge that occurred was **resistance to training**. Although we were able to create a training culture within the W.E.S.T. project that was inclusive, accessible, and supportive in nature, we were surprised to be met with resistance at both the management and employee levels. Management-level resistance often showed itself in passive-aggressive patterns, such as continually canceling training dates, inability to commit to training outcomes, and ongoing requests that seemed beyond the scope of the project. For employees, it can be embarrassing to self-identify their shortcomings in Essential Skills due to fears of job loss or possible limitations to future advancement (Sidhu, 2013).

As was anticipated, we were able to readily address resistance at the employee level with change efforts by preparing in advance and taking a proactive approach to ensuring confidentiality and building trust.

By conducting ongoing assessments, we were able to conclude that resistance to change can exist at all levels. Taking a proactive approach to assessing such possible resistance, at all levels, is critical for training implementation.

2. The **logistics of scheduling training** was another challenge and although expected, it significantly shifted training delivery plans.

Factors such as finding coverage for staff that participated in training, selecting times within a day to deliver training, finding champions to assist with delivery, locating training space, etc.—all affected our ability to deliver training according to a logical and timely schedule within the project plan. As a result—our "lesson learned" and a great success of the program—was creating a variety of delivery methods including:

- Classroom instructor-led training;
- E-learning—facilitated;
- E-learning—self-paced;
- Blended learning; and
- Self-paced independent learning (see Table 1)

Efforts within the project that will further contribute to capacity building, community awareness, and access include:

- Creation of a **website** with numerous training tools including lesson plans and slide presentations, assessment tools, Essential Skills resources, articles, and the final resource guide at www.westproject.ca. The W.E.S.T. website provides over forty Essentials Skills tools including:

  - Lesson plans and slide presentations for various Essential Skills training workshops,
  - Assessment tools,
  - Evaluation tools, and
  - Essential Skills articles and resources (also provided in a CD along with the *Resource Guide*) (Sidhu, 2013).
- Creation of the final *Resource Guide for Small Businesses*
The *Resource Guide* is designed to:

  - Describe "literacy" and "Essential Skills";
  - Bring focus to the fact that employees' Essential Skills issues can affect a business's productivity, effectiveness, adaptability, creativity, and success either positively or negatively;
  - Help decision makers in an organization identify the business benefits and understand why addressing and improving

employee Essential Skills can lead to improvements in daily operations and increased profitability; and

- Support managers of small businesses in assessing, developing, and delivering appropriate training to enhance the skills and effectiveness of their workers (Sidhu & Weaver, 2013).

Embedding Essential Skills Training and Development in College and University Programs to Better Prepare Graduates for the Workplace: Drawing from the W.E.S.T. Pilot Project

According to the National Association of Colleges and Employers (NACE, n.d.), in addition to a solid knowledge of the new grad's field, noted by earning a good GPA and participation in internships, employers are looking for grads who have a number of "soft" skills (NACE, 2012). During a recent City University Advisory Board meeting for the business degree programs, a list of skills that graduates need to master to land and keep a job were identified. Board members agreed that graduates must be competent in their major subject and also possess the necessary theory and knowledge to master the technical part of the job. Essential Skills that contribute to competency in technical skills include document use, numeracy, and computer skills.

According to a study of what corporations seek when they hire MBAs, "the three most desired capabilities are communication skills, interpersonal skills and initiative—all of which are elements of emotional intelligence" (Goleman, 2000, p. 13).

Examples of the skills that were identified by the City University Advisory Board are listening, a sense of humor, manners, social pleasantries, ability for small talk, acceptable social communications, respect for one another and their superiors, phone etiquette, and understanding office politics. *Soft skills* is a more encompassing term for required work skills that involve communication, working with others, continuous learning, and thinking. The Essential Skills include some literacy and technical skills as well as soft skills. In short, in addition to subject matter knowledge, graduates need the Essential Skills of communicating, working with others, thinking and continuous learning, and soft skills to be successful in the workplace.

> *According to a study of what corporations seek when they hire MBAs, "the three most desired capabilities are communication skills, interpersonal skills, and initiative—all of which are elements of emotional intelligence" (Goleman, 2000, p. 13).*

We argue that Essential Skills development is critical and should be integrated into educational programs at the postsecondary level. As many students are expected to demonstrate competence in both technical knowledge and soft skills development, should postsecondary programming not foster such skill development?

The framework from the W.E.S.T. pilot project can be adapted to meet the needs of Essential Skills, including soft skills training in the classroom. Educators can create learning activities that integrate the required workplace Essential Skills to further prepare students for their careers. Teaching skills related to communications, working with others, and thinking and then encouraging continuous learning will better equip students to be prepared for the competitive workforce. Many instructors already foster and encourage these skills in their classrooms and some schools include special program orientation courses or tutorials to enhance and develop skills in their students to better prepare them for learning while at college or university, which of course, leads to graduates who are better prepared to enter the workforce.

Teaching Essential Skills: Adapting the Framework

Let's explore how the W.E.S.T. model can be adapted in an academic setting.

Step 1: ASSESS—Conduct Initial and Ongoing Assessments

A critical component of designing any skill development program is the needs analysis. Educators need to learn more about their students, including current skill levels, the skills required for future work, and the skills required for academic course work. Learning about students, their needs, and their goals early in the learning journey will assist with knowledge and skill acquisition.

In a college or university setting, conducting a needs analysis should be done at both the admissions stage by assessing students' Essential Skills upon entry to the program, and assessment can also be done at an individual course level to determine needs specific to the course.

At the **admissions or program level**, needs analysis for program development can be conducted in a variety of methods:

- Conducting one-on-one information interviews with the students;
- Creating online surveys;
- Engaging in focus groups or small group discussions;
- Inviting students to interview each other;
- Inviting learners to conduct self-assessments of skill levels;
- Formal testing/assessments to determine skill levels (such as TEFOL for English language development or math assessments for numeracy development); or
- Human Resources and Skills Development Canada offers several tools and resources for Essential Skills assessment.1

Part of the needs analysis should also include a review of the particular skills students need to be successful in the workplace upon graduation. An educator may decide to select two to three core skills he or she believes are critical for workplace success. Human Resources and Skills Development Canada developed Essential Skills profiles for over 350 jobs outlining the top three Essential Skills of that profession.

Although teaching Essential Skills (or soft skills) may seem like a daunting task, especially in courses that are already content-heavy, at a **course level**, skills development can be achieved with small adaptations to activities that already exist in course work by starting with one of the two end goals in mind:

1. Conduct a needs analysis to determine *what skills need to be developed.*
2. Conduct a needs analysis on a *particular skill to assess skill gaps.*

Methods to assess students' skill levels at the course level might include:

- Creating activities and conducting observations from a "distance" (i.e., observing students as they participate in group activities)
- Reviewing past course assignments/exams/assessments (looking for trends/themes)

Case 1. *Needs Analysis*

Needs Analysis in Action

In a Practical Nursing program, the department head (DH) questioned the high failure rate in the Pharmacology course. After careful review of student exams, quizzes, and assignments, it was evident that most students were failing in the medication conversion tables. After further review, the DH realized students were unable to complete basic mathematical operations with fractions (multiplying, dividing, adding, and subtracting fractions).

As a result, the Pharmacology course integrated a numeracy section to teach basic operations with fractions.

At the individual course level, start with the course syllabus. What assessments, activities and tasks are expected of students? What are the learning outcomes? What skills do students require to successfully complete the course outcomes? What challenges have students presented in the past in completing the course requirements? This is an excellent way of initiating a skill development program. Draw on existing course requirements and identify the *specific tasks* required to complete the expected assessment. Take a look at the sample course assessment outline below:

Table 2. *Sample Course Assessment*

Course Assessment	Overall Course %	Required Essential Skills
Group Presentation	30	Working with Others Oral Communication Thinking Skills (plan and organize job tasks)

243

Final Essay	20	Thinking Skills (plan and organize job tasks, finding information, use critical thinking) Writing and Reading Skills Document Use Computer Use
Midterm Exam	20	Document Use Reading and Writing Skills
Final Exam	30	Document Use Reading and Writing Skills

Conduct a skills assessment. For the purpose of this discussion, let's explore the first assessment—group presentation (worth 30% of the final mark). Ask yourself:

- In the past, how often did you deal with group dynamic issues? Student complaints about peers? Personality conflicts?
- How often have you observed presentations and noticed that not all group members contributed during the presentation?
- Did students complain about the amount of time required to complete the task?

Regardless of the clear assignment expectations, grading rubrics, and ongoing instructor support, it is inevitable that educators will deal with ongoing Essential Skills gaps if such skills are not developed. To expect a student to engage in group tasks without teaching the core skills required to function within a group, educators will continually burden themselves with ongoing student challenges and students will continue to feel the strain of poor group functioning. Furthermore, employers will find themselves challenged with such dynamics in the workplace. Group work requires students to:

- Understand group dynamics including the stages of group formation
- Recognize and appreciate personality styles
- Demonstrate an ability to use and manage time effectively
- Implement priority management skills

- Identify and resolve problems including conflict management skills
- Demonstrate an ability to give and receive feedback effectively
- Plan and organize job tasks

Just as a nursing student needs to divide fractions to complete a medication conversion, students require each of the skills presented to complete a group presentation, yet such skills are often not taught in a classroom setting.

Step 2: TRAIN AND EVALUATE: Creating Task-Related and Specific Training, and Evaluating Effectively

Similar to the example of the nursing department head, it is important to create skill development programs that are directly connected to the specific tasks related to the skill. Teaching calculus or topics in numeracy that are not *directly connected* to the conversion chart in the Pharmacology course would not serve the students' needs. In fact, it would likely deter students from participating at all! Adults must be able to identify the reason for learning something. It must be applicable to their personal or professional lives if it is to be of any value (Barnes, 2005). As educators, in defining program objectives, we must make sure that the theories and concepts are relevant to the learners' needs.

Drawing from the data collected in the needs analysis will assist in creating specific, focus-based skills programs. Program directors can design program-wide orientation programs or credit courses that enhance essential skills by including training that teaches students how to work on teams, how to access and use documents in the library, how to use the online course platform, business writing courses, professionalism and ethics courses, organizational culture courses, etc. Instructors can use the information to create training objectives and determine learning outcomes for their specific courses. The information gathered will further assist educators in identifying the optimal delivery methodology—ensuring programs that are engaging and student-centered in their approaches.

Clearly communicating learning outcomes to students is an important step in skill development. The article "The Effects on Students of Pre-Announced Learning Objectives and Immediate Performance Feedback"

(Kothare, 1993) reports interesting research on the effect of being clear about learning outcomes—students will be more focused and their learning will be strengthened with clearly communicated outcomes.2

Case 2. *Specific and Task-Related Training*

Specific and Task-Related Training

A psychology instructor in a 100-level course decides to implement a group assignment valued at 30 percent of the overall course mark. The students are expected to write a paper and present their findings to the class in a presentation at the end of the term.

After explaining the details of the assignment, the instructor presents a thirty-minute lesson on team development. She outlines the various stages of team formation and connects the topic to the experience students will have as they work in their groups.

A few weeks later, the instructor engages in a class discussion about the stages of team formation. She invites the students to share their thoughts, challenges, and next steps to overcome the challenges. She may initiate a team contract so that students develop an agreement with each other about their roles, responsibilities, and desired outcomes for the team project.

At the end of the term, the instructor invites students to reflect on the stages of team formation and connects this discussion to a workplace setting, inviting students to discuss how their experience in their groups can be transferred to the workplace.

A similar application is to provide students with a peer evaluation form to complete after working on a group assignment. This allows students to give and receive feedback on their ability to work in a group. When this skill is tied to grading rubrics, it reinforces the importance of working well with others

Application: Skills Training in the Classroom

There are endless possibilities when it comes to skill development; the challenge is how to start and how much to integrate skill development into the classroom. Of course, skills-training integration (or embedding) will depend on the course, the instructor, the students, and the institution, but there are simple steps that educators can take to enhance skill development that might not be as intimidating as a skills development program. Reviewing the course syllabus is a great start, but here are some examples of simple applications:

- Creating classroom codes of conduct that outline professional expectations of the group, including appropriate interpersonal behaviors;
- Providing links or information that invite learners to learn more about group formation, personality styles, and working with others (or other topics);
- Creating team-building activities early in a course that are "fun and interactive" yet teach core group processing skills;
- Including active-listening workshops that include feedback;
- Modeling and demonstrating active-listening skills that include feedback skills;
- Clearly communicating the core skills required to successfully complete class assessments (prompting continuous learning and inviting students to seek support as needed);
- Engaging in reflective practice activities and ongoing student self-assessment;
- Providing a scaffold approach to writing assignments (invite students to submit parts of an overall essay to assess and offer feedback on writing skills);
- Teaching appropriate research skills (i.e., document use—provide a one-page article and invite students to identify and retrieve key information);
- Assigning journal article reviews to give students an opportunity to use documents, read and understand them;
- Including role playing (practicing skills);

- Incorporating and encouraging classroom or online discussions to practice oral or written communication and assimilation of ideas and concepts from class reading;
- Applying Bloom's taxonomy of learning domains to ensure that students practice all three domains (cognitive, affective, and psychomotor) to be able to improve their thinking Essential Skill (cognitive domain) and their interpersonal-emotional (soft) skills (affective domain), etc. (Bloom et al., 1956).

Step 3: EVALUATE—Evaluating Programs as an Integral Part of Program Development

Critical to any effective program is evaluation. Evaluation exists at every level and should be used to determine the effectiveness and effect on student performance, course expectations and requirements, and overall effectiveness of programs implemented. Just as presented in the pilot project, the question to ask is:

> *Did we accomplish what we set out to do?*

Assessing student progress of skill development can be conducted in a variety of methods including:
- Pre- and post-assessments (conducted formally though tests or surveys or informally through observations);
- Student feedback indicating skill development;
- Comparisons based on historical data (i.e., are the classes able to work more effectively in groups compared to previous classes?);
- Grading rubrics for assignments that require students to demonstrate Essential Skills in their work, such as points for writing, grammar, spelling and punctuation, or computer skills (e.g., developing a graph or chart to demonstrate an idea or concept).

Step 4: EMPOWER—Educate and Empower

The student is the center of any skill development program. Creating, delivering, and initiating a skills program develops the whole student—beyond technical skills training. It assists students in effectively completing course requirements and better prepares graduates for the workforce. Student skills development is a joint, ongoing effort of both the educator and the student. Similar to workplace training, consider the following factors when creating programs for skill development among students:

- Provide opportunities to put learning acquired during training into use in the actual class activities/assessments;
- Support students to use the skills acquired in training; give students a chance to demonstrate new skills;
- Encourage active student participation in decision making about training goals as a whole.

Conclusion

Creating a culture of lifelong learning and student development will contribute to a workforce that is competent in Essential Skills, eager to learn, adaptable to change, and responsive to business flexibility. Graduates who are competent in Essential Skills will be sought after by recruiters and will favorably influence the reputations of the universities from which they graduate (Sidhu & Weaver, 2013). The W.E.S.T. model that embeds Essential Skills in training and emphasizes Train, Develop, Evaluate, and Empower with ongoing assessment and continuous improvement can be adapted to an academic environment to achieve these results and better prepare students for the world beyond the doors of our classrooms.

References

Bacal & Associates. (n.d.). *The training and development world*, retrieved November 7, 2012, from http://thetrainingworld.com/

Barnes, L. (2005). *Achieving success with adult learners*. Retrieved March 12, 2013, from Thomson-Delmar Learning Web site: http://emarketing. delmarlearning.com/milady/milady_news_fall05_classroom.asp

Bloom, B. S., Engelhart, M. D., Furst, E. J., Hill, W. H., & Krathwohl, D. R. (1956). *Taxonomy of educational objectives: The classification of educational goals.* New York: Longman's Green.

Brown, Tris. (2008, April 2). *Top 10 training best practices for effective learning and development programs,* retrieved November 10, 2012, from http://www.articlesbase.com/management-articles/top-10-training-best-practices-for-effective-learning-and-development-programs-376420.html

BusinessDictionary.com, retrieved from http://www.businessdictionary.com/definition/stakeholder.html on August 2, 2013.

Canadian Construction Sector Council. (2009). *Mentorship program.* Ottawa, Ontario.

Canadian Literacy and Learning Network. (n.d.). *All about literacy in Canada,* retrieved December 20, 2012, from http://www.literacy.ca/literacy/literacy-sub/

Canadian Manufacturers & Exporters Ontario. (2008). *Business results through essential skills and literacy guidebook,* retrieved March 12, 2013, from www.cme-mec.ca/pdf/Business_Results_Through_Essential_Skills_and_Literacy.pdf

Clark, D. (n.d.). *Bloom's taxonomy of learning domains,* retrieved March 30, 2013, from http://www.nwlink.com/~donclark/hrd/bloom.html

Daft, R. L. (2005). *Management* (7th ed.). Mason, OH: Thomson Southwestern.

Donovan, M. *Concepts in mentoring series,* ARG Australia.

Douglas College. (n.d.). *Essential Skills: The building blocks for success.* Retrieved October 15, 2012, from http://www.douglas.bc.ca/training-community-education/essentialskills.html

Goleman, D. (2000). *Working with emotional intelligence.* New York, NY: Bantam Dell.

Hayes, A. (n.d.). *If you only understood your customer's personality style.* Retrieved June 30, 2011, from AH Digital FH Studios, Inc. Web site: http://www.ahfx.net/weblog/37

Human Resources and Skills Development Canada (HRSDC). (n.d.). *Literacy and Essential Skills*, retrieved March 12, 2013, from www.hrsdc.gc.ca/eng/workplaceskills/LES/index.shtml

Human Resources and Skills Development Canada (HRSDC). (2007, November). *Readers' guide to Essential Skills profiles*, retrieved March 12, 2013, from http://www.hrsdc.gc.ca/eng/jobs/les/profiles/readersguide.shtml

Human Resources and Skills Development Canada (HRSDC). (n.d.). *Building Essential Skills in the workplace*, retrieved March 12, 2013, from http://www.hrsdc.gc.ca/eng/jobs/les/tools/awareness/building_es.shtml

Kibbee, K., & Gerzon, J. (2008). *MIT training delivery guide.* Retrieved November 8, 2012, from Massachusetts Institute of Technology Web site: http://web.mit.edu/training/trainers/guide/deliver/train-guide-matrix.pdf

Kirstein, K., Hinrichs, J., Olswang, S. (2011). *Authentic instruction and online delivery: Proven practices in higher education.* Seattle, WA: City University of Seattle.

Kothare, U. (Fall 1993). The effects on students of pre-announced learning objectives and immediate performance feedback**,** *College Quarterly,* *1***(1),** retrieved March 30, 2013, from www.senecac.on.ca/quarterly/1993-vol01-num01-fall/kothare.html

Lane J., & Hirsch, T. (2011, September 6). Mind the gap: No "people skills," no job, *Globe and Mail*, retrieved March 12, 2013, from http://m.theglobeandmail.com/commentary/mind-the-gap-no-people-skills-no-job/article550966/?service=mobile

Moran, G. (2011). *How to make employee training a winning investment*, retrieved October 17, 2017, from http://www.msnbc.

msn.com/id/45187680/ns/business-small_business/t/how-make-employee-training-winning-investment/

National Assessment of Adult Literacy (NAAL). (2011, July 12). *Required reading: A look at literacy in America*. Retrieved December 20, 2012, from NBC News Education Nation Web site: www.educationnation.com/index.cfm?objectid=DB931940-AC95-11E0-8358000C296BA163

National Association of Colleges and Employers (NACE). (October 4, 2012). *What employers want to see on a resume*. Retrieved March 30, 2013, from https://www.naceweb.org/press/releases/what-employers-want-to-see-on-a-resume.aspx

Office of Literacy and Essential Skills. (2011). *What are Essential Skills?* Retrieved March 12, 2013, from www.hrsdc.gc.ca/eng/workplaceskills/LES/tools_resources/tools_audience/what_are_essential_skills.shtml

Rabemananjara, R., & Parsley, C. (2006, Oct.). *Employee training decisions, business strategies and human resource management practices: A study by size of business*. Retrieved October 17, 2012, from Small Business Branch, Industry Canada Web site: http://www.ic.gc.ca/eic/site/061.nsf/eng/h_rd02058.html

Seibert, Wang G., & Courtright, S. (2011, Sept.). Antecedents and consequences of psychological and team empowerment: A meta-analytic review, *Journal of Applied Psychology, 96*(5).

Sidhu, L. (2011). *How does a company empower its staff? Part III: Don't just train…empower,* retrieved July 28, 2011, from www.westproject.ca

Sidhu, L. (2011). *How is workplace training and business success connected? Part II: Training and development,* retrieved July 28, 2011, from www.westproject.ca

Sidhu, L. (2011). *Take your training to a new level of success: Go W.E.S.T.—Part I: Train, develop and empower,* retrieved July 28, 2011, from www.westproject.ca

Sidhu, L. (2013, March 3). *Final project review: W.E.S.T.*

Sidhu, L., & Weaver, C. (2011). *Train, develop, empower: PowerPoint presentation.* Surrey, BC: Sources BC.

Sidhu, L., & Weaver, C. (2013). *Train, develop, empower: A resource guide for small businesses.* Surrey, BC: Sources BC. Retrieved March 13, 2013, from http://issuu.com/sourcesbc/docs/sources_w.e.s.t._resource_guide?mode=window

Simmons, B. (2011, April 15). *Employee empowerment: Why it matters and how to get it,* retrieved June 4, 2013, from http://www.bretlsimmons.com/2011-04/employee-empowerment-why-it-matters-and-how-to-get-it/

SkillPlan. (2010). *Six steps to mentoring,* Burnaby, BC: Author. Retrieved from http://www.skillplan.ca/

Stillwagon, A. (2010, August 2). Employee training: A wise investment, *Small Business CEO.* Retrieved October 17, 2012, from http://www.smbceo.com/2010/08/02/employee-training/

Stolovitch, H., & Keeps, E. (2002). *Telling ain't training,* Alexandria, VA: ASTD Press.

The Construction Sector Council. (2009). *Mentorship program,* Ottawa, ON.

Workplace Education, Manitoba. *The 9 Essential Skills,* retrieved October 15, 2012, from http://www.wem.mb.ca/the_9_essential_skills.aspx

Endnotes

1. To learn more visit: www.hrsdc.gc.ca/eng/workplaceskills/LES/tools_resources/tools.shtml.

2. To review the article visit: www.senecac.on.ca/quarterly/1993-vol01-num01-fall/kothare.html.

Made in the USA
San Bernardino, CA
03 July 2017